Political Behavior of
the American Electorate

Political Behavior of
the American Electorate
Tenth Edition

William H. Flanigan
University of Minnesota

Nancy H. Zingale
University of St. Thomas

CQ PRESS

A Division of Congressional Quarterly Inc.
Washington, D.C.

CQ Press
A Division of Congressional Quarterly Inc.
1255 22nd Street, N.W., Suite 400
Washington, D.C. 20037

(202) 822-1475; (800) 638-1710

www.cqpress.com

⊗ The paper used in this publication meets the minimum requirements of the American National Standard for Information Sciences— Permanence of Paper for Printed Library Materials, ANSI Z39.48-1992.

Cover design: Rich Pottern

Composition: G&S Typesetters, Inc.

Printed and bound in the United States of America

06   05   04   03   02   5   4   3   2   1

Library of Congress Cataloging-in-Publication Data

Flanigan, William H.
    Political behavior of the American electorate / William H. Flanigan, Nancy H. Zingale—10th ed.
        p. cm.
    Includes bibliographical references and index.
    ISBN 1-56802-741-9 (alk. paper)
        1. Voting—United States.   I. Zingale, Nancy H.   II. Title.

JK1967 .F38 2002
324.973—dc21

2002000173

To
Amy K. Hill
and to the memory of
Ruth M. Flanigan
Edwin N. Flanigan
James S. Hill

Contents

Tables and Figures

Tables

Figures

Acknowledgments

THE ANALYSIS and description of the American electorate presented in this book depend heavily on the work of others. Until 1960 analyses of the research findings and data collected by social scientists were limited to an examination of published tables, but there have been significant changes since then. The major studies of American public opinion and voting behavior are now accessible to scholars throughout the world for further examination and analysis.

These developments in political analysis resulted from the cooperation of many individuals, but the efforts of two men associated with the Institute for Social Research at the University of Michigan deserve special mention. The late Angus Campbell first opened the archives of the Survey Research Center to outside scholars. The late Warren Miller of the Center for Political Studies directed the organization and further expanded these archival activities through the creation of the Inter-university Consortium for Political and Social Research (ICPSR). The ICPSR, composed of more than 370 academic and research institutions, has made available to an extensive clientele not only the archives of the Survey Research Center but thousands of other major data collections as well. Scholars in the field of political behavior have benefited in incalculable ways from this work.

This book is highly dependent on the ICPSR in two ways. First, our analyses are based primarily on the large quantities of material collected by the National Election Study (NES), the high-quality biennial election survey originated by the Survey Research Center, and the ICPSR Historical Archive. Both are distributed by the ICPSR. Second, several generations of the scholars whose work we cite have similarly benefited from the availability of these resources. We are pleased to acknowledge our great debt to the individuals in both the ICPSR and the NES who have contributed to the establishment of these resources and services.

We must hasten to add that neither organization bears any responsibility for the analysis and interpretation presented here. Indeed, the hazard of their efforts in providing open archives is the sort of reinterpretation and reanalysis that follow. We can only hope that any weaknesses of this work will not reflect on the general worthiness and excellence of the ICPSR and the NES.

We also wish to thank our editors at CQ Press—Brenda Carter, Shana Wagger, Charisse Kiino, Kerry Kern, Tracy Villano, Ann O'Malley, Debbie Hardin, Christopher Karlsten, and Talia Greenberg—for their shepherding of the last four editions of this book to publication. It is a pleasure to work with such competent and pleasant people.

W. H. F.
N. H. Z.

Introduction

THE TERRORIST ATTACKS on Tuesday, September 11, 2001, were a watershed event for American society and the U.S. political system. Very few things happen in our lifetimes that cause us to think "nothing will ever be the same," but this was just such an event. It may not be literally true that *everything* changed, but an event this traumatic leaves us unsure of so much that we were once confident of that it might as well be true. This book describes past attitudes and behavior and we have some confidence in that account. We are much less confident in our ability to extrapolate these characteristics of the American political system in the future. Regardless of the uncertainty about the future, this is the past we will build on and evolve out of.

Even before September 11 a strange year was unfolding after the November 2000 election. Very soon after the election, events overwhelmed any recollections of the campaign. To begin with, the presidential election was the closest in more than a hundred years. More remarkable, the election remained undecided because of the uncertainty of the outcome in Florida. Not since 1876 had a presidential election remained undecided for more than a few hours after the polls closed. In 2000 the uncertainty lasted more than a month. In Florida the voting was extremely close, and an alarming number of irregular procedures and events occurred both before and after the election that called into question the validity of many of the votes. An unprecedented series of political and legal steps eventually led to a five to four U.S. Supreme Court decision that ended the recount then in progress and effectively gave an extremely narrow electoral college victory to George W. Bush.

Other electoral oddities abounded. For the first time since 1884 the popular vote winner was not the electoral college winner. Vice President Al Gore was the popular vote winner by a margin of more than 500,000

votes, but he lost the electoral college by four votes. Ralph Nader, a minor party candidate with a very small percentage of the popular vote, denied the presidency to a candidate who would have otherwise won. This
had not happened since 1912.

Dead heats were not limited to the presidential election. The results of the 2000 election left the U.S. Senate evenly divided between the
Democrats and Republicans, with the vice president holding the tie-
breaking vote. Until Dick Cheney was sworn in on January 20, 2001,
Gore ironically held the tie-breaking vote, although the Democrats did
not attempt to organize the Senate during that period to take advantage
of that fact. The Senate was to witness yet another unprecedented event
in the late spring. Sen. James Jeffords of Vermont switched from Republican to independent and denied the Republicans control of the
Senate. So in June following the election the Democrats reorganized the
Senate. It was the first time that party control of the Senate had changed
during a session.

With all of this happening after election day it is easy to forget the
events of the campaign leading up to the election. The Democratic Party
approached the 2000 campaign with clear strengths and weaknesses.
Democrats had made an unusually strong showing in the 1998 midterm
elections. President Bill Clinton's popularity was extremely high for a
president in his second term. The economy was strong, unemployment
was low, and the federal budget was showing a surplus. President Clinton's popularity, however, was limited to the job he was doing as president; there was widespread disapproval of his personal behavior. The
Democratic candidate, therefore, could not campaign on "more of
the same."

Gore as vice president was the front-runner for the Democratic
nomination throughout the campaign. He was challenged by former
senator Bill Bradley, but not very effectively. Vice President Gore was
never in danger of losing the support he needed to secure the nomination. In the early primaries there was substantial media attention directed at the contest between Gore and Bradley, but the public never
took as much interest in this race as they did in the Republican primary
contests.

George W. Bush as governor of Texas was able to distance himself
from the Republican leadership in Congress, and this was an advantage
given the unfavorable image the Republicans had after their unsuccessful attempt to remove Clinton from office. The Bush campaign through
old ties and a fresh face was able to raise an enormous amount of money
a year before the election. This seemingly unassailable position was,
nonetheless, effectively challenged by Sen. John McCain (Ariz.) for a
time. If Bush was not close to the Republican Party leadership, McCain
was at odds with the leadership at every turn. Senator McCain mounted

a surprisingly strong campaign during the early weeks of the primary season and stimulated a great deal of interest in the race and in his candidacy.

By mid-spring it was obvious the contest for president would be between Gore and Bush. The race was close from the beginning, with poll after poll showing the differences in their support within sampling error. Neither candidate was able to do anything during the campaign that garnered substantial new support. The rather undramatic debates and public appearances were accompanied by a huge advertising campaign. Partisans on both sides remained remarkably loyal throughout the election year, leaving the balance of power to independents.

The public was relatively satisfied with the candidates and the campaign. Overall evaluations were not as negative as in recent years. Still nothing in the campaign prepared the public or the candidates and their staffs for the events that followed election day. Indeed, it is hard to imagine how one *would* prepare for the postelection ordeal.

The first edition of this book was published in 1967. The plan of the book then, as now, was to present basic analysis and generalizations about the political behavior of Americans. What was unknowable at the time was that a decade of political trauma was beginning for the American polity in the late 1960s. Not only would some basic changes in political life take place, but these changes would call into question some of the things political scientists thought they knew about the way Americans behave politically. The 1980s were a quieter time. Many of the trends that began or were accelerated by the crises of the late 1960s and early 1970s tapered off but did not reverse during the Ronald Reagan and George Bush Sr. years.

If nothing else, the elections of the 1990s demonstrated once again the capacity of the electorate to surprise and confound political pundits and public opinion analysts. The election of 2000, however, outdid all elections in living memory for the unexpected and bizarre. But it was the electoral system, not the electorate, that supplied the surprises.

Following the tragic events of September 11, 2001, the political system entered an uncertain period. Much has changed drastically, but it is unclear what this means for the trends that are examined in this book. Over the years since that first edition, however, we have been impressed with the overall continuity in the behavior of the electorate, even in the midst of significant changes in the political environment.

In this tenth edition we continue to focus attention on the major concepts and characteristics that shape Americans' responses to politics: Are Americans committed to upholding basic democratic values? Who votes and why? How does partisanship affect political behavior? How and why does partisanship change? How do economic and social characteristics influence individuals' politics? How much influence do the mass media have on our attitudes and political choices? How do party loyalties, candidates' personalities, and issues influence our choices among candidates?

Throughout the book we will place the answers to these and other questions in the context of the changes that have occurred in American political behavior over the past fifty years. Wherever possible, we place these recent trends in the broader context of political change over the two hundred years of the Republic. Specifically, we are concerned with the decline in voter turnout, the drop in voter attachment to political parties, and the loss of trust in government that many citizens have expressed. These trends, and their implications for American democracy, have been the subject of much discussion by political analysts and commentators.

A second major focus of this book is to illustrate and document these trends in American political behavior with the best longitudinal data available. We rely heavily, although not exclusively, on data from the National Election Studies (NES) as distributed through the Interuniversity Consortium for Political and Social Research (ICPSR). These surveys, covering a broad range of political topics and offering the best time-series data available, have been conducted during the fall of every election year since 1952. Unless otherwise noted, the data come from this extraordinarily rich series of studies. We hope that the numerous tables and figures contained in this book will be used not only for documenting the points made in the book but also for learning to read and interpret data. Students can also explore a much wider range of data from the NES on its Web site at www.umich.edu/~nes/. The data from the NES and other studies are available for classroom use through the ICPSR. (To see the full range of political studies available to the academic community, visit the Web site of the ICPSR at www.icpsr .umich.edu.) One of our purposes is to provide an impetus for obtaining high-quality data to answer questions prompted, but not answered, by this book.

As this edition goes to press, full, continuing support for the NES by the National Science Foundation is in doubt. Indeed, support was sufficiently limited for the 2000 study that half of the interviewing was conducted by telephone. The reader may notice in some tables there are many fewer respondents for 2000 than for earlier years. We have used data only from the traditional face-to-face interviews in our analysis in this edition, so we have only half as many cases as we would otherwise. Every scholar using the 2000 study will have to make a difficult decision about what to do with the telephone interviews. Our decision was to maintain the comparability of interview data both within the 2000 study and over time.

All of the decisions to cut support for the NES were made before September 11. Along with all the other changes brought by the terrorist attacks, perhaps there will be a renewed interest in the scholarly study of American public opinion and, in particular, the impact of the public's reaction to September 11 on the midterm elections of 2002.

Political Culture and American Democracy

SUCCESSFUL DEMOCRACIES rest on the consent of the governed and widespread public support. In representative democracies we look for regular, free, and fair elections to choose political leaders and, when necessary, to turn these leaders out of office. A democratic system of government, at a minimum, affords its citizens the opportunity to organize, to speak freely, and to select its leaders.

Beyond this simple, widely agreed on view, which assumes a crucial role for the people in choosing their representatives and emphasizes the individual as an autonomous actor with inherent political rights, there is less consensus on what is required of citizens. On the one hand are visions of a well-informed electorate making decisions based on rational calculations of its own best interest or, possibly, a public good. On the other, some critics see a deluded public, manipulated by political elites to hold views and support policies that are in the interests of the elites rather than the people. Somewhere in between is the view that the electorate responds to generalized policy promises and symbolic issues in selecting its leaders, setting broad and rather vague outer limits on decision makers. Specific policies, however, are negotiated between public officials and subsets of the attentive public who are unrepresentative of the general public, both in terms of their degree of interest in a particular policy and in the political resources available to them with which to exert influence. In the chapters that follow, you will have the opportunity to judge for yourself the level of information and capacity for rational decision making that the American public displays.

In this chapter we consider two topics. First, we examine an issue brought starkly into focus by the unusual election of 2000. What are the requirements for fair and free elections in a democracy and how closely does our system come to meeting that standard? Second, we look at the cultural and attitudinal requirements for instituting and sustaining a democratic system and examine the extent to which those requirements are met in the United States: How widespread is support for democratic values in the United States and how are these values learned and transmitted from generation to generation? How confident are American citizens that their government is playing by democratic rules? How confident are they that a democratic system is the best route to satisfactory policy outcomes?

Fair, Free, and Competitive Elections

Elections are a basic component of a democratic political system. They are the formal mechanism by which we maintain or alter the existing political leadership. At occasional intervals, competitive elections give ordinary citizens the power to choose their leaders and, just as important, to throw them out of office. Although the choices available to voters in a general election may not be numerous or even particularly dissimilar, democratic systems *must* provide for competition, usually by means of political parties, in presenting alternative candidates.

If elections are to be competitive, political leaders and organizations must be able to compete for the support of voters, and voters should have leaders competing for their support. (If some voters have no leaders competing for their support, the system must be open to the entry of new leaders who will seek the support of these unrepresented voters.)

Competitive elections require that all citizens must be free to participate fully in campaign activities before the election itself. These campaign activities include the freedom to express one's views and the freedom to organize with others during the nominating phase and the campaign to express preferences and persuade others. Implicit in this is the freedom to receive information about the choices before the voters.

Citizens must be free to vote, and the right to vote should not be undermined by substantial economic or administrative barriers. Certainly there should not be physical or social intimidation. Citizens legally eligible to vote should have full and convenient access to polling places. The right to vote and the right to express one's choices freely require a secret ballot. In fair elections the ballots cast should reflect the intention of the voters, and the votes should be counted accurately and weighted equally. Votes should be weighted equally in translating votes into representation.

Finally, the requirements of free, fair, and competitive elections should be established in law and be enforceable through the judicial system. Both citizens and leaders must enjoy equal treatment under the law.

The 2000 presidential election gives us an opportunity to reassess the extent to which the election met the requirements for a fair and free election. In retrospect, the 2000 election certainly appears to have been competitive. It may be that some potential voters were ignored, but by most standards the political parties and the candidates seem to have campaigned aggressively for every possible vote. Indeed, the excesses of the campaign might reasonably be linked to the high degree of competitiveness and the belief that the outcome was in doubt. The challenge in a democratic electoral system is to be highly competitive without compromising the integrity of the election process.

Despite the tight competition between the two major-party candidates, we need to bear in mind the barriers to entry into the competition by other candidates. Although two other candidates—Pat Buchanan and Ralph Nader—were on the ballot in virtually every state in 2000, and Buchanan had access to public financing, the obstacles to effectively competing are serious. Both these candidates were denied a place in the nationally televised debates, and the electoral college arrangements encourage voters to see a vote for such candidates as a wasted vote. Many of the rules governing elections in the United States are designed to weed out nuisance candidates to limit attention to those with some degree of public support. Public financing, participation in the debates, and place on the ballot all require demonstration of some minimum level of support. On an informal level, coverage of a candidate's campaign by the mass media also requires such a demonstration. Unfortunately, minor candidates are faced with a chicken-and-egg dilemma. They cannot gain access to these important resources unless they are competitive, but they cannot become competitive unless they have access to these resources.

With this serious caveat in mind, we can conclude that elections in the United States are reasonably competitive, with considerable opportunity for citizens and groups to organize, campaign, express their views, and receive information about the candidates and their positions.

It has become easier to register to vote in most states in recent years, and in fact there has been increased registration. (We will treat the topic of voter registration and turnout more fully in Chapter 2.) Administrative problems remain, however, and these fall unevenly on the citizenry. In many states, officials have been slow to process new registrations, so that individuals who have correctly followed registration procedures find themselves not registered when they get to the polling place. This problem can rarely be solved in a timely fashion by the election judges at the polling place. (Hence there are various proposals to connect all polling places with central election officials to settle such problems or have voters with registration problems cast "provisional ballots" that could be held until the matter is resolved.)

There was an unusual registration problem in Florida in 2000 that has received a considerable amount of attention from the U.S. Commission on Civil Rights.[1] Because there had been significant fraud in some recent Florida elections, before the 2000 election the state legislature enacted legislation to purge the registration lists of ineligible voters (such as the dead or otherwise departed). The state contracted with a private firm to purge from the registration lists felons, who are not eligible to vote in Florida; this was done by computer-matching lists of felons from Florida and elsewhere with the voter registration lists. This led many nonfelons to be removed from the lists because the lists were inaccurate and the computer match did not have to be perfect—the computer purged names if there was a 90 percent match of letters. Some people were informed that they had been purged before the election, but the procedures for reinstatement were confusing. Others were not informed beforehand and arrived at their polling place only to be told that they were ineligible to vote.

The Civil Rights Commission also heard testimony of black citizens in Florida who reported being stopped by state police on the way to the polls. To the extent these reports were true, it would be an obvious denial of fair access to a polling place. Simple administrative bungling can have the same effect—for example, providing incorrect or conflicting information to would-be voters.*

Because so much information is available on the vote-counting process in Florida in the aftermath of the 2000 election, we can use it as a test of the requirement that votes be counted accurately. (Focusing on Florida may create unfairly the impression that everywhere else elections are trouble-free. That is certainly not the case; we simply have little information on most other states.)

The 2000 election in Florida demonstrated that voting procedures themselves can deny voters their vote. Voting devices fail to record votes in various ways: On "punch hole" ballots the paper "chad" may not be dislodged, and therefore would not be counted; on scanned ballots the choices may not be detected; on most voting devices the voter can in-

---

*On primary day 2001 in Minnesota—a state known for its "clean" elections—we went to vote for local offices, only to find that the polling place had been moved to the opposite end of the precinct, a mile away. Most voters were not informed of this change until they arrived at the "old" polling place. The Web site for the county office in charge of elections showed no change. For motivated voters with transportation and flexible schedules this was only a minor annoyance; however, it does not take great imagination to think what kinds of voters—in a diverse, urban neighborhood—would be disadvantaged by such cavalier administrative action.

advertently void the ballot by various kinds of inappropriate marking. (In party primary elections where voters are required to vote in only one party's races but the ballot form allows voting in more than one party primary, large percentages of the ballots are invalidated for this reason.) [2] There are voting machines that detect these errors and give the voter another chance to cast a ballot correctly, but these machines are relatively expensive and not widely used.

The marked ballot should accurately reflect the voter's intention. In Broward County in Florida, for example, the "butterfly ballot," which was enlarged to help elderly voters read it better, seems to have resulted in a considerable number of voters mistakenly casting their votes for Buchanan when they intended to vote for Gore. Election officials in different counties used different rules for determining the "voter's intent" on flawed ballots during the various phases of the recount. Some officials allowed votes to be counted if the voter's intention could be reasonably inferred from the marks or punches on the ballot. In other counties, even ballots with a clear declaration of intent—such as that of the frustrated voter who wrote "I want to vote for Gore" on the ballot—were disallowed.

The counting of votes is overseen by representatives of the competing political parties, and they are expected to keep each other honest. Even so it is extremely difficult to standardize procedures in different election districts.** For example, in Florida in 2000 the counting of the overseas ballots attracted a great deal of attention. It was not until many months after the election that it was revealed that the Republican Party had pursued a two-part strategy: In Republican counties they insisted that all ballots be counted even if the ballots were flawed in various ways; however, in Democratic counties Republican officials followed the strict letter of the law to disallow identically flawed ballots.

Although it has never been a major theme in democratic theory, a fair election must allow for a thorough and accurate recount to ensure that the official results faithfully reflect the voters' choices. All vote-counting procedures are susceptible to error and fraud, so the occasional authentication of official returns is crucial to maintaining the legitimacy of elections in general. Typically in the United States recounts have uncovered a certain amount of clerical error and very little fraud.

**Following the Florida election controversy, a consortium of eight news organizations was formed to recount the presidential vote for the entire state. They used a number of different rules for counting disputed ballots. They found that systematically following the rules advocated by the Gore advisors would have led to a Bush victory, and following the rules preferred by the Bush organization would have produced a Gore victory. All major newspapers, including the *New York Times* and the *Washington Post*, carried stories on the recount project on November 9, 2001.

As a consequence, the failure to have a full recount in Florida fueled questions about the legitimacy of the election. Finally, the partisan overtones to the involvement of the Florida Supreme Court (which ruled to benefit the Democrat) and the U.S. Supreme Court (which ruled to benefit the Republican) in deciding the election raise questions about the extent to which elections in the United States are subject to the rule of law.

It is perhaps too early to determine how much the election of 2000 undermined the confidence of the public in the fairness of the electoral system. In the short run, partisan sympathies colored reactions. A few months after his inauguration, only half the public reported believing that George W. Bush "won fair and square."[3] On the other hand, 80 percent of the public said they were very or fairly satisfied with U.S. democracy after the 2000 election. This was about the same percentage as in 1996.

Political Culture

Elections operate within the context of political values and beliefs that form the political culture. The political culture provides the setting in which political processes operate. The political culture constrains electoral activities and the actions of elected leaders but rarely determines election or legislative outcomes.

The political culture is a fundamental element of any democratic political system. The values and opinions of the people are the foundation of democracy. To a large extent the achievement of political goals in a democracy depends on the public. A critical look at American democracy includes assessment of the public's support for political institutions and its attitudes toward political leadership.

In recent years, much has been made of Americans' increasing disenchantment with their political system and how it operates. Most noteworthy has been a long-term decline in the level of trust Americans have for their political institutions as well as a decline in citizens' belief in their ability to influence governmental decisions.

The primary focus of this chapter is on a broad pattern of beliefs that form part of the political culture; the secondary focus is on the acquisition of these beliefs. We examine the content of American political culture as a foundation for democracy. We will also make a distinction, where appropriate, between the beliefs of political leaders and those of the mass public, because a basic finding is that the beliefs of these two groups about the political system are quite dissimilar. The discussion of political culture will cover attitudes regarding the role of individual participants in the system and the implications of these attitudes for political action. We will of necessity focus attention on the values of the dominant national culture, though we must keep in mind that political subcultures exist that may support contrary values and attitudes.

Democratic Beliefs and Values

A major thrust of the analysis of democratic political systems, and the U.S. system in particular, has been the search for a fundamental, underlying set of widely supported values. Presumably, the commitment to these principles holds a democratic society together in the presence of conflict and provides support and legitimacy for the functioning of its political institutions. These beliefs and values are variously referred to as the *American creed,* the *American consensus,* or the *American ethos.*[4] Among the most important values making up this creed are beliefs in *freedom, equality,* and *individualism.*

Social and political theorists make a distinction between the economic system and the political system. Most would say that the United States has, as an ideal, a democratic political system and a capitalist or free market economic system. Ordinary citizens are more likely to mix the two and view freedom as a basic value in both. The freedom to own property, fundamental to a capitalist economic system, is considered by ordinary citizens of the United States to be as important as the right to vote, for example.

Although highly valued in American culture, freedom is not considered an absolute. People in fact accept all kinds of limitations on freedom. For example, when given a choice between government intervention and a wholly free market, the American public is clearly in favor of strong government activity. In the 2000 National Election Study, by a ratio of more than three to two, the public preferred government intervention to handle economic problems rather than depending solely on free-market operations. Similarly, majorities of the public support limiting the freedom to read pornography, to own guns, and to smoke cigarettes.

The widespread belief in equality similarly needs to be qualified. Americans believe in "equality before the law" and in "equal opportunity" but are largely uninterested in using government to promote economic and social equality. For example, the public agrees overwhelmingly with the proposition that "our society should do whatever is necessary to make sure that everyone has an equal opportunity to succeed."[5] But at the same time a substantial minority of the public believes "we have gone too far in pushing equal rights in this country."[6] In many respects, the value placed on individualism undermines the commitment to equality. There is widespread support in most social groups for the idea that people can and should get ahead by virtue of their own hard work.

A distinction often is made between democratic *goals,* such as equality and individual freedom, and democratic *procedures,* such as majority rule; protection of the political rights of freedom of speech, press, and assembly; and due process of law. The distinction is an important one when the extent to which these ideals are supported in the political culture of a system is under consideration, because democratic goals can quite possibly be pursued through undemocratic means or democratic procedures can be used for antidemocratic ends. Likewise, mass support may exist for democratic goals but not for democratic procedures or vice versa.

A widely held and perfectly plausible expectation is that the American public supports both these kinds of democratic values. At an abstract level this is true enough. American citizens overwhelmingly subscribe to the basic rules and goals of democracy when this commitment is kept vague. But, as we have seen, the near unanimous support for the democratic goals of freedom and equality disappear when we consider specific applications of these concepts. The same has been true for specific applications of democratic procedures, such as protection of free speech. Majorities historically have been happy to infringe on the right to speak, to organize, and to run for office of unpopular groups such as atheists, Communists, and the Ku Klux Klan.

Rising educational levels in the United States brought an increased willingness on the part of the public to allow free speech on unpopular points of view and permit books with distasteful perspectives to remain in public libraries. Numerous studies document this shift in attitudes occurring from the mid-1950s to the 1970s, and without exception they find a strong relationship between increased tolerance and higher levels of education.[7]

Several important qualifications are in order. First, the electorate's responses are attitudes that may have little meaning for it and are not measures of its behavior or of its attitudes under crisis or threat to democratic principles. Second, it may not be that people are more tolerant but that the focus of their intolerance has shifted. People now tolerate speeches by Marxists but object to those of fascists or racists.[8] More broadly, the desire for censorship may have shifted from political speech to other forms of expression, such as art and music, particularly those involving sexual or sacrilegious themes.

Third, it is essential to keep in mind the distinction between mass attitudes and those of the political, social, and economic leaders in American society who consistently support these democratic principles more strongly than the general public. Support among leaders is usually so high that it is possible to conclude that the leaders in society defend and maintain democratic procedures. This consensus among leaders on democratic rights and values makes the weakness of the general public's support less crucial.

National studies by both Samuel Stouffer in the 1950s and Herbert McClosky in the 1960s support the view that leaders are stronger than the public in support of the "rules of the game."[9] The degree to which leaders support these rules compared with the public can be seen in Table 1-1. Political influentials—in this study delegates and alternates to the Democratic and Republican national conventions in 1956—were consistently more likely to agree with the rules of the game than was a sample of the electorate. It may not be reassuring to discover that 7 percent of the political influentials agreed that "the majority has the right to abolish minorities if it wants to" or that 13 percent agreed that "almost any unfairness or brutality may have to be justified when some great purpose is being carried out." But in both examples substantially *greater* percentages of the general electorate, 28 percent and 33 percent, respectively, supported these views.

In 1972 Jeane Kirkpatrick studied the attitudes of political leaders, focusing on delegates to the Democratic and Republican national conventions.[10] Although this study was concerned primarily with issues rather than principles, her findings suggest that the earlier pattern still existed in the 1970s. For example, Kirkpatrick found that among leaders, 17 percent endorsed abridging the rights of the accused to stop criminal activity, and among the public as a whole 46 percent supported stopping crime even at the risk of reducing rights.[11]

Presumably, leaders are recruited and educated in such a way that they come prepared with, or develop, agreement on democratic procedures. Leaders apparently make decisions that maintain democratic practices, even without widespread public support. A somewhat less comforting possibility is that political elites are simply sophisticated enough to understand what the "correct" answer is to attitude questions dealing with democratic beliefs. The seemingly greater adherence to these values by the politically active would attest to the prominence of such norms in the mass political culture but would not necessarily suggest any great commitment to or willingness to abide by these values. A third possibility exists such that political leaders, like ordinary citizens, are willing to violate the rights of groups and individuals whom they particularly dislike or fear. Enough incidents of undemocratic behavior by public officials have occurred in recent decades—harassment of dissidents during the Vietnam War, "dirty tricks" to undermine the electoral process in 1972, surreptitious aiding of the Nicaraguan contras in violation of the law in the 1980s—to suggest no great depth of appreciation of democratic principles on the part of elites of either political party.

The 2000 election appears to offer examples of elites adhering to the rules of the game in some instances and abandoning the rules in others. Certainly there was evidence of pressure from some members of

TABLE 1-1   Political Influentials versus the Electorate, Responses to Items
Expressing Belief in Democratic Values

Item	Percentage agreeing with item	
	Political influentials	General electorate
There are times when it almost seems better for people to take the law into their own hands rather than wait for the machinery of government to act.	13	27
The majority has the right to abolish minorities if it wants to.	7	28
If congressional committees stuck strictly to the rules and gave every witness his rights, they would never succeed in exposing the many dangerous subversives they have turned up.	25	47
I don't mind a politician's methods if he manages to get the right things done.	26	42
Almost any unfairness or brutality may have to be justified when some great purpose is being carried out.	13	33
People ought to be allowed to vote even if they can't do so intelligently.	66	48
The true American way of life is disappearing so fast that we may have to use force to save it.	13	35
(N)	(3,020)	(1,484)

Source: Adapted from Herbert McClosky, "Consensus and Ideology in American Politics," *American Political Science Review* 58 (June 1964): 365, Table 1.

Note: Because respondents were forced to make a choice on each item, the number of omitted or "don't know" responses was, on the average, fewer than 1 percent and thus has little influence on the direction or magnitude of the results reported in this table.

the elite to abide by the result of the election (whatever that might be) and the rule of law (however interpreted) and a desire to be seen as following democratic rules. At other times, the operating principle seemed to be "do whatever you can get away with."

To take another example, reaction to the Supreme Court's decisions on flag burning illustrates several aspects of the role of political elites in supporting democratic values. Political dissidents have occasionally burned the American flag to protest policies or governmental actions with which they disagree. In retaliation, Congress and some state legislatures have passed laws making it a crime to "desecrate" the flag. The Supreme Court has consistently ruled these laws to be an unconstitutional infringement on free speech—classifying flag burning as "symbolic speech" and therefore protected by the First Amendment. Inevitably, these decisions provoke a public outcry and calls to amend the Constitution as a means to circumvent the Court's decision and punish those who would burn the flag. In these circumstances, various political elites—the Court itself and some congressional leaders—support democratic values by resisting the popular passion for punishing flag burners. At the same time, other political leaders see an opportunity to exploit an issue that plays well among the public, because polls consistently show the public believes, by majorities of three or four to one, that there should be no right to burn or deface the U.S. flag.[12] The relatively easy defeat of the most recent proposed constitutional amendment to ban flag burning, once the issue became rephrased as "tampering with the Bill of Rights," demonstrates the generalized, if vague, support the public has for democratic values and the critical nature of elite leadership in these areas.

The widespread interest of political analysts in public opinion and democratic beliefs has been based partly on a somewhat mistaken impression. Stable democratic political systems have been assumed to rest on a nearly universal commitment to fundamental principles and their application, but the evidence on this point is inconclusive. Certainly, a democratic system cannot long survive widespread, intense hostility to democratic values, but positive belief in particular operating procedures among the public is probably unnecessary. Hostility to democratic procedures is fatal, whether among the leaders or the public, but support of specific procedures may prove essential only among leaders. Perhaps the public need not agree on basic principles so long as it does not demand disruptive policies and procedures.

System Support

Feelings of strong national loyalty may or may not be narrowly political in content, but they are likely to provide support for the political system, whether the system is democratic or not. Patriotism may provide system support when other attitudes do not. When people are dissatisfied with public policies or the economy, for example, strong feelings of national loyalty may suppress hostile attitudes or disruptive behavior. Democratic as well as authoritarian leaders have used a foreign enemy or an external crisis to rally support and distract the public from troubles at home.

In response to questions in public opinion polls, Americans express a strong pride in their country: Of those questioned, 96 percent say that they are proud to be American; 89 percent say they are very patriotic; 80 percent characterize their love of America as "very" or "extremely strong"; and 71 percent say their feelings about the flag are "very" or "extremely good."[13]

When people are asked about their pride in the United States, they tend to offer political factors as examples. In other countries people are much more likely to give nonpolitical reasons for their pride: their country's economy, culture, or physical beauty. They are not nearly so likely to say they are proud of their political system.[14] Americans not only give political reasons for their pride in the United States but also cite "freedom" or "liberty" as the aspect of their political system that makes them proud. Thus, not only is there strong patriotic pride in the nation, but a central democratic value is a prominent feature of that sentiment.

This pride in the nation and its democratic form of government translates into high levels of political system support. Of the respondents to a national survey 85 percent say that "whatever its faults, the United States still has the best system of government in the world." More than half of the public "would not change anything" in the American political system.[15]

As we noted previously, vague principles may be widely endorsed even though, at the same time, specific applications may be opposed. So it should not be surprising that respondents will agree to vague statements of system support and at the same time endorse contradictory specifics as well. Eighty percent of the public say the Constitution should not be amended.[16] However, majorities also believe that the Constitution should be amended to abolish the electoral college, mandate a balanced budget, or adopt the Equal Rights Amendment. Almost certainly none of these answers tells us how people would behave if actually faced with choices on amending the Constitution.

In general, the public has considerable confidence in the *institutions* of government but not much confidence in the *individuals* charged with operating these institutions. Thus, there is virtually no popular support for abolishing the presidency or the Supreme Court or Congress, although there is simultaneous and widespread disenchantment with the way the nation's political leadership is performing in these major branches of government. At the end of the year 2000, a little more than 10 percent of the public had "a great deal" of confidence in Congress, and roughly one quarter had "a great deal" of confidence in the presidency and the Supreme Court.[17] These low levels of confidence, with some variations, have existed since the early 1970s and represent a noticeable drop from the levels of confidence characteristic of earlier years.

John Hibbing and Elizabeth Theiss-Morse argue, in their book, *Congress as Public Enemy*, that it is the very openness to public scrutiny of congressional activities that generates distaste.[18] This may explain the higher level of confidence in the more secretive executive and Supreme

Court decision making. In short, when the people see democracy in action, they do not like it very much.

Figure 1-1 shows another indicator of declining public confidence in the political system. For years, the National Election Study has asked respondents whether they thought "the government in Washington could be trusted to do the right thing." Figure 1-1 shows an overall decline from high levels in the 1950s and early 1960s to the point in the early 1990s where only a third of the public believed the government will do what is right "all of the time" or "most of the time." Short-term reversals in this downward trend have been associated with policy successes or popular incumbents. President Ronald Reagan created an upbeat mood in the 1980s that translated into a modest restoration of confidence in government, as did the booming economy in the mid-1990s. After the terrorist attacks on the World Trade Center and Pentagon on September 11, 2001, a *Washington Post* poll reported an upward spike in the level of trust in government, shown at the right of Figure 1-1. Of the people questioned, 64 percent of the public said they trusted the government all or most of the time.[19] This level has not been seen since the 1960s. Whether it will be sustained for any length of time is yet to be seen.

FIGURE 1-1   Trust, Cynicism, and Efficacy, 1952–2001

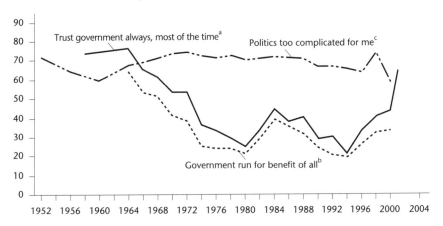

Sources: National Election Studies. Data provided by the Inter-university Consortium for Political and Social Research. Data point for 2001 "trust," *Washington Post*, September 30, 2001.

[a] "How much of the time do you think you can trust the government in Washington to do what is right—just about always, most of the time, or only some of the time?"
[b] "Would you say the government is pretty much run by a few big interests looking out for themselves or that it is run for the benefit of all the people?"
[c] Agree that "Sometimes politics and government seem so complicated that a person like me can't really understand what's going on."

Because the steepest decline in trust in government officials occurred between 1964 and 1976, it is easy to blame the Vietnam War and the Watergate scandal. Although no doubt contributing factors, the decline in trust had already begun before Vietnam became an issue and continued after Richard Nixon's departure from office. Furthermore, this pattern of declining trust extends to many nongovernmental institutions, such as the news media, schools, the professions, and indeed to people in general. It is paralleled by similar trends outside the United States in many of the developed nations of the world.

These general attitudes of distrust of and dissatisfaction with political leaders and institutions are not paralleled by a decline in the confidence of individuals in their own ability to participate effectively in the political process. Figure 1-1 shows no long-term decline in the individual's *sense of political efficacy*—that is, the individual's belief about his or her ability to understand government. Other indicators of political efficacy, such as questions about confidence in one's ability to influence government, often show a decline. However, it seems likely this is a reflection of lack of confidence in government's willingness to listen rather than in the individual's lack of the necessary skills to command attention. There are, of course, differences among individuals in their sense of political efficacy, differences that are strongly related to education, general self-confidence, and experience with political participation.

Citizen Roles and Political Participation

American citizens have a strongly developed sense of obligation to inform themselves, to participate in elections, and, to a lesser extent, to participate in other forms of political activity. About 90 percent of all adults believe it is the duty of good citizens to vote in elections, although obviously many of them do not act on that commitment at every election. Although Americans also believe in the importance of informing themselves about political and governmental affairs, they readily concede that in most cases they personally are not as well informed as they should be.

The most common form of political participation is exercising the right to vote. We will discuss voter turnout in Chapter 2, including the impact of declining levels of trust on citizens' willingness to participate. Maintaining a representative democracy involves more than voting, however. Becaus_ the message or mandate of an election is seldom clear, specific policy concerns must be communicated to one's elected representatives; organizing with like-minded individuals increases the chances that one's interests will be heard. Participation in voluntary associations—political and nonpolitical—has long been

noted as an important contributor to democratic politics. Alexis de Toc-
queville, writing in the nineteenth century, commented on Americans'
proclivity toward joining organizations of all sorts. Not only do participants in voluntary associations learn useful political skills, the existence
of many organizations with overlapping memberships tends to moderate conflict. People whose interests conflict on one set of issues may find
themselves working together as allies on some other set of issues. Membership in organizations links people to each other and to their communities. In a study of Italian states, Robert Putnam showed that the
most significant difference between those with effective democratic politics and those without was the existence of a strong associational life.[20]

Putnam has recently raised the alarm over what he refers to as the
"declining social capital" in the United States. Americans, he argues, are
now less likely to join organizations of all kinds—from bowling leagues
to labor unions to political parties. This he attributes to women in the
workforce, increased residential mobility, and technological innova-
tions, such as television, the personal computer, and the VCR, all of
which allow individuals to work and play in isolation.[21]

In a major study of political participation in the United States,
Verba, Schlozman, and Brady seem to counter Putnam's claim, finding
organizational participation in America "lively and varied."[22] In a comparison with a similar study in 1967, they find a decline in some forms
of political activity, such as voting and membership in political clubs, but
similar levels of participation in community activities and sizable increases in political contributions and contacting public officials about
issues. Putnam would agree with the last contention, also noting increases in the membership in "tertiary"—or mass membership—organizations. Such organizations, however, usually do not involve the
face-to-face interaction that fosters cooperation and builds community.

Verba et al. also conclude that the pattern of participation in America distorts the voice of the people. Those with education and money
participate; the poor and uneducated do not. As a consequence, the interests of the affluent are well represented in government, and those of
the less advantaged are not. It is interesting to note that participation in
religious institutions does not have this social class bias, and Verba et al.
conclude that religious organizations are an important mechanism for
developing political skills among the less advantaged citizenry.[23]

More intense forms of political activity, such as working on political
campaigns, have remained much the same over this time period—although the levels of involvement have never been high. Many individuals who contribute financially to campaigns are not involved in any
other way. When all forms of campaign activity, including financial contributions, are counted, slightly more than 10 percent of the electorate
is involved in some way.

There are many forms of political activity that ordinary citizens engage in beyond campaigning in elections. Active, interested individuals with political concerns call and write public officials, become involved in interest groups dedicated to influencing public policy, circulate petitions, and even occasionally take to the streets to demonstrate. The general decline in positive feelings toward politics and government discussed in the preceding section is not necessarily paralleled in the behavior of the most active, concerned members of the public.

Childhood Socialization

Most social groups, particularly those with distinctive sets of norms and values, make some effort to teach these attitudes and expected behaviors to their new members. In most societies this process of socialization is focused primarily on the largest group of new members: children. Through the process of political socialization the political culture of a society is transmitted from one generation to the next, but this socialization is also an important mechanism through which change in the political culture can take place.

In societies in which most learning about politics takes place in the home, the prevailing political culture probably changes no faster than the attitudes of the adult population as a whole, in response to varied personal experiences and changing circumstances in the environment. In modern societies other agents of political socialization also are involved, particularly the educational system and, increasingly, the mass media. To the extent that these institutions instill a different set of values and norms compared with those held by the adult population as a whole, there is an opportunity for changing the political culture. Under the Communist regimes in the People's Republic of China and, formerly, the Soviet Union, the official ideology dominated both the schools and the mass communications system. Massive changes in values took place within the span of a generation. (The fact that contrary attitudes survived this indoctrination attests to the multiplicity of agents of socialization, even in totalitarian states.) More diversity in views is permitted in the United States, but the prevalence of middle-class values among both teachers and the media guarantees that these orientations will continue to be widespread in the population as a whole.

Given the importance of the socialization process in the transmission of the fundamental beliefs and values of the political culture, it is surprising that socialization studies have not paid much attention to the development of attitudes supportive of democratic goals and procedures. Data collected by David Easton and Robert Hess in the 1950s show that children develop an affective attachment to the term *democracy* very early (by about the third grade), but the concept acquires

FIGURE 1-2   Children's and Teachers' Understanding of the Concept of
Democracy

Percentage agreeing that the phrase
is part of the definition of democracy

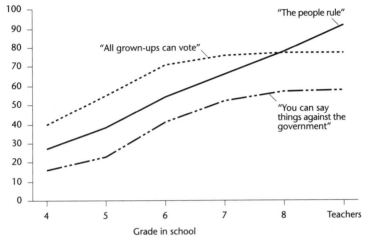

Source: Adapted from Robert D. Hess and Judith V. Torney, *The Development of Political Attitudes in Children* (New York: Anchor Books, 1968), 75, Table 13.

meaning much more slowly.[24] The progress of this learning from the
fourth grade to the eighth grade is shown for several concepts in Figure 1-2. Perhaps the most interesting aspect of this figure is the high
level of disagreement among teachers over the correctness of including
the right of dissent in the meaning of democracy. Other studies have
shown that adolescents are somewhat more likely than their parents to
endorse democratic values, but the process through which these ideals
are learned and the extent to which children learn to apply them to
concrete situations remain to be studied.

More emphasis has been placed on the development of the child's
thinking about the institutions of government and about his or her own
role as a citizen. The child's first view of government and governmental
leaders casts the leaders as all-powerful and benevolent, undoubtedly
the result of the twin objectives of parents and teachers to instill an
acceptance of authority and to shield young children from the harsher
realities of political life. Gradually, the child acquires a more realistic
and more cynical view of the world. Children also begin with a very personalized view of government; government means the president or,
for some, the police officer. In time these images are replaced or supplemented with more abstract ideas about Congress and the election
process.[25]

Throughout the socialization process, there are important differences in development associated with social class and intelligence as measured by IQ tests. In general, this takes the form of brighter students learning and adopting the values of teachers more quickly, often with rather intriguing results. Taking a partisan stance would be considered taboo in most American classrooms, but advocating nonpartisanship is not. An overwhelming majority of the teachers in the Easton and Hess sample thought it preferable to "vote for the person" than to join a political party. Children progressively adopt this view as they move through the elementary grades, and middle-class and high-IQ children do so at higher rates.[26] Some 87 percent of the teachers saw the United Nations as more influential than the United States in keeping world peace, and, by a margin of two to one, teachers believe Congress has more to do with "running the country" than the president. Children learn these perceptions, inaccuracies and all, with the better students absorbing them faster.

During the elementary grades, children also develop a set of attitudes toward their own roles as citizens. Initially, the emphasis is on obedience: The good citizen obeys the law, just as good children obey their parents. In the American socialization process, this is gradually replaced by a view of oneself as a more active participant in the political system: The good citizen is one who votes. Still later, the child adds to this the notion that the government can be influenced through the voting process. Data from *The Civic Culture* by Gabriel Almond and Sidney Verba suggest that the socialization process in the United States instills this set of attitudes in its citizens more successfully than in some other Western democracies.[27] Americans are more likely to view themselves as "participants" as opposed to "subjects" than are citizens of the United Kingdom, Germany, Italy, or Mexico. In all the countries studied, experiences with democratic decision making, in the schools or in the family, were related to adult participation in politics and to the belief that the individual can influence government. Other studies have documented that, within the United States, children's attitudes toward their own possible effectiveness with regard to government are related to social class; social class, in turn, is related to differences in the attitude toward authority within the home. Working-class parents are more likely to demand obedience and allow less input from children in the familial decision-making process than are middle-class parents. As a result, their children are less likely to see themselves as able to influence authority or to participate successfully in politics.

As with other attitudes, the development of confidence in one's own ability to influence government is related to social class and intelligence among children, just as it is related to social class and education in adults. Some other aspects of the view of the citizen's role that children develop in the later elementary years might conceivably hinder their effectiveness or willingness to participate in the real world of politics later. The role of the individual in influencing government is stressed; the role of organized group activity in politics is downgraded. In the same way, American children develop a low tolerance for conflict, believing, for example, that it hurts the country when the political parties disagree.

In the past, the youngest voters were typically the most trusting of government, a tendency one would expect, given their recent exposure to an educational process that tries to build support for the system. In the 1950s and early 1960s, when most of the major socialization studies were undertaken, young people entered adulthood with strong affective feeling toward the government and a positive orientation toward themselves as participants in it.

A study of high school seniors and their parents, carried out in 1965 by M. Kent Jennings, showed that trust and confidence in government were fairly high among the students.[28] As learning continues into adulthood, substantial modification of attitudes can occur through a variety of personal experiences with politics, new group membership, and the like. When the students in the Jennings study were interviewed again in 1973, their level of trust had declined markedly and was accompanied by an increase in cynicism.[29] These changes were considerably greater than the changes in their parents' attitudes over the eight years, although the young people were still somewhat more supportive than their parents. A third interview of these individuals in 1982 showed an additional drop in trust.

The 1972 National Election Study showed that the young people in the sample were the least trusting of government of any age group, a stark reversal of findings in earlier years when young people were generally the most trusting. It is possible that when dramatic changes occur, as they did in the late 1960s and early 1970s, they are felt most intensely among those groups with the least firmly established attitudes. These patterns have fluctuated over the years, but since the 1970s young people have not been consistently more or less trusting than older people.

Maintaining a Democracy

Belief in democratic ideals is essential to the preservation of a democratic system, both because such beliefs inhibit citizens from undemocratic actions and because the public will demand proper behavior on the part of political leaders. Belief that the system and its leaders meet democratic expectations in adhering to democratic procedures and responding to the wishes of the public is also important. A third factor is perhaps less obvious. A democratic system must also meet some standard for effectiveness in solving societal problems. If not, the public may conclude that democracy does not work, that some other form of government—like a dictatorship—is needed to maintain order, fend off an enemy, or provide economic well-being.

When expectations are not met in the behavior of political leaders or in the experiences individuals have in the political process, disappointment, cynicism, or hostility may result. Americans come to hold rather high expectations for the political system and, as a consequence, are subject to considerable disenchantment with the performance of government and their own role in politics. Although no direct evidence on this point is available, nothing has been found to suggest that the value Americans place on the ideals of democracy, majority rule, or the importance of participation in politics has declined. Rather, events over the past thirty years have led to a larger perceived discrepancy between the specific American political institutions (and their incumbents) and the ideal.

These ideals, combined with the generally high expectations Americans hold for the political system, can lead to cynicism and mistrust of political leadership when scandals occur or policies appear not to work. But there is another form of disenchantment that operates at the individual level. The American ethos and the content of the political culture lead individuals to expect a wide range of conditions and values. They expect to enjoy freedom, justice, and equality; they expect to enjoy personal economic success; and they expect to be safe from violence.

If individuals find that what is happening to them is far different from these expectations, they may react with resentment. Many individuals, to be sure, respond to adversity in personal terms and do not view their problems from a collective or political perspective. Others, however, may engage in disruptive political activities. In a society such as the United States, the people who suffer economic hardship or are victims of social injustice are often times minorities that are isolated by race, ethnicity, sexual orientation, or some other identifiable characteristic. Under these circumstances such a group may develop a set of subcultural values that is quite different from the values of the dominant culture. The group may passively withdraw from political activity or it may become actively disruptive of the system. The bombing of the federal building in Oklahoma City in 1995 and the 1992 rioting in Los Angeles in the wake of the Rodney King verdict illustrate that a disruptive, antisystem sentiment can emerge. The rioting in Seattle at the World Trade Organization meetings in 2000 may represent a new capacity to mobilize large numbers of people with quite different agendas. In any case, the Internet has created an unprecedented opportunity for communication and mobilization of individuals who would not have been so well connected in the past.

Public opinion polls indicate considerable variation in Americans' assessment of their society. One general question that has been used for many years asks whether the country is going in the "right direction" or has gotten on the "wrong track." For most of the last three decades, the public has been more dissatisfied than satisfied with the way the country is going. In December 2000, 49 percent of the public said the country was going in the "right direction" and 41 percent said the country was on the "wrong track," a relatively positive assessment by historical standards.[30] At the same time, when asked to agree or disagree with the statement, "Whatever its faults, the United States still has the best system of government in the world," 89 percent agreed—and most of those agreed strongly.[31]

Given the lack of sophistication in the public's understanding of democratic values and procedures, along with the declining levels of trust in government and its leaders, there is some uneasiness about public support for American democracy—and perhaps for any democratic regime. It is possible to view the United States as a democratic system that has survived without a strong democratic political culture because governmental policies have gained continual, widespread acceptance. If that satisfaction erodes, however, the public has no deep commitment to democratic values and processes that will inhibit support of antidemocratic leaders or disruptive activities.

Democratic theory implies that the public should demand values and procedures embodying democratic principles. There is the hope or expectation that the public in a democratic society will insist on certain values and processes. Certainly, a mass public demanding democratic values and procedures would provide strong support for a democratic regime. It may be, however, that a democratic system can survive with much lower levels of support, given other conditions.

In our view, a distinction should be made between the factors necessary for establishing a democracy and those contributing to maintaining one. The example of contemporary Russia, to mention only one case, suggests that stronger public support probably is required for the successful launching of a democracy than it is for maintaining an already established democracy. Possibly, preserving a regime simply requires that no substantial proportion of the society be actively hostile to the regime and engage in disruptive activities. In other words, absence of disruptive acts, not the presence of supportive attitudes, is crucial.

On the other hand, leaders' positive support for a political system is essential to its existence. If some leaders are willing to oppose the system, it is crucial that there be no substantial number of followers to which such leaders can appeal. The followers' attitudes, as opposed to their willingness to act themselves, may provide a base of support for antisystem behavior by leaders. In this sense, unanimous public support for democratic principles would be a firmer basis for a democratic system.

The high levels of dissatisfaction, accompanied by a lack of strong commitment to democratic values in the American public, appear to create some potential for public support of undemocratic leaders. As we shall see in subsequent chapters, many Americans feel an attachment to one or the other of the established political parties, an attachment that inhibits their embracing new political leaders. The parties and the public's attachment to them are often seen as preventing political change; they can also be seen as encouraging stability and preserving a democratic system by lessening the likelihood of a demagogue's rise to power.

Notes

1. U.S. Commission on Civil Rights, "Voting Irregularities in Florida during the 2000 Presidential Election." See especially chap. 5, "The Reality of List Maintenance." Located at www.usccr.gov/vote2000/stdraft1/main.htm.
2. In party primary elections voting in both primaries invalidates up to one third of the ballots.
3. Gallup Poll, April 20–22, 2001. Roper Center, accession number 0381385.
4. For a major effort to capture this fundamental aspect of political culture, see Herbert McClosky and John Zaller, *The American Ethos* (Cambridge: Harvard University Press, 1984).
5. 2000 National Election Study.
6. Ibid.
7. For the major study of the 1950s, see Samuel Stouffer, *Communism, Conformity and Civil Liberties* (Garden City, N.Y.: Doubleday, 1955); for a more recent work, see C. Z. Nunn, H. J. Crockett, and J. A. Williams, *Tolerance for Nonconformity* (San Francisco: Jossey-Bass, 1978).
8. John L. Sullivan, James Piereson, and George E. Marcus, *Political Tolerance and American Democracy* (Chicago: University of Chicago Press, 1982), and George E. Marcus, John L. Sullivan, Elizabeth Theiss-Morse, and Sandra L. Wood, *With Malice toward Some* (Cambridge: Cambridge University Press, 1995).
9. Stouffer, *Communism, Conformity and Civil Liberties;* and Herbert McClosky, "Consensus and Ideology in American Politics," *Public Opinion* 58 (June 1964): 361–382.
10. Jeane Kirkpatrick, *The New Presidential Elite* (New York: Russell Sage Foundation and the Twentieth Century Fund, 1976).
11. These data are recomputed from Kirkpatrick, *The New Presidential Elite,* Table 10.3, 302.
12. Most recently, in April 2000 the Freedom Forum found 25 percent agreed that "people should be allowed to burn or deface the American flag as a political statement" and 74 percent disagreed. The public is rather evenly divided on amending the Constitution to prohibit desecration of the flag. Roper Center, accession numbers 0367822 and 0367832.
13. *The Public Perspective* 3 (May/June 1992): 7–9; Center for Political Studies National Election Studies, 1991, 1992.

14. Gabriel Almond and Sidney Verba, *The Civic Culture* (Princeton: Princeton University Press, 1963). These patterns have been evident in cross-national public opinion polls since Almond and Verba first recorded them in 1963.
15. "Opinion Roundup," *Roundup Opinion* (July 1979): 35.
16. Ibid.
17. Data taken from the 2000 General Social Survey. Data provided by the Inter-university Consortium for Political and Social Research.
18. John Hibbing and Elizabeth Theiss-Morse, *Congress as Public Enemy* (Cambridge: Cambridge University Press, 1995), chap. 3.
19. Stephen Barr, "Trust in Government Surges During Crisis," *Washington Post,* September 30, 2001.
20. Robert D. Putnam, *Making Democracy Work: Civic Traditions in Modern Italy* (Princeton: Princeton University Press, 1993).
21. Robert D. Putnam, "Bowling Alone: America's Declining Social Capital," *Journal of Democracy* 6 (January 1995): 65–78.
22. Sidney Verba, Kay Lehman Scholzman, and Henry E. Brady, *Voice and Equality: Civic Voluntarism in American Politics* (Cambridge: Harvard University Press, 1995), 509.
23. Ibid., chap. 17.
24. The results of this study have been reported in several articles and in Robert D. Hess and Judith V. Torney, *The Development of Political Attitudes in Children* (New York: Anchor Books, 1968); and David Easton and Jack Dennis, *Children in the Political System: Origins of Political Legitimacy* (New York: McGraw-Hill, 1969).
25. David Easton and Jack Dennis, "The Child's Image of Government," in *Socialization to Politics: A Reader,* ed. Jack Dennis (New York: Wiley, 1973), 67.
26. Hess and Torney, *The Development of Political Attitudes in Children,* 186.
27. Almond and Verba, *The Civic Culture.*
28. The findings of this study are most extensively reported in M. Kent Jennings and Richard G. Niemi, *The Political Character of Adolescence: The Influence of Families and Schools* (Princeton: Princeton University Press, 1974); and *Generations and Politics* (Princeton: Princeton University Press, 1981).
29. These observations are based on data provided with an instructional workbook by Paul A. Beck, Jere W. Bruner, and L. Douglas Dobson, *Political Socialization: Inheritance and Durability and Parental Political Views* (Washington, D.C.: American Political Science Association/Inter-university Consortium for Political and Social Research, 1974).
30. ABC News/*Washington Post* Poll, December 14–15, 2000. Roper Center, accession number 0375835.
31. Ibid., accession number 0375554.

Suggested Readings

Almond, Gabriel, and Sidney Verba. *The Civic Culture.* Princeton: Princeton University Press, 1963. A classic study of political culture in five nations, including the United States.
Hibbing, John R., and Elizabeth Theiss-Morse. *Congress as Public Enemy.* Cambridge: Cambridge University Press, 1995. An analysis of the public's attitudes toward American political institutions.
Marcus, George E., John L. Sullivan, Elizabeth Theiss-Morse, and Sandra L. Wood. *With Malice toward Some.* Cambridge: Cambridge University Press, 1995. An innovative study of the public's tolerance of unpopular groups.

McClosky, Herbert, and John Zaller. *The American Ethos.* Cambridge: Harvard University Press, 1984. An analysis of the public's attitudes toward democracy and capitalism.

Putnam, Robert. *Bowling Alone: The Collapse and Revival of American Community.* New York: Simon & Schuster, 2000. An analysis of the decline of participation in civic affairs.

Rosenstone, Steven J., and John Mark Hansen. *Mobilization, Participation and Democracy in America.* New York: Macmillan, 1993. An analysis of the interaction between the strategic choices of political elites and the choices of citizens to participate in politics.

Skocpol, Theda, and Morris P. Fiorina, eds. *Civic Engagement in American Democracy.* Washington, D.C.: Brookings Institution, 1999. A collection of readings on civic engagement in historical perspective.

Verba, Sidney, Kay L. Schlozman, and Henry E. Brady. *Voice and Equality: Civic Voluntarism in American Politics.* Cambridge: Cambridge University Press, 1995. A survey of various forms of political participation, their determinants, and the impact on representative democracy.

Internet Resources

The Web site of the National Election Studies, www.umich.edu/~nes/, offers extensive data on topics covered in this chapter. Click on "Support for the Political System." Some of the attitudinal data cover 1952 to the present. For all items there is additional information on numerous social groupings in each election year.

If you have access to LEXIS-NEXIS through your school, click on "Academic Universe," then "Reference," and then "Polls and Surveys." This will give you access to the Roper Center for Public Opinion Research, which has a keyword search capability. Hundreds, perhaps thousands, of items related to political culture can be found there from surveys taken in the 1930s to the present.

c h a p t e r   t w o

Suffrage and Turnout

In 2000, A LITTLE MORE THAN 50 percent of the eligible electorate voted in the presidential election, one of the lowest percentages in seventy years. This continued a four-decade decline in voter turnout from a high of more than 60 percent in 1960. Only the brief jump to 55 percent in the three-candidate contest in 1992 was a significant departure from this downward trend.

The decline in the voting turnout rate since 1960 has occasioned a great deal of commentary and more than a little concern about the future of American democracy. The decline in turnout is paradoxical, because it has occurred at a time when the legal impediments to voting have been eliminated or eased and the education levels of American citizens are reaching all-time highs. Despite greater opportunities to vote, Americans seem to be doing so less frequently. A favorite theme of editorial writers has focused on the declining turnout rate as a symbol of the growing disenchantment of voters with the political system.

In this chapter we will put this recent trend in voter turnout into a broader historical context. We will look at the factors that make some individuals more likely to vote than others and examine how changes in the political environment can affect whether people vote. In doing so we will come to some conclusions about what the decline in turnout, and its brief reversal in 1992, does and does not mean about the current state of the democratic process.

Extensions of Suffrage

Suffrage, or the *franchise,* means the right to vote. Originally, the U.S. Constitution gave the determination of who should have the right to vote entirely to the states. Later, various amendments were added to the Constitution that restricted the states' abilities to deny the right to vote on the basis of such characteristics as race, gender, or age. However, the basic constitutional provision that gives states the right to set the qualifications for voting remains, and over the years states have used such things as the ownership of property, literacy, or length of residency as criteria for granting or withholding the right to vote.

During the colonial period and the early years of the Republic, suffrage was commonly restricted to white males possessing varying amounts of property; in effect, only a small proportion of the adult population was eligible to vote. The severity of the impact of property requirements varied from state to state, and their enforcement varied perhaps even more. Gradually, the required amount of property held or the amount of taxes paid to obtain suffrage was reduced. Sometimes these changes were hard-won reforms enacted by state legislatures or by state constitutional changes; at other times practical considerations led to substantial reforms. For example, delays in acquiring final title to land holdings in the western frontier areas during the 1800s made it impractical to establish property requirements for suffrage. Often during the very early years of American history, candidates in local elections would simply agree among themselves that all white males could vote rather than try to impose complicated restrictions on the electorate. Only in more settled communities could complex restrictions on suffrage be effectively enforced. In sections of the East, however, wealthy landlords sometimes supported the enfranchisement of their poorer tenants with the expectation of controlling their votes.[1]

After the eventual granting of suffrage to all white males, the next major change was the enfranchisement of black males by constitutional amendment following the Civil War. Even though this change was part of a set of issues so divisive that it had led to war, the numerical impact of adding black males was actually rather slight in the nation as a whole. However, unlike other changes in suffrage, this one had a geographical bias: The impact of enfranchising black males was felt almost entirely in the South. (Their subsequent disfranchisement in the South will be discussed later.) The next major constitutional extension of voting rights was suffrage for women in 1920. This created by far the most dramatic increase in the number of eligible voters, roughly doubling the size of the potential electorate. In the early 1970s, through a combination of federal statutory law and state laws followed by constitutional amendment, the definition of citizenship for purposes of voting was lowered to age eighteen, accomplishing another major extension of suffrage.

These extensions of suffrage, which have not been easy or inevitable, may be explained by the existence of certain political forces. In stable political systems such as the United States, the extension of suffrage will result from (1) a widely shared commitment to moral principles that entail further grants of suffrage, and (2) the expectation among political leaders that the newly franchised will support the political preferences of the leaders.

As discussed in Chapter 1, the political culture and political rhetoric of America carries strong themes of individualism and equality. These values are reinforced in the educational system, in the media, and throughout popular culture. As a result, the commitment most Americans have to equality, individualism, and democracy has provided a basis for supporting extensions of voting rights.

But more than idealism contributed to the expansion of the electorate. In the two most dramatic extensions of suffrage, to blacks and to women, political leaders obviously expected the newly enfranchised to support certain policies. Republicans—the party of abolition—anticipated that black voters in the South after the Civil War would help to secure Republican domination of the southern states, and perhaps most southern states passed through a period during which at least some chance existed of combining the votes of blacks and poor whites into a governing majority. The intense prejudice of whites and the difficulty in maintaining the enfranchisement of blacks kept this strategy from working under most circumstances, but a significant element in Republican enthusiasm for black suffrage was the knowledge that Republican voters were being added to the rolls.

The same mixture of idealism and self-interest that was behind the efforts to enfranchise blacks appears to have supported suffrage for women as well. Women were expected to clean up politics once they had the vote; they were seen optimistically as the cure for corruption in government, as unwavering opponents of alcohol, and as champions of virtue in the electorate. Reformers of all sorts encouraged the enfranchisement of women as a means of promoting their own goals.

No doubt similar factors were at work in the most recent extension of suffrage to eighteen- to twenty-year-olds, but perhaps more important was the widespread feeling that a system drafting young people to fight in the unpopular Vietnam War ought to extend to them the right to participate in the electoral process.

A unique aspect of the extension of suffrage in the United States was the addition of states in the frontier expansion across the continent. During the decades immediately preceding the Civil War, the politics of slavery dominated political decisions about additions of states, with accompanying expectations about the policy impact of expansion. Here, too, the question of the expansion of the electorate was dominated largely by concern over the political persuasion of the newly enfranchised voters.

Because throughout American history different state and local election practices have existed, no single set of eligibility requirements can be used as a basis for deciding exactly who belonged to the electorate at any one time. For example, individual states had granted suffrage to blacks, women, and young voters, either in law or in practice, before these groups' nationwide enfranchisement. In some states, women had previously been allowed to vote in local and school elections but not in statewide or federal contests. Thus, there were many different eligible electorates with different characteristics.

Restrictions on Suffrage

Under the provisions of the U.S. Constitution, the states set the qualifications for voters; the three extensions of suffrage by constitutional amendment did not alter this but rather prohibited the states from using certain criteria (race, gender, or age) to deny the right to vote. Because states retained the right to impose other restrictions, they have at times used these restrictions to prevent whole classes of people from voting. The most notorious of these efforts was the effective disfranchisement of blacks in the southern states during the late nineteenth and early twentieth centuries.

Several techniques for disfranchising blacks have been used during the past century in the South, and from time to time some of these techniques were applied in the North on a more limited basis to restrict the electoral participation of immigrants. The most common methods included white primaries, the poll tax, literary tests, discriminatory administrative procedures, and intimidation. In some southern states only whites were allowed to vote in party primaries (the crucial election in one-party states), under the rationale that primaries to nominate candidates were internal functions of a private organization. The Supreme Court ruled such white primaries unconstitutional in 1944 on the grounds that the selection of candidates for election is a public function in which discrimination on the basis of race is prohibited. The now illegal poll tax, whereby each individual was charged a flat fee as a prerequisite for registration to vote, was used for years and no doubt disfranchised both poor blacks and poor whites. In some states the effect was cumulative, because poll taxes had to be paid for all previous years in which the individual had not voted. The poll tax eventually became unpopular with the white voters who had to pay it whereas the blacks, disfranchised by other means, did not. The literacy test gave local officials a device that could be administered in a selective way to permit registration of whites and practically prohibit the registration of blacks. The "standards of literacy" applied to blacks in some cases—for example, reading and interpreting the state constitution to the satisfaction of the white registrar—made it impossible for even highly educated blacks to register, whereas whites might only be required to know how to sign their names. To remain effective over long periods of time, these and other similar administrative devices probably depended on intimidation or the use of violence against blacks. Detailed analysis by Jerrold Rusk and John Stucker of the impact of the poll tax and literacy tests from 1876 to 1916 suggests that the poll tax was the more effective device, and its efficacy was greatest where the tax rate was highest and its application most cumulative.[2]

A study of black registration in 1958 by Donald Matthews and James Prothro indicated that southern states using poll taxes and literacy tests still inhibited black voter registration after World War II.[3] The poll tax has since been outlawed by amendment to the U.S. Constitution, and the use of federal voting registrars in the South under the terms of the Voting Rights Act of 1965 has eliminated the worst excesses in the application of literacy tests. Registration rates in the South for whites and blacks were approximately equal by 1980, and turnout rates have concurrently increased to the point that there is now little difference in turnout between the North and South in presidential voting.

The outlawing of the poll tax through constitutional amendment and the suspension of literacy tests by the Voting Rights Act of 1965 and its extensions have eliminated two important restrictions on the right to vote. Other state restrictions on suffrage remain, although there is great variation from state to state. In all but four states, prison inmates cannot vote. In many states, convicted felons cannot vote until they have served their entire sentence—in other words, completed probation or parole; in some, a felony conviction entails a permanent forfeiture of voting rights. With the prison population growing, this amounts to a sizable restriction of the franchise. Because of longer sentences and higher rates of incarceration among blacks, this restriction falls more heavily on the black population. A recent study by The Sentencing Project estimates that 15 percent of black males are disfranchised under these requirements.[4]

Residency requirements are another common restriction on suffrage. In the past such requirements were often highly restrictive; some states mandated up to two years of residence in the state before one was eligible to vote. Highly mobile segments of the population were thus often disfranchised intermittently as each move required a reestablishment of residence. In the 1970s the Middle Atlantic states, with their mobile populations and traditionally rigorous residency requirements, had as high a rate of unregistered citizens as did the states of the former Confederacy with their legacy of racial discrimination.

In 1972 the Supreme Court linked the imposition of a residency requirement to the length of time needed to prepare lists of registered voters before an election, suggesting that thirty days was sufficient to do this. Since then the Court has allowed state laws requiring fifty days to stand.

By the early 1990s the legal barriers to voting had been reduced, for the most part, to the requirement that voters be registered to vote in advance of an election. The inconvenience of administrative arrangements for voter registration and the frequent need to reregister have offered greater obstacles to voting than has the imposition of other eligibility standards. Some states have moved toward "same-day" registration in an effort to remove impediments to voting and increase electoral turnout.

Nevertheless, as was discussed in Chapter 1, the aftermath of the 2000 presidential election in Florida revealed an impressive array of means whereby voters were denied the right to vote. After its investigation following the election in Florida, the U.S. Commission on Civil Rights wrote that its "findings make one thing clear: widespread voter disenfranchisement—not the dead-heat contest—was the extraordinary feature in the Florida election."[5] It is clear from the Florida example that there are at least as many forces trying to use suppression of turnout for partisan advantage as there are efforts to increase turnout.

Turnout in American Elections Historically

One of the most persistent complaints about the American electoral system in the twentieth century is its failure to achieve the high rates of voter turnout found in other countries and common in this country in the nineteenth century. Voter turnout in the United States was close to 80 percent before 1900 (see Figure 2-1); modern democracies around the world frequently record similarly high levels. Turnout in the United States during the twentieth century, in contrast, has exceeded 60 percent only in presidential elections, and in recent years the figure has been closer to 50 percent.

These unfavorable comparisons are somewhat misleading. The *voting turnout rate* is the percentage of the eligible population that actually votes in a particular election. This is ideally calculated as the number of votes cast divided by the total number of eligible adult citizens. The definition of *eligible adult* takes into account the historical changes in eligibility occasioned by the extension of suffrage to blacks, women, and eighteen-year-olds, but it does not take into account state restrictions on eligibility, such as residency requirements. As we have seen, these restrictions may be substantial. Thus, some of those included in the eligible population are not really able to vote; the turnout rate, when calculated in this manner, appears lower than it actually is. And in some states, blacks, women, and eighteen-year-olds were given the right to vote before suffrage was extended to them by amendment to the U.S.

FIGURE 2-1   Estimated Turnout of Eligible Voters in Presidential Elections
in the South, Non-South, and the Nation, 1860–2000

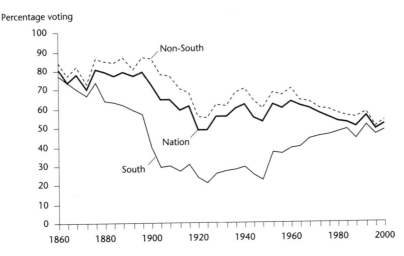

Sources: Robert Lane, *Political Life* (New York: Free Press, 1965), 20; Walter Dean Burnham, "The Changing Shape of the American Political Universe," *American Political Science
Review* 59 (March 1965): 11, Figure 1; U.S. Bureau of the Census, *Historical Statistics of
the United States, Colonial Times to 1970,* bicentennial ed. (Washington, D.C.: U.S. Government Printing Office, 1975), 1078–1080; U.S. Bureau of the Census, *Statistical Abstract of
the United States, 1996,* 116th ed. (Washington, D.C.: U.S. Government Printing Office,
1996), 287; Office of the Clerk, U.S. House of Representatives, clerkweb.house.gov;
www.census.gov.

Constitution; not including them in the denominator makes the turnout rate in earlier years appear higher than it actually was.

Even today in the United States, the calculation of the voting turnout rate is difficult. We do not know the total number of ballots cast
throughout the country; we only know the total vote for particular races.
For example, we do not include the people who went to the polls but
skipped the presidential race. Nor can we count the numbers who inadvertently invalidated their ballots. Even worse, we have no official count
of citizens, because the census no longer asks about citizenship. Thus,
all noncitizens are counted as if they were eligible to vote. An analysis by
Ruy Teixeira suggests an underestimate of turnout of about 4 percent
in 1988.[6]

Nevertheless, from Figure 2-1 it is apparent that some dramatic
changes have occurred historically in the rate of voter turnout. Each
major extension of suffrage—in 1868, 1920, and 1971—was marked by
a drop in the proportion of the electorate voting. Perhaps this is not surprising, because the newly eligible voters might be expected to take
some time to acquire the habit of exercising their right to vote. It should

also be noted that the drop in the turnout rate occasioned by the extension of suffrage was, in each case, the continuation of a downward trend.

During the nineteenth century, national turnout appears to have been extremely high—always more than 70 percent. The decline in national turnout from shortly before 1900 to 1916 is in part attributable to the restriction of black voting in the South. This decline in voting in the South also resulted from the increasing one-party domination of the region. In many southern states the "real" election was the Democratic primary, with the Republicans offering only token opposition, or none at all, in the general election. Turnout was often extremely low in the general election—far lower than can be accounted for simply by the disfranchisement of blacks.

Explaining the voting record shown in Figure 2-1 for the northern states presents a more difficult problem. There was a substantial decline in turnout in the first two decades of the twentieth century, and turnout has never returned to its previous levels. The disfranchisement of blacks and whites in the South cannot account for northern nonvoting.

There are two quite different explanations for the decline in voting in the North that commenced in the late 1890s. A persuasive set of arguments has been made by E. E. Schattschneider and Walter Dean Burnham in their individual studies of this period.[7] They contend that a high level of party loyalty and political involvement during the last quarter of the nineteenth century caused high turnout and great partisan stability. Then, during the 1890s, electoral patterns shifted in such a way that the South became safely Democratic, and most of the rest of the nation came under the domination of the Republican Party. Schattschneider's analysis emphasizes the extent to which this alignment enabled conservatives in both regions to dominate American politics for many years. According to this line of argument, one consequence of declining competition and greater conservatism throughout the electoral system was a loss of interest in politics accompanied by lower turnout and less partisan loyalty in the early twentieth century. Burnham emphasizes the disintegration of party voting with more ticket-splitting and lower turnout in off-year elections.

Some elements of this account are undeniably accurate. Electoral patterns did change somewhat around the turn of the century, with many regions of the nation changing from competitive to one-party areas. Throughout areas previously characterized by high turnout, straight-ticket voting, and stable voting patterns, turnout and partisan stability suffered greater fluctuations.

An alternative set of arguments gives these patterns a different interpretation.[8] The high rate of turnout in the nineteenth century may not have resulted from political involvement by an interested, well-informed electorate; on the contrary, it may have been possible only because of low levels of information and interest. During the last half of the nineteenth century, a largely uninformed electorate was aroused to vote by means of extreme and emotional political appeals. Presumably, in the absence of more general awareness of the political situation, these alarmist arguments produced firm commitments to vote. By and large, the parties manipulated the electorate—a manipulation possible because the electorate was not well informed.

Furthermore, proponents of this argument allege that the party organizations "delivered" or "voted" substantial numbers of voters during this period, by party loyalists casting multiple votes, "voting tombstones," or buying votes. Thus the remarkable stability of party voting may be a testimony to the corruption of the party organizations. The decline of stable party voting in the early twentieth century coincides with various attacks on political corruption and party machines. The resultant weakening of party machines and increased honesty in electoral activities could have reduced turnout. In fact, the apparent hostility of the electorate to the parties throughout this period seems inconsistent with strong party loyalty. A study by Jerrold Rusk shows dramatic changes in voting patterns associated with electoral reform laws, especially the introduction of the Australian ballot.[9] Before the introduction of electoral reforms, voting was often not secret; distinctively colored ballots prepared by the political parties and limited to one party were distributed to voters, marked, and openly placed in the ballot box. The Australian ballot provided for secret voting and an official ballot with all candidates' names appearing on it.

Another of the reforms instituted during the early twentieth century to combat corruption was the imposition of a system of voter registration. Besides limiting the opportunity for fraudulent voting, registration requirements created an additional barrier to the act of voting that had the effect of causing the least motivated potential voters to drop out of the electorate. Many states introduced permanent or semipermanent forms of registration that only involved a one-time effort by the voter; however, in others, like New York, where annual registration was required in many cities, the barrier to voting could be formidable.

After reaching an all-time low in the early 1920s, turnout in national elections increased steadily until 1940. There was a substantial drop in turnout during World War II and immediately thereafter, and since 1960 there has been a gradual decline. Great differences in turnout among the states are concealed within these national data. Rates of voting in the South, as shown in Figure 2-1, were consistently low until recently when they nearly converge with northern turnout. Regional differences in turnout in presidential voting have almost disappeared; state variation within regions, however, is still considerable.

High- and Low-Stimulus Elections

Elections vary in the amount of interest and attention they generate in the electorate. As can be seen in Figure 2-2, presidential elections draw higher turnout, whereas off-year congressional elections are characterized by lower levels of turnout. Even in a presidential election year, fewer people vote in congressional elections than vote for president. The most dramatic decline in turnout is the 10 to 20 percent drop in voting experienced in off-year elections. Primaries and local elections elicit still lower turnout. Some of these differences can be accounted for by the lower visibility of these latter elections; when less information about an election is available to the voter, a lower level of interest is produced.

A number of elements would seem to influence the amount of interest in an election. The differences in level of interest from presidential elections to congressional elections to local elections can be viewed as a result of five factors:

1. Differences in media coverage given the election,
2. Significance attached by voters to the office,
3. Importance of issues raised in the campaign,
4. Attractiveness of the candidates,
5. Competitiveness of the contest.

Variation in these factors leads to what Angus Campbell called *high-stimulus* and *low-stimulus elections*.[10]

Newspapers and television give far more coverage to the activities and speeches of presidential candidates than to those of congressional candidates. Even the most indifferent citizen comes to possess impressions and some information about presidential candidates and their campaigns. Such bombardment through the mass media awakens the relatively uninterested and often provides them with some reason to vote. This is not nearly so likely to happen in other election campaigns, where only the motivated citizens will become informed and concerned to any degree. Even so, a week or so after the election, a substantial proportion of the voters will not recall the name of the congressional candidate for whom they voted.

The factors of media coverage, the significance of the office, and the importance of the issues do a better job of explaining the differences in the levels of turnout in presidential elections versus other kinds of elections than they do among presidential elections themselves. None of these factors can account for the decline in turnout in presidential voting over the past four decades. Media coverage and campaigning through the media have increased; there is no evidence that the significance attached to the presidency has declined; and critical issues have

FIGURE 2-2   Turnout of Eligible Voters in Presidential and Congressional
Elections, 1868–2000

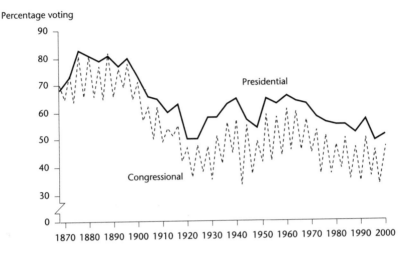

Sources: Historical Data Archive, Inter-university Consortium for Political and Social Research; U.S. Bureau of the Census, *Historical Statistics of the United States, 1973,* 94th ed. (Washington, D.C.: U.S. Government Printing Office, 1973), 379; U.S. Bureau of the Census, *Statistical Abstract of the United States, 1996,* 116th ed. (Washington, D.C.: U.S. Government Printing Office, 1996), 287; Office of the Clerk, U.S. House of Representatives, clerkweb.house.gov; www.census.gov.

been intensely debated, such as civil rights and the Vietnam War in 1968, the Vietnam War again in 1972, and the Iranian hostage crisis and inflation in 1980. Yet a steady erosion in turnout occurred throughout these years.

The lack of attractiveness of the presidential candidates has often been cited as a possible explanation, contrasting the enormously popular Dwight D. Eisenhower in 1952 and 1956 with the "lesser of two evils" contests of later years. In 1988 George Bush and Michael Dukakis illustrated the point as two candidates who were viewed by many as relatively unattractive ran in an election with the lowest turnout in three decades. Similarly, the 1996 contest between incumbent Bill Clinton and Bob Dole also offered relatively unattractive candidates, especially Dole, and turnout hit another record low. In 2000 the major-party candidates were viewed slightly more positively than in recent presidential elections, and turnout increased by a small amount. On the other hand, the 1992 election challenged this conventional wisdom. None of the three major contenders, George Bush, Bill Clinton, or Ross Perot, was viewed as especially attractive by the public, yet turnout was at its highest level in some years. In the case of 1992, the availability of a third alternative may well have brought to the polls some voters who were disenchanted with the major parties and their candidates.

Another factor often thought to raise the level of turnout in an election, perhaps by increasing the level of interest, is the degree of competition between the parties. Presumably, the closer and more uncertain the outcome, the more people will see their vote as potentially decisive. Undeniably, the virtual absence of party competition in the South during the period of black disfranchisement was associated with extremely low levels of turnout, even among white voters. Both turnout and competition in the South have increased since blacks joined the electorate.

However, the elections of 1968, 1976, 1980, and 1988 suggest that the expectation of a close race does not invariably lead to heightened turnout, whereas the 1984 election that reelected the popular Ronald Reagan shows that the expectation of a landslide does not necessarily depress turnout. On the other hand, the expectation that Clinton would easily win in 1996 is widely interpreted as having depressed turnout in that election. The 2000 election was the closest in many years and certainly too close to call beforehand. The closeness of the race surely contributed as much to turnout as the appeal of the candidates.

Another aspect of competitiveness probably has more relationship to the level of turnout. The decision to allow a race to remain uncontested or to offer only a "sacrificial lamb" can dramatically reduce turnout. In contrast, a hotly contested race with strenuous activity by party organizations is likely to get more voters to the polls on election day, even though the final outcome may not be particularly close.

Voters and Nonvoters

All but a small proportion of the eligible electorate vote at least occasionally, but individuals vary in the regularity with which they cast their ballots. Certainly, individual interest in politics is one factor creating such differences. In the previous section, the level of interest in a campaign was treated as a characteristic of the political environment, generated by the importance of the office at stake, the amount of media coverage, and so on. But interest and involvement in politics are also characteristics of individuals, and individuals vary substantially in the attention they pay to politics, their involvement in politics, and the amount of information about candidates and issues they acquire. As one would expect, the probability of voting increases at each level of expressed interest and involvement in political campaigns. This relationship is illustrated in Figure 2-3: The highly interested, involved, and informed citizens (a combination of characteristics highly valued in the

FIGURE 2-3   Relationship between Electoral Participation and Interest, Involvement, and Information

		Low	High
Level of interest, involvement, and information	High	Alienation or intimidation	Model citizenship
	Low	Apathy	Manipulation

Likelihood of voting

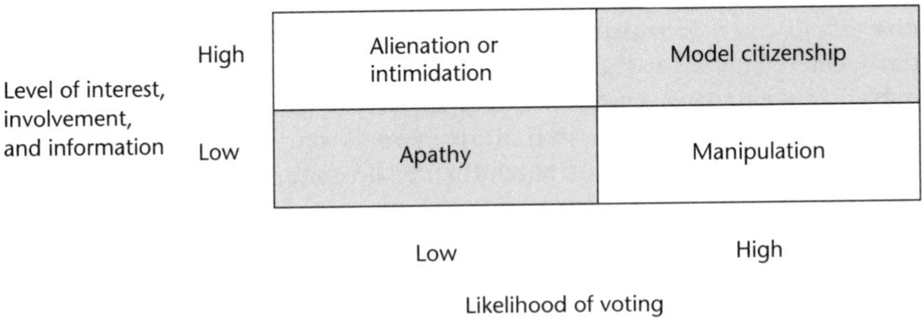

belief system of a democratic society) turn out to cast their ballots on election day, whereas the apathetic, uninvolved, and ill-informed stay at home.

Two deviant cases that run contrary to the expected pattern can also be seen in Figure 2-3. The first deviant condition, *alienation,* describes voters characterized by high interest and low turnout. The situation may be one of voluntary alienation in which individuals withdraw from political participation purposefully. Their high level of interest and information implies some reason for their withdrawal; they are dissatisfied with, or offended by, the political system. *Nonvoluntary alienation* refers to situations in which interested potential voters are prevented from participating, perhaps through intimidation. Both situations are dangerous to the political system because highly interested and informed citizens who do not participate have the potential for extremely disruptive activities. Alienation in this form is thought to be uncommon in American politics. In the United States, the interested and informed are consistently the most likely to participate even though they are somewhat more cynical about the political system. Furthermore, a study focusing primarily on the causes of nonvoting in the 1976 election found voters and nonvoters to be quite similar in their levels of alienation and cynicism toward politics; for only 6 percent of the nonvoters was rejection of politics the main explanation of their nonvoting.[11] Studies have consistently shown no relationship between cynicism or alienation and nonvoting in elections.

The second deviant case, *manipulation,* describes voters characterized by low interest and high turnout. It refers to a situation in which individuals with little information or interest become involved in voting. Presumably, this manipulation is achieved by getting individuals to vote either through coercion or by highly stimulating and arousing appeals. Coercive methods for ensuring turnout may range from police-state orders to fines for failure to vote. More common in the American political system are exceptionally moving or alarming appeals, bringing to the polls people so unsophisticated that they are easily swayed. Very high levels of turnout can be inspired by emotional, inflammatory appeals; indeed, this is one possible explanation for the high turnout levels in the United States for many years after the Civil War. Campaigns were marked by extreme appeals, and, because education levels were low, it is reasonable to suspect that there were lower levels of interest, involvement, and information than during the campaigns of the twentieth century.

Even though interest in politics is strongly correlated with voting, about half of those who say they have "not much" interest do in fact vote in presidential elections, suggesting that still other factors are also at work. One of these is a sense of civic duty—the attitude that a good citizen has an obligation to vote, that it is important to vote, regardless of the expected impact on the outcome. Because such feelings are usually a prime focus of the political socialization carried on in the American educational system, turnout is the highest among those with the longest exposure to this system. Length of education is one of the best predictors of an individual's likelihood of voting.

Because education is so closely associated with relative affluence and social status, people who vote are usually slightly better off in socioeconomic terms than the population as a whole. This bias is likely to increase in low-stimulus elections as greater numbers of occasional voters drop out of the electorate, leaving the field to the better educated and more affluent who rarely miss an election. In analyzing voting in presidential primaries, Barbara Norrander found voters in the 1988 Super Tuesday primaries to be older, better educated, and wealthier than their counterparts who did not vote. However, the common assumption that this leads to drastic political differences between primary voters and the general electorate is unfounded. In studying the 1980 presidential primaries, she discovered no substantial ideological or issue differences between primary voters and general election voters.[12]

Another important factor contributing to nonvoting is age; a relatively large proportion of young people pass up their first opportunities to vote. This situation has been magnified in presidential elections since 1972. The extension of the franchise to eighteen-year-olds enlarged the pool of eligible voters, yet since then turnout has gradually declined to its lowest point since 1948. Figure 2-4, based on survey data from the 2000 presidential election, shows that the likelihood of voting increases from young adulthood through middle age.* In most presidential years,

---

*The reported vote obtained in surveys, including surveys by the Bureau of the Census, is consistently higher than that of official statistics. Validation studies suggest

FIGURE 2-4   Percentage of the Electorate Reporting Having Voted in the
2000 Presidential Election by Age

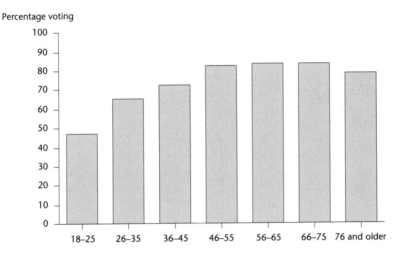

Source: 2000 National Election Study. Data provided by the Inter-university Consortium for Political and Social Research.

including 2000, there is a slight decline in turnout among the most elderly portion of the population.

The tendency of young people not to vote is partially offset by their generally higher levels of education. Although the turnout of middle-aged people is higher at each educational level than that of young adults, the gap narrows among the better educated (see Figure 2-5).

Much of the nonvoting among young people may be attributed to the unsettled circumstances of this age group rather than to simple disinterest in politics, although young people are slightly less interested than older people of similar educational levels. Military service, being away at college, geographic mobility with the possible failure to meet residence requirements, and the additional hurdle of initial registration all create barriers to voting for young citizens that are less likely to affect older ones. Efforts to promote voter registration have affected the young, with about two thirds of the youngest members of the electorate having registered to vote. But registering is not the same as turning

---

that more than 10 percent of the respondents claim to have voted when they did not. Bias in survey samples—that is, interviewing disproportionate numbers of voters—is also a factor contributing to the difference. See U.S. Bureau of the Census, "Current Population Reports," Series P-23, No. 168, *Studies in the Measurement of Voter Turnout* (Washington, D.C.: U.S. Government Printing Office, 1990).

FIGURE 2-5   Turnout in the 2000 Presidential Election by Age and
Education

Percentage voting

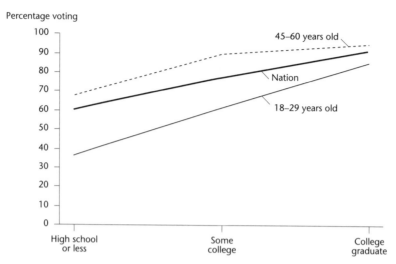

Source: 2000 National Election Study. Data provided by the Inter-university Consortium for Political and Social Research.

out to vote. On election day in November 2000, three times as many young people who were registered failed to vote as older people who were registered.

By age thirty-five, most people have joined the voting population at least on an occasional basis. A small proportion of the middle-aged and older group remains outside the voting public. These habitual nonvoters, who have passed up several opportunities to vote, are less than 5 percent of the total electorate, according to current survey research estimates.**

This group has been steadily decreasing in size, and the social forces that brought about this decrease will likely reduce it still further. In the past, this group of habitual nonvoters was disproportionately southern, black, and female. Restrictions against black suffrage, coupled with a traditional culture that worked against active participation of women in civic life, meant that as recently as 1952 in the South large proportions of blacks of both genders, as well as white women, had never voted in a presidential election. The percentages of respondents

---

**This "best estimate" of individuals outside the political system is unquestionably low. First, a disproportionately large number of people outside the political system would not even be included in the population of households from which the sample is drawn. Second, many of those in the sample who were never contacted or who refused to be interviewed would probably be classified as outside the political system.

in surveys from 1952 to 1980 who reported never having voted are shown in Figure 2-6. It is clear that dramatic changes took place in southern voting patterns during this time. By the late twentieth century, turnout patterns were quite similar in the North and South.

FIGURE 2-6   Percentage of Adults Who Have Never Voted by Race and Gender for the South and Non-South, 1952–1980

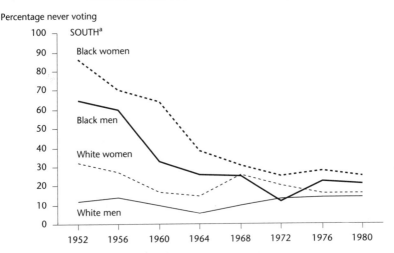

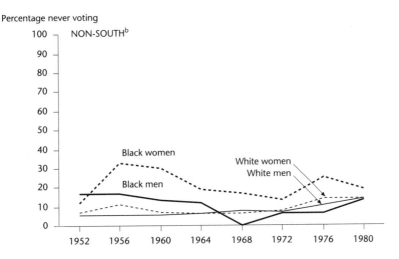

Sources: National Election Studies. Data provided by the Inter-university Consortium for Political and Social Research.

[a]The states included in the South are Alabama, Arkansas, Florida, Georgia, Kentucky, Louisiana, Maryland, Mississippi, North Carolina, Oklahoma, South Carolina, Tennessee, Texas, Virginia, and West Virginia.

[b]The states included in the non-South are the remainder.

Registration as a Barrier to Voting

We have observed that registration requirements are the last major legal impediment to voting. Registration poses barriers to voting in several ways. In most parts of the country, an unregistered citizen must go to the courthouse several weeks before the election, during working hours, and fill out a form. This is not a horrendous burden, but it does take time and some ability to deal with a governmental bureaucracy. Regulations also typically cancel the registration of people who fail to vote in a few consecutive elections. In addition, residential mobility annually relocates millions of citizens in new precincts in which they must reregister. All of these circumstances raise the costs of political involvement, costs that a significant number of citizens will choose not to assume. Furthermore, voter registration is not always purely an electoral matter: An unknown number of Americans prefer to remain off registration lists to avoid jury duty or bill collectors or a former spouse.

Not surprisingly, individuals with little or no interest in politics lack the motivation to overcome registration barriers on their own. Voter registration drives, in which volunteers go door to door or register voters at shopping malls and on college campuses, capture many politically uninvolved people. A certain proportion of these people will not have the interest or incentive to bear the additional costs of getting to the polls on election day. In 2000, the Federal Election Commission reported registration close to an all-time high of 73 percent of the eligible electorate. One out of three of these registered voters failed to vote in the presidential election.[13]

Table 2-1 illustrates differences between unregistered citizens, registered nonvoters, and registered voters in terms of their level of interest in the election campaign and their partisanship. The registered nonvoters are in between the two larger groups and are somewhat more similar to the unregistered than to the registered voters. When it comes to personal characteristics such as social class and education, registered nonvoters are also similar to the unregistered. In 2000, a clear partisan impact can be seen in the failure of large numbers of potential voters to vote. Whereas Democrats outnumber Republicans among all three categories, the difference is considerably greater among the nonvoters, both registered and unregistered. Clearly, the Democrats have potentially more to gain from mobilizing nonvoters.

In recent years, various plans have been introduced to reduce the difficulty in registration as a way to boost voter turnout. Some state governments have implemented "same day registration," whereby individuals can register at the polls on election day. Most notably, in 1993 Congress passed, and President Clinton signed into law, the "motor voter" bill, which provides that registration forms will be available at a variety

TABLE 2-1   Interest and Partisanship of Registered Voters and Nonvoters
            and Unregistered Citizens, 2000

		Registered	
	Unregistered	Nonvoters	Voters
Very much interested	7%	8%	32%
Somewhat interested	38	43	53
Not interested at all	54	49	15
Total	99%	100%	100%
Strong Democrat	10%	11%	23%
Weak Democrat	14	22	16
Independent Democrat	16	35	13
Independent	21	14	8
Independent Republican	18	8	14
Weak Republican	10	7	11
Strong Republican	5	1	14
Other, Don't know, Apolitical	8	1	1
Total	102%	99%	100%
(*N*)	(155)	(97)	(582)

Source: 2000 National Election Study. Data provided by the Inter-university Consortium for Political and Social Research.

of governmental agencies that citizens visit for other purposes. These include agencies where motor vehicles are registered and driver's licenses are obtained, though because of a Republican-sponsored amendment, states are not required to provide them at unemployment and welfare offices. The purpose of the bill is clearly to make it easier for all citizens to exercise their right to vote, but Democratic support and Republican concerns point to a potential side-effect. Because the unregistered tend to be poorer and less well educated, Democrats, who traditionally represent such groups, hope (and Republicans fear) that reducing registration obstacles will increase the number of Democratic voters. As in the historical extensions of the suffrage, this effort to facilitate voter registration mixes philosophical concerns with political motivations.

Registration requirements are one reason why the United States has significantly lower turnout rates than other western democracies, where governments take responsibility for maintaining registration lists rather than placing the burden of registration on the individual.[14] Reducing registration requirements is a logical and fairly easy means to increase the turnout rate, but we should not expect it to have an astounding effect. The best estimate of the impact of reducing registration barriers suggests it will increase turnout about 8 percentage points.[15] Although this is obviously significant, the resulting turnout rate would still be substantially below that of other industrialized nations. Similarly, the Federal Election Commission estimates that the 1993 motor-voter law resulted in an increase of less than 2 percent in registration in 1996 over 1992.[16] In part, the impact was so small because many states had already implemented aspects of the law so their practices and procedures did not change. During 1995 and 1996, almost one third of all registrations were by mail and one third came through some form of motor-voter program. Public assistance offices were the source of a little more than 6 percent of the registrations, even though not all states provided registration forms in these offices.

Despite Republican fears that easing registration requirements would bring more Democrats to the polls, the main impact of making it easier to register seems to have been a decline in the proportion of the officially registered who actually vote. Failure to register prohibits voting, but registering does not ensure turnout. More of those only casually interested in politics and government register—because it is so easy. But when election day arrives, it takes the same amount of energy to get to the polling place as it always did.

The minimal impact of lessening registration requirements has led some states to experiment with easing the act of voting itself—by mailing ballots to registered voters and allowing them to vote by mail. A study of Oregon's experience with mail-in voting in its special Senate election in 1996 suggested that turnout was higher than usual for a special election. Those who voted by mail were much like traditional voters, although younger, busier people were more likely to take advantage of the vote-by-mail opportunity.[17]

Politically unmotivated individuals may still find it not worth the effort to go to the polls to cast a ballot even though it is easy enough to get registered and to vote. Clearly, the overall decline in turnout during the past four decades, even as education levels increased and registration restrictions were relaxed, calls for further explanation.

Recent Changes in Turnout

How can we account for the overall decline in turnout over the past four decades? As we have seen, legal restrictions on voting have eased and education levels have increased; these circumstances should be expected to increase turnout, yet they have apparently been more than offset by other factors. One explanation has focused on the expansion of the electorate in 1971 to include eighteen-year-olds. Because young people are less likely to vote than older people, their inclusion in the electorate would be expected to decrease turnout, other things being equal. Apparently, however, this can account for only a small portion of the decline.

Another possibility, raised by political commentators in 1972, 1980, and 1984, is that "calling the election" early in the evening, before the polls have closed in all states, especially western states, reduces turnout. Once potential voters learn that a television network has declared a winner in the race for president, the argument goes, they will no longer be interested in voting for president or any other office. On the other hand, the 1976 and 2000 elections were so close that the winner was not known until long after the polls had closed in all fifty states, and there was no appreciable impact on turnout. Public concern about calling the election too early, together with congressional threats of regulation, led the networks to restrict their reporting voluntarily in 1988 and thereafter. However, if public opinion polls before the election all point to a clear winner, as they did in 1996, the impact on turnout may be the same. Persuasive as the idea is, the evidence on this matter is inconclusive, and no one has clearly demonstrated that these factors have influenced turnout in a significant way.[18]

A somewhat more sweeping form of this argument—and one harder to test—suggests that the style of media coverage of campaigns has turned elections into a "spectator sport" that voters watch with varying degrees of interest but feel no need to engage in. The prediction of the winners in polls, the focus in presidential debates on who "won" rather than on substance, the attention to the "horse race" aspects of the primary campaigns, and the networks' race to call the election first are all alleged factors in this withdrawal of the voter from active participation.

In a major study of nonvoting, Ruy Teixeira establishes two general explanations for the decline in turnout since 1960.[19] First, he cites a set of circumstances that he calls *social connectedness*—that is, the extent to which individuals are socially integrated into their community. This is similar to Putnam's idea of *social capital,* which was discussed in Chapter 1. Older people, married people, those who attend church and are settled in the community are more socially connected than young, single, mobile people who do not belong to community organizations. Over the past few decades, the proportion of socially unconnected people has increased; Teixeira estimates that about one third of the decline in turnout is associated with this decline in social connectedness.

The second factor is the extent of "political connectedness"—that is, the degree to which people feel interested and involved in government and believe government is concerned and responsive to them. The decline in political connectedness over the past three decades is manifested in a loss of trust in government, a lower sense of political efficacy, a decline in interest in politics, and a diminished sense of civic duty, many of the same trends noted in Chapter 1. These changing attitudes toward government and politics account for more than half of the decline in turnout, according to Teixeira's estimates.

It appears that the sharp bounce in turnout in 1992 was a temporary deviation from the downward trend. Still, it is worthwhile to look at the possible reasons for it. There is little doubt that the presence of Perot in the 1992 presidential race contributed to the higher turnout. An atypically high level of turnout emerged among those voters most attracted to Perot's candidacy: the young, the nonpartisan, and those disenchanted with government and political leadership. These groups, in fact, are the socially and politically disconnected whose increased numbers, Teixeira argues, have been responsible for the recent declines in turnout. Perhaps Perot's candidacy gave these voters an alternative that allowed them to connect with the political world, at least temporarily. By 1996, Perot looked less like the outsider who could fix the system and he drew fewer of the unconnected into the electorate.

Beyond this, the 1992 campaigns of Perot, Clinton, and to a lesser degree George Bush Sr., used new means for reaching the voters. Talk show appearances, Perot's infomercials, town meetings, and MTV's Rock the Vote initiative were all efforts to establish connections with the public in the age of cable television. In subsequent elections, this trend has continued, with candidates making multiple appearances on the talk shows hosted by Jay Leno, David Letterman, and Oprah Winfrey. Presidential candidates clearly differ in how well they come across in these venues, but none can now avoid them. In a book on electoral participation, Rosenstone and Hansen[20] make the point that the opposite side of the coin to participation is *mobilization*. If candidates and parties fail to mobilize potential voters—or fail to find appropriate means to reach them—then it is not surprising that people do not vote. The declining turnout rate may be a failure of party elites rather than a "fault" of citizens.

Throughout this discussion of turnout, we have implied the need for an explanation of nonvoting; we have assumed voting is "normal" or to be expected. However, this topic could be approached quite differently. The question could be asked, "Why do people bother to vote?" as if nonvoting were the natural pattern or expected behavior and voting required explanation. The answer that one vote can determine the outcome of an election and that most people vote anticipating that their vote may be crucial is not reasonable, even after an extremely close election such as in 2000. One vote rarely decides an election, although many races are close, and no v ter should expect to cast the deciding vote in an election. There is, however, another sense in which "votes count" in an election, and that is as an expression of preference for a candidate or for a party, regardless of whether that candidate ultimately wins or loses.

Elections are more than simply a mechanism for selecting public officials; they are also a means for communicating, albeit somewhat dimly, a set of attitudes to the government. For most Americans, voting remains the only means of influence regularly used. Many see it as the only avenue open to ordinary citizens to make the government listen to their needs. The desire to be counted on one side of the fence or the other and the feeling that one ought to be so counted are perhaps the greatest spurs to voting. If this is true, then perhaps the most disturbing lesson that comes from examining electoral procedures in Florida in 2000 was the realization that your vote may not even get counted—let alone make a difference.

Notes

1. Chilton Williamson, *American Suffrage from Property to Democracy: 1760–1860* (Princeton: Princeton University Press, 1960), especially 131–181.
2. Jerrold D. Rusk and John J. Stucker, "The Effect of the Southern System of Election Laws on Voting Participation," in *The History of American Electoral Behavior*, ed. Joel Silbey, Allan Bogue, and William Flanigan (Princeton: Princeton University Press, 1978). For a treatment of these and many additional topics, see also J. Morgan Kousser, *The Shaping of Southern Politics* (New Haven: Yale University Press, 1974).
3. Donald R. Matthews and James W. Prothro, "Political Factors and Negro Voter Registration in the South," *American Political Science Review* 57 (June 1963): 355–367.
4. *Minneapolis Star Tribune*, January 30, 1997, 12.
5. U.S. Commission on Civil Rights, "Executive Summary" of "Voting Irregularities in Florida during the 2000 Presidential Election," at www.usccr.gov/vote2000/stdraft1/exsum.htm.
6. Ruy A. Teixeira, *The Disappearing American Voter* (Washington, D.C.: Brookings Institution, 1992), 10.
7. E. E. Schattschneider, *The Semisovereign People* (New York: Holt, Rinehart and Winston, 1960), especially chap. 5; and Walter Dean Burnham, "The Changing Shape of the American Political Universe," *American Political Science Review* 59 (March 1965): 7–28.
8. The most general statement of this argument is found in Philip E. Converse, "Change in the American Electorate," in *The Human Meaning of Social Change*, ed. Angus Campbell and Philip E. Converse (New York: Russell Sage Foundation, 1972), 263–337. For an analysis that alters the estimates of turnout, see Ray M. Shortridge, "Estimating Voter Participation," in *Analyzing Electoral History*, ed. Jerome M. Clubb, William H. Flanigan, and Nancy H. Zingale (Beverly Hills: Sage Publications, 1981), 137–152.
9. Jerrold D. Rusk, "The Effect of the Australian Ballot Reform on Split Ticket Voting: 1876–1908," *American Political Science Review* 64 (December 1970): 1220–1238.
10. Angus Campbell, Philip E. Converse, Warren E. Miller, and Donald E. Stokes, eds., *Elections and the Political Order* (New York: Wiley, 1966), 40–62.
11. Arthur T. Hadley, *The Empty Polling Booth* (Englewood Cliffs, N.J.: Prentice-Hall, 1978), 20, 41.

12. Barbara Norrander, *Super Tuesday: Regional Politics and Presidential Primaries* (Lexington: University of Kentucky Press, 1992); Norrander, "Ideological Representativeness of Presidential Primaries," *American Journal of Political Science* 33 (August 1989): 570–587.

13. "Executive Summary of the Federal Election Commission's Report to the Congress on the Impact of the National Voter Registration Act of 1993 on the Administration of Federal Elections," June 1997, at www.fec.gov/votregis/ (taken on September 18, 1997).

14. G. Bingham Powell Jr., "American Voter Turnout in Comparative Perspective," *American Political Science Review* 80 (March 1986): 17–44.

15. Teixeira, *The Disappearing American Voter*, chap. 4.

16. "Executive Summary of the Federal Election Commission's Report to the Congress on the Impact of the National Voter Registration Act of 1993 on the Administration of Federal Elections."

17. Priscilla Southwell and Justin Burchett, "The Effect of Vote-by-Mail on Turnout: The Special Senate Election in the State of Oregon" (Paper presented at the annual meeting of the American Political Science Association, San Francisco, 1996).

18. See Laurily K. Epstein and Gerald Strom, "Election Night Projections and West Coast Turnout," *American Politics Quarterly* 9 (October 1981): 479–491; and Raymond Wolfinger and Peter Linquiti, "Tuning In and Turning Out," *Public Opinion* (February–March 1981): 56–60.

19. Teixeira, *The Disappearing American Voter*.

20. Steven J. Rosenstone and John Mark Hansen, *Mobilization, Participation, and Democracy in America* (New York: Macmillan, 1993.)

Suggested Readings

Conway, M. Margaret. *Political Participation in the United States,* 3d ed. Washington, D.C.: CQ Press, 2000. A good introduction to the study of turnout and other forms of political participation.

Powell, G. Bingham, Jr. "American Voter Turnout in Comparative Perspective." *American Political Science Review* 80 (March 1986): 17–44. A careful analysis of the institutional and attitudinal factors that depress American turnout rates compared with those of other industrialized democracies.

Rosenstone, Steven J., and John Mark Hansen. *Mobilization, Participation and Democracy in America.* New York: Macmillan, 1993. An analysis of the interaction between the strategic choices of political elites and the choices of citizens to participate in politics.

Rusk, Jerrold D., and John J. Stucker. "The Effect of the Southern System of Election Laws on Voting Participation." In *The History of American Electoral Behavior,* edited by Joel Silbey, Allan Bogue, and William Flanigan. Princeton: Princeton University Press, 1978. A sophisticated analysis of the disfranchisement of voters in the South in the nineteenth century.

Teixeira, Ruy A. *The Disappearing American Voter.* Washington, D.C.: Brookings Institution, 1992. A sophisticated and thorough analysis of the factors that have contributed to the decline in turnout in the United States and a discussion of the impact of proposed reforms.

U.S. Bureau of the Census. *Voting and Registration in the Election of November 1992.* Series P-20, No. 466. Washington, D.C.: U.S. Government Printing Office, April

1993. A report of findings on turnout and registration based on a huge survey that allows complex analysis of many subgroups within the U.S. population.

Internet Resources

The Web site of the National Election Studies, www.umich.edu/~nes/, offers data on turnout in both presidential and off-year elections since 1952. Click on "Political Involvement and Participation in Politics." It is also possible to examine turnout in numerous social groups from 1952 to the present.

Recent turnout and registration data for the nation and the states are available at the Federal Election Commission Web site, www.fec.gov.

More information is available at the Census Bureau Web site, www.census.gov. Click on "V" under the subject headings and then find "Voting."

c h a p t e r   t h r e e

Partisanship

THE DIVISION OF POWER between the political parties in the
United States could hardly be closer. The Republicans have a narrow
majority in the House of Representatives. The Senate was evenly divided
at the start of the new Congress in January 2001, first with outgoing Vice
President Al Gore and then new Vice President Dick Cheney holding
the tie-breaking vote. Within a few months, Republican senator James
Jeffords of Vermont declared himself an independent who would vote
with the Democrats for organizational purposes. Control of the Senate
switched to the Democrats. George W. Bush won the presidency in the
electoral college by a four-vote margin while losing the popular vote by
less than one half of 1 percent. (This was the closest vote in the electoral
college since 1876, an even more bizarre election than 2000.)

These circumstances reflect *partisanship*—the sense of attachment
or belonging that an individual feels for a political party. In this and the
next two chapters we will explore the concept of partisanship and its implications for political behavior. In this chapter we will discuss the meaning of partisanship and how the partisanship of Americans has changed
over the course of the country's political history. In Chapter 4 we will examine the impact of partisanship on the way people act politically and
how partisanship changes over the lifetime of the individual and between generations. In Chapter 5 we will consider the social characteristics of partisans and independents.

Party Loyalty

For more than one hundred years the U.S. electorate has supported
a two-party system in national politics. This remarkable stability is unknown in other democracies. Within this stable party system, however,

FIGURE 3-1   Partisan Division of the Presidential Vote in the Nation, 1824–2000

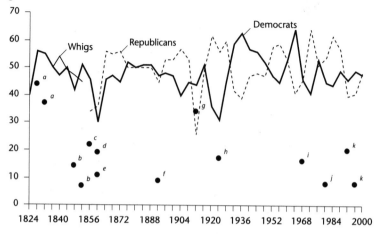

Sources: Historical Data Archive, Inter-university Consortium for Political and Social Research; Office of the Clerk, U.S. House of Representatives, clerkweb.house.gov.

Note: In presenting these data, we have not drawn attention to the wide range of errors that may exist. There are errors in collecting and recording data, as well as errors in computation. The presidential election of 1960 provides an illustration of another form of uncertainty that enters into these data—choices made among alternative ways of presenting the data. It is customary to list the popular vote in such a way that Kennedy appears a narrow winner over Nixon in 1960. Actually, to reach this distribution of the total vote, it is necessary to exaggerate the Kennedy vote from Alabama, because on the slate of Democratic electors in Alabama there were uncommitted electors. Eventually six of the uncommitted electors voted for Harry Byrd; five electors voted for Kennedy. If the Kennedy popular vote in Alabama is reduced to a proportion, say 5/11 in this case, of the vote for Democratic electors and if only this reduced popular vote is added to his national total, Nixon, not Kennedy, has the larger popular vote total nationally in 1960. In percentages these are negligible changes, but symbolically such differences can become important. In these tables we have followed the usual practice of presenting the augmented Kennedy total.

Other parties gaining at least 5 percent of the vote: [a]National Republican; [b]Free Soil; [c]American; [d]Southern Democratic; [e]Constitutional Union; [f]People's; [g]Bull Moose; [h]Progressive; [i]American Independent; [j]Anderson Independent Candidacy; [k]Perot Independent Candidacy, Reform Party. Ralph Nader's 2.7 percent in 2000 falls below this minimum and is not shown.

voter support for Republicans and Democrats has fluctuated widely, and significant numbers of voters occasionally, as in 1992, abandon the traditional parties to support third-party or independent candidates. The aggregate vote totals for presidential elections, shown in Figure 3-1, reveal a wide range of party fortunes, even in elections close together in time. Some of the more dramatic fluctuations have involved the appearance of strong third-party candidates, such as Theodore Roosevelt in 1912, George Wallace in 1968, and Ross Perot in 1992 and, to a lesser degree, 1996. Perot's 1992 showing of 19 percent was the largest percentage won by a third-party candidate since 1912. Although Ralph Nader can accurately be seen as denying the presidency to Gore in 2000, his 2.7 percent of the popular vote was an unimpressive figure for a third-party candidate in recent years.

Despite these variations in election outcomes and despite the demonstrated capacity of American voters for highly selective and differentiated support for candidates offered them by the political parties, most voters have a basic and quite stable loyalty to one party or the other. This tendency of most individuals to be basically loyal to one political party makes the idea of partisanship, or *party identification* as it is often called, one of the most useful concepts for understanding the political behavior of individuals. After good survey data became available in the late 1940s, party identification assumed a central role in all voting behavior analysis.[1]

Party Identification

Party identification is a relatively uncomplicated measure determined by responses to the following questions:

- Generally speaking, do you usually think of yourself as a Republican, a Democrat, an independent, or what?

- (If R or D) Would you call yourself a strong (R), (D), or a not very strong (R), (D)?

- (If independent) Do you think of yourself as closer to the Republican Party or to the Democratic Party?

Leaving aside for the moment the people who do not or cannot respond to such questions, we have seven categories of participants in the electorate according to intensity of partisanship:

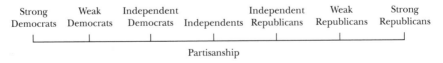

Because this self-identification measure of party loyalty is the best indicator of partisanship, political analysts commonly refer to *partisanship* and *party identification* interchangeably. Partisanship is the single most important influence on political opinions and voting behavior. Many other influences are at work on voters in U.S. society, and partisanship varies in its importance in different types of elections and in different time periods; nevertheless, no single factor compares in significance with partisanship.

Partisanship represents the feeling of sympathy for and loyalty to a political party that an individual acquires—sometimes during childhood—and holds through life, often with increasing intensity. This self-image as a Democrat or a Republican is useful to the individual in a special way. For example, individuals who think of themselves as Republicans or Democrats respond to political information partially by using party identification to orient themselves, reacting to new information in such a way that it fits in with the ideals and feelings they already have. A Republican who hears a Republican Party leader advocate a policy has a basis in party loyalty for supporting that policy, quite apart from other considerations. A Democrat may feel favorably inclined toward a candidate for office because that candidate bears the Democratic label. Partisanship orients individuals in their political environment, although it may also distort their picture of reality.

This underlying partisanship is also interesting to political analysts because it provides a base against which to measure deviations in particular elections. In other words, the individual voter's longstanding loyalty to one party means that, "other things being equal," or in the absence of disrupting forces, he or she can be expected to vote for that party. However, voters are responsive to a great variety of other influences that can either strengthen or weaken their tendency to vote for their usual party. Obvious variations occur from election to election in such factors as the attractiveness of the candidates, the impact of foreign and domestic policy issues, and purely local circumstances. These current factors, often called *short-term forces*, may move voters away from their usual party choices.

These ideas can also be used in understanding the behavior of the electorate as a whole. If we added up the political predispositions of all the individuals in the electorate, we would have an "expected vote" or "normal vote."[2] This is the electoral outcome we would expect if all voters voted their party identification. Departures from this expected vote in actual elections represent the impact of short-term forces, such as issues or candidates.

In assessing the partisanship of the American electorate historically, we will not be able to add up individual party identifications to find an expected vote. Survey data of this type have only been available for the past sixty years or so. For the period from 1824 to 1968, we base our estimates on the only available data—election returns for aggregate units.[3] These data cannot, of course, reveal voting patterns of individuals; but they do allow one to make assessments of party loyalty and temporary deviations from party by collections of voters. Even though the same set

FIGURE 3-2a   Democratic Expected Vote in Presidential Elections, 1840–1968

Percentage of the vote

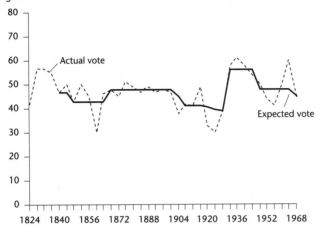

Source: Jerome M. Clubb, William H. Flanigan, and Nancy H. Zingale, *Partisan Realignment* (Beverly Hills: Sage Publications, 1980), 92–93, Table 3.1a.

FIGURE 3-2b   Republican Expected Vote in Presidential Elections, 1872–1968

Percentage of the vote

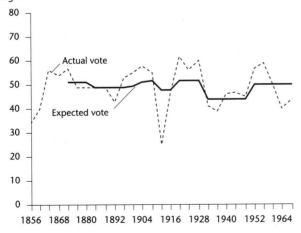

Source: Jerome M. Clubb, William H. Flanigan, and Nancy H. Zingale, *Partisan Realignment* (Beverly Hills: Sage Publications, 1980), 92–93, Table 3.1a.

of individuals does not turn out to vote in each election, we use the election returns over the years to indicate the collective partisanship of the electorate. From these data an estimate is made of the expected vote for the Democratic and Republican Parties. It is then possible to say, for example, that the electorate deviated from its normal voting pattern in favor of the Republican Party in 1904 or that the voters departed from their normal Democratic loyalty in 1952.

Our estimates of the expected vote nationwide in presidential voting for the Democratic Party from 1840 to 1968 and for the Republican Party from 1872 to 1968 are shown in Figures 3-2a and 3-2b. The actual vote in these elections is also shown to indicate the amount of departure from underlying partisan patterns that occurred in each election.

For the more recent period we can use something similar to the normal vote technique developed by Philip Converse that uses individual-level survey data to create an expectation about vote choice in the absence of short-term forces. This technique uses party identification and expected defection rates to generate an estimate of the normal vote. The Democratic and Republican normal votes, along with the actual vote for president, from 1968 to 2000 are shown in Figures 3-3a and 3-3b. (Because normal vote calculations depend on party identifications

FIGURE 3-3a   Democratic Normal Vote, 1968–2000

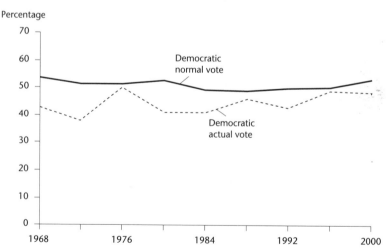

Source: Office of the Clerk, U.S. House of Representatives, clerkweb.house.gov.

Note: The normal vote calculations are a simplified version of Converse's original analysis. See Philip E. Converse, "The Concept of a Normal Vote," in *Elections and the Political Order,* ed. Angus Campbell, Philip E. Converse, Warren E. Miller, and Donald E. Stokes (New York: Wiley, 1966), 9–39.

FIGURE 3-3b   Republican Normal Vote, 1968–2000

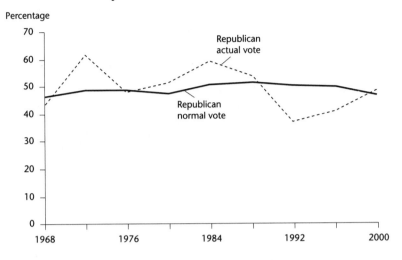

Source: Office of the Clerk, U.S. House of Representatives, clerkweb.house.gov.

Note: The normal vote calculations are a simplified version of Converse's original analysis. See Philip E. Converse, "The Concept of a Normal Vote," in *Elections and the Political Order,* ed. Angus Campbell, Philip E. Converse, Warren E. Miller, and Donald E. Stokes (New York: Wiley, 1966), 9–39.

and identifications with third parties are trivial, note that the Republican normal vote is a mirror image of the Democratic normal vote.) The deviation of the actual Democratic vote meanders under the Democratic normal vote line, meaning that Democratic presidential candidates since 1968 have rarely done as well as we would expect, given the distribution of party identification. In elections in which a third party candidate won a significant number of votes—1968, 1992, and 1996—both the Democratic and Republican candidates performed below what the normal votes would predict.

Types of Electoral Change

As we have said, the utility of the concept of the expected vote in part lies in providing a base against which to measure and analyze departures from the expected pattern. One type of departure is usually referred to as *deviating change:* the temporary deviations from normal party loyalty attributable to the short-term forces of candidate images or issues.[4] The amount of deviating change in an election tells how well a candidate or party did relative to the party's normal performance. In these terms, the Eisenhower victories or the Nixon landslide appear even more dramatic because they represent big Republican margins during a time when the Democratic Party held an advantage in party loyalists. These "deviating elections" involved substantial departures from the underlying strength of the two parties in the electorate.

These temporary deviating changes may be dramatic and reflect important electoral forces, but another type of change is of even greater interest. On rare occasions in American national politics, a permanent or *realigning change* in voting patterns occurs. In such instances the electorate departs from its expected voting pattern but does not return to the old pattern afterward. On occasion these changes are large enough to alter the competitive balance between the parties, with significant consequences for the policy directions of the government. Such a period of change is usually referred to as a *partisan realignment.*[5]

Electoral analysts usually discuss three major realignments in American history: One occurred during the time of the Civil War and the emergence of the Republican Party; another followed the depression of 1893 and benefited the Republicans; and the most recent followed the depression of 1929 and led to Democratic Party dominance. These abrupt changes in the expected votes of the parties can be seen in Figures 3-2a and 3-2b. Each realignment of partisan loyalties coincided with a major national crisis, leading to the supposition that a social or economic crisis is necessary to shake loose customary loyalties. But major crises and national traumas have not always led to disruptions of partisanship, suggesting that other political conditions must also be present for a crisis to produce a realignment. The nature of the realignment crisis has political significance, however, because it generally determines the lines along which the rearrangement in partisan loyalties will take place, as different segments of the electorate respond differently to the crisis and to attempts to solve it.

In general, realignments appear to happen in the following way. At a time of national crisis, the electorate rejects the party in power, giving a decisive victory to the other party, a victory that includes not only the presidency but also large majorities in both houses of Congress. Armed with this political mandate, the new party in office acts to meet the crisis, often with innovative policies that are sharp departures from the past. *If* the administration's policy initiatives are successful in solving the nation's problems (or at least if they are widely perceived as successful), then significant numbers of voters will become partisans of the new administration's party and continue voting for this party in subsequent elections, thus causing a lasting change in the division of partisan strength in the electorate. If, on the other hand, the administration in power is *not* perceived as successful in handling the crisis, then in all likelihood the voters will reject that party in the next election, and its landslide victory in the previous election will be regarded, in retrospect, as a deviating election.

In a realignment it is very likely that the people who actually become partisans of the new majority party are the independents and previously uninvolved members of the electorate, not partisans of the other party. In other words, in a realignment few Democrats or Republicans switch parties; it appears more likely that independents drop their independent stance and become partisan. Thus, for a realignment to occur, a precondition may be a pool of people without partisan attachments who are "available" for realignment. This, in turn, suggests that there may be a longer sequence of events that forms a realignment cycle.

First there is the crisis that, if successfully handled, leads to a realignment. This initiates a period of electoral stability during which the parties take distinct stands on the issues that were at the heart of the crisis. Party loyalty is high during this period, both within the electorate and among the elected political leaders in government. However, as time passes, new problems arise and new issues gradually disrupt the old alignment and lead to greater electoral instability. During this period, often referred to as a *dealignment,* voters are much more susceptible to the personal appeals of candidates, to local issues, and to other elements that might lead to departures from underlying party loyalty. As the time since the last realignment lengthens, more and more new voters come into the electorate without attachments to the symbols and issues of the past that made their elders party loyalists. This group of voters without strong attachments to either party may provide the basis for a new realignment should a crisis arise and one or the other of the parties be perceived as successfully solving it.

Party Systems and Realignments

Political historians often divide American electoral history into five *party systems*—eras that are distinguished from each other by the different political parties that existed or by the different competitive relationships among the parties.[6] The transition from one party system to another has usually been marked by a realignment.

The first party system, which extended from the 1790s until about 1824, saw the relatively rapid formation of two parties, the Federalists and the Jeffersonian Republicans. The issue that divided these parties most clearly was their attitude toward the power of the central government. The commercial and financial interests supported the Federalist position of increasing the authority of the central government, whereas Jeffersonian Republicans distrusted the centralizing and, in their view, aristocratic tendencies of their rivals. These parties began as factions within

Congress, but before long they had gained organizations at the state and local level and had substantially broadened the base of political participation among the voting population. After 1815, competition between the two parties all but ceased as the Jeffersonian Republicans gained supremacy, moving the country into the so-called Era of Good Feelings.

The second party system is usually dated from 1828, the year of the first presidential election with substantial popular participation, which marked the resurgence of party competition for the presidency. Emerging ultimately from this renewed competition were the Democrats and the Whigs, parties that competed almost evenly for national power until the 1850s. Mass political participation increased and party organizations were strengthened as both parties sought electoral support from the common people. Although the Democratic Party had come to prominence led by frontiersman Andrew Jackson, by the 1850s both Democrats and Whigs had adherents in all sections of the nation. Thus, when the issue of slavery broke full-force on the nation, the existing parties could not easily cope with the sectional differences they found within their ranks. As the Whigs and Democrats compromised or failed to act because of internal disagreements, a flurry of minor parties appeared to push the cause of abolition. One of these, the Republican Party, eventually replaced the floundering Whigs as one of the two major parties that would dominate party systems thereafter.

The intense conflicts that preceded the Civil War led to the basic regional alignment of Democratic dominance in the South and Republican strength in the North that emerged from the war and that characterized the third party system. But the extreme intensity and durability of these partisan loyalties were also significantly dependent on emotional attachments associated with the war. The strength of these partisan attachments after the Civil War was not lessened by the sharp competitiveness of the two parties throughout the system. Electoral forces were so evenly balanced that the Republican Party could effectively control the presidency and Congress only by excluding the southern Democrats from participation in elections. Once Reconstruction relaxed enough to permit the full expression of Democratic strength, the nation was narrowly divided, with the slightest deviation determining the outcome of elections.

The most dominant characteristic of the Civil War realignment was the regional division of party strongholds, but there was considerable Republican vote strength throughout much of the South and Democratic strength in most of the North. Especially in the North, states that regularly cast their electoral votes for Republican presidential candidates did so by very slim margins. Within each region persistent loyalty to the minority party was usually related to earlier opposition to the war. The intensity of feelings surrounding the war overwhelmed other issues, and the severity of the division over the war greatly inhibited the emergence of new issues along other lines. Thus, a significant feature of the Civil War realignment is its "freezing" of the party system.[7] Although later realignments have occurred and, indeed, a fourth and fifth party system can be identified, after the Civil War the same two parties have remained dominant. New parties have found it impossible to compete effectively (although they may affect electoral outcomes). The subsequent realignments only changed the competitive position of these two parties relative to each other. Thus, although the choices were frozen following the Civil War, the relative strength of the parties was not.

Toward the end of the nineteenth century, Civil War loyalties weakened enough to allow new parties, particularly the Populists in the Midwest and South, to make inroads into the votes of both major parties. Following the economic recession of 1893 for which the Democrats suffered politically, the Republican Party began to improve its basic voting strength. In 1896 the formation of a coalition of Democrats and Populists and the unsuccessful presidential candidacy of their nominee, William Jennings Bryan, resulted in increased Republican strength in the East and a further strengthening of the secure position of the Democratic Party in the South. Republican domination was solidified in the Midwest by the popularity of Theodore Roosevelt in the election of 1904. By the early twentieth century, competitive areas were confined to the border states and a few mountain states.

It is appropriate to view the realignment of 1896 and the fourth party system that followed as an adjustment of the Civil War alignment. Few areas shifted very far from the previous levels of voting; most individuals probably did not change their partisanship. The issue basis of this alignment was economic. The Republicans advocated development and modernization while opposing regulation of economic activity. The Democrats supported various policies intended to provide remedies for particular economic hardships. At a minimum these issues led the more prosperous, more modern areas in the North to shift toward the Republicans and the more backward, more depressed areas in the South to shift toward the Democrats. These tendencies are based on normal vote patterns and should not obscure the considerable variation in the vote for president during these years, particularly in the elections of 1912 and 1916.

Following the onset of the Great Depression of 1929 under a Republican president, Democrat Franklin D. Roosevelt rode the reaction to economic hardship to a landslide victory in 1932. In his first administration, Roosevelt launched a program of economic recovery and public assistance called the New Deal. The Democrats emerged as the majority party, signaling the start of the fifth party system. The New Deal realignment resulted in far greater shifts than the earlier realignment of

1896, because it shifted many of the northern states from Republican to Democratic status. This most recent realignment has more present-day interest than the others and is reflected most prominently in present voting patterns. Because the policies of the Democratic administration during the New Deal appealed more to the working class than to the middle class, more to poor farmers than to more prosperous farmers, these groups responded differently to Democratic candidates. The New Deal and the electorate's response to Roosevelt's administration considerably sharpened the social class basis of party support. Especially for younger voters during these years, class politics was of greater salience than it had been before or has been since.

This realignment resulted in adjustments in previous loyalties, but it did not override them completely. The New Deal coalition was based on regional strength in the South, which was independent of social class, and further reinforced an already overwhelming dominance there. Perhaps the most incompatible elements in the New Deal coalition were southern middle-class whites, mainly conservative, and northern liberals, both white and black. Although the New Deal era established the basic pattern of partisanship that has led to the present alignment, changes have occurred in several major components of this pattern of party loyalties. Most notably, southern whites have moved away from the Democratic Party, first in presidential contests and, increasingly, in voting for Con-

TABLE 3-1   Party Identification of the Electorate, 1947–2000

	1947	1952	1954	1956	1958	1960	1962	1964	1966	1968	1970	1972	1974
Democrats	46%	47%	47%	44%	47%	46%	47%	51%	45%	45%	44%	40%	38%
Independents	21	22	22	24	19	23	23	22	28	29	31	35	36
Republicans	27	27	27	29	29	27	27	24	25	24	24	23	22
Nothing; don't know	7	4	4	3	5	4	3	2	2	2	1	2	4
Total	101%	100%	100%	100%	100%	100%	100%	99%	100%	100%	100%	100%	100%
(N)	(1,287)	(1,799)	(1,139)	(1,762)	(1,269)	(1,954)	(1,317)	(1,571)	(1,291)	(1,557)	(1,507)	(2,705)	(2,523)

	1976	1978	1980	1982	1984	1986	1988	1990	1992	1994	1996	1998	2000
Democrats	39%	39%	41%	44%	36%	40%	35%	39%	35%	34%	38%	37%	36%
Independents	36	38	35	30	34	33	36	35	38	35	32	35	42
Republicans	23	21	22	24	28	26	28	24	25	31	29	26	20
Nothing; don't know	2	3	2	2	2	2	2	2	2	1	1	2	2
Total	100%	101%	100%	100%	100%	101%	101%	100%	100%	101%	100%	100%	100%
(N)	(2,872)	(2,283)	(1,614)	(1,418)	(1,989)	(2,166)	(2,040)	(2,000)	(2,485)	(1,795)	(1,714)	(1,281)	(977)

Sources: For 1947, National Opinion Research Center; for all other years, National Election Studies. Data provided by the Inter-university Consortium for Political and Social Research.

gress and in state and local elections. To a degree, working-class whites in the North also have been attracted to the Republican Party on occasion, and middle-class voters have sometimes shifted toward the Democrats.

Survey data on party identification over the past fifty years also yields evidence of the New Deal alignment, as well as its recent deterioration (see Table 3-1). During these years, the Democrats have held an advantage over the Republicans, ranging from a high of 2 to 1 in 1964 to a low of 4 to 3 since 1988. This means, among other things, that in the nation as a whole the Democratic Party has begun campaigns with more supporters than has the Republican Party. Broadly speaking, the Democrats have tried to hold on to their following during a campaign, whereas the Republicans have attempted to win over a following.

In the early years of this period, the advantage that the Democrats enjoyed nationwide was largely a result of having an overwhelming Democratic majority in the South, as shown in Table 3-2. Today, Democrats are about equally strong in the North and South, and the proportion of Republicans in the South has increased to about the same level as in the North. In both the South and the North, independents hold the balance of power between Democrats and Republicans.

An interesting change reflected in these data is the increase beginning in 1966 in the proportion of independents. Supporters of George Wallace in the South represented part of this increase initially, but an even larger portion is composed of young voters who are not choosing sides in politics as quickly as their elders did. This increase appears to have leveled off in the 1970s, and although the proportions have fluctuated, the number of independents remains near its highest point since the era of survey research began. The 42 percent independent in 2000 is the largest proportion of independents in the history of the National Election Study. This general loosening of party loyalties is widely suggested as the possible forerunner of a major realignment in partisanship, or, alternatively, as an indication that the public has lost its capacity for party loyalty.

The disintegration of the New Deal coalition occurred first in presidential voting. In 1964 the states of the Deep South were the only states carried by Republican candidate Barry Goldwater, a stark reversal of 100 years of history. This pattern continued in subsequent presidential elections; only when the Democratic candidate was a southerner (Jimmy Carter in 1976 and Bill Clinton in 1992 and 1996) did the Democrats have a chance to carry some southern states. In 2000, Gore, also a southerner, was given a chance of winning only two southern states, Florida and his home state of Tennessee. Ultimately, he won neither. (Of course, he was running against another southerner.)

The New Deal partisan realignment established in the 1930s remained intact longer in congressional voting. However, by the 1970s ad-

TABLE 3-2   Party Identification of the Electorate for the Nation, the Non-South, and the South, 1952–2000

The Nation

	1952	1956	1960	1964	1968	1972	1976	1980	1984	1988	1992	1996	2000
Strong Democrats	22%	21%	20%	27%	20%	15%	15%	18%	17%	17%	18%	19%	19%
Weak Democrats	25	23	24	25	25	26	25	23	20	18	17	20	17
Independents	22	23	22	22	29	35	36	34	34	36	38	32	42
Weak Republicans	14	14	14	13	14	13	14	14	15	14	14	16	10
Strong Republicans	13	15	15	11	10	10	9	8	13	14	11	13	10
Apolitical, other	4	4	5	2	2	2	2	2	2	2	2	1	2
Total	100%	100%	100%	100%	100%	101%	101%	99%	101%	101%	100%	101%	100%
(N)	(1,799)	(1,762)	(1,954)	(1,571)	(1,557)	(2,705)	(2,872)	(1,614)	(1,989)	(2,040)	(2,485)	(1,714)	(977)

The Non-South

	1952	1956	1960	1964	1968	1972	1976	1980	1984	1988	1992	1996	2000
Strong Democrats	18%	17%	18%	23%	17%	13%	12%	15%	15%	16%	16%	17%	18%
Weak Democrats	22	19	20	23	24	22	22	22	18	16	17	20	17
Independents	26	26	25	25	28	37	38	37	33	36	39	32	44
Weak Republicans	16	16	16	16	17	16	17	14	17	16	15	17	11
Strong Republicans	17	18	17	12	12	12	10	9	14	15	12	14	9
Apolitical, other	2	2	4	1	1	1	2	2	2	2	1	1	1
Total	101%	98%	100%	100%	99%	101%	101%	99%	99%	101%	100%	101%	100%
(N)	(1,290)	(1,249)	(1,293)	(1,087)	(1,076)	(1,799)	(1,623)	(1,050)	(1,352)	(1,322)	(1,650)	(1,123)	(642)

The South

	1952	1956	1960	1964	1968	1972	1976	1980	1984	1988	1992	1996	2000
Strong Democrats	31%	29%	23%	36%	26%	17%	19%	23%	19%	21%	21%	22%	21%
Weak Democrats	32	32	33	30	28	32	30	25	23	21	18	19	15
Independents	14	15	17	15	30	29	32	29	35	35	37	32	38
Weak Republicans	8	9	8	8	8	10	11	13	11	10	12	14	10
Strong Republicans	6	8	12	8	4	9	7	7	9	11	9	13	12
Apolitical, other	9	9	6	3	2	2	2	3	3	2	3	0	4
Total	100%	102%	99%	100%	98%	99%	101%	100%	100%	100%	100%	100%	100%
(N)	(509)	(513)	(661)	(484)	(481)	(906)	(780)	(564)	(596)	(718)	(835)	(591)	(335)

Sources: National Election Studies. Data provided by the Inter-university Consortium for Political and Social Research.

FIGURE 3-4   Democratic Vote for Congress, North and South, 1936–2000

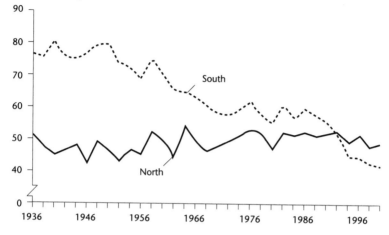

Sources: U.S. Bureau of the Census, *Statistical Abstract of the United States, 1993*, 113th ed. (Washington, D.C.: U.S. Government Printing Office, 1992); "Election '96," *Congressional Quarterly Weekly Report*, February 15, 1997, 444; Office of the Clerk, U.S. House of Representatives, clerkweb.house.gov.

ditional shifts in the New Deal alignment became evident, as conservative Republicans began to show strength in races for other offices in many parts of the South. Long-standing southern Democratic incumbents in Congress were safe from competition; however, as they stepped down, their seats have been won, more often than not, by Republicans. On the other hand, in some areas of the North moderate Republicans have been replaced by liberal Democrats, reflecting a weakness in long-established Republican support. These trends are shown in Figure 3-4, plotting the Democratic vote for Congress in the North and South since 1936. Obviously, Democratic strength in the South was crucial for the Democrats' control of the House of Representatives for much of this period.

We should be clear about what is changing and what is not. White southerners have always been conservative, especially on racial matters. From the Civil War until the 1960s, the Democratic Party was at least as conservative as the Republican Party on the crucial issue of race. When the national Republican Party took the more conservative position on race in 1964, white southerners began to vote for Republican presidential candidates. They continued to vote for southern conservative Democratic candidates in state and local races. Meanwhile, for the same reasons in reverse, newly enfranchised black southern voters were moving into the Democratic Party. Over the years, the positions of the two parties have become more clearly distinguished—the Democratic Party as the more liberal party on racial as well as economic issues, the Republican Party as the more conservative party. Particularly in the South, but also in the North, some voters have changed their partisanship and their votes accordingly. The congressional elections of 1994 were perhaps the culmination of this process; as the Republicans took control of the House of Representatives and Senate, their leadership was predominantly southern.

Has There Been a Realignment?

Some analysts have argued that the movement of white southerners into the Republican Party and the movement of blacks and some northern whites toward the Democratic Party constitutes a realignment and should be regarded as the start of a new party system. Disagreement arises about when this realignment occurred. Some date it from the 1960s, with the start of Republican dominance in presidential voting. Others view it as a "Reagan realignment" of the 1980s.

There is no question that there has been a lot of voter movement and electoral volatility since the 1960s. It is also true that much of this movement has been a sorting-out process whereby some voters are finding their natural home in a political party that shares their views on issues that concern them most. It is equally true, however, that over this same time period, a sizable number of voters have found neither political party a congenial place to be and have demonstrated this by becoming independent, or not adopting a party identification in the first place, or supporting an independent candidate such as Perot. Although major changes have taken place—like the turning out of the long-time Democratic majority in the House of Representatives—neither party has had control of all the branches of government for any significant period of time. As a consequence, if there are policy initiatives, neither party can claim exclusive credit for them nor assert its status as the new majority party. In these circumstances, we find it more useful to consider the current situation as a continuation of a period of *dealignment*.

The Future of the Two-Party System

Americans are far from enchanted with the two major political parties or with political parties in general. Only a little more than half of the

TABLE 3-3　Public Support for the Two-Party System, 1994–2000

	1994	1996	1998	2000
Continue two-party system of Democrats and Republicans	38%	42%	38%	39%
Candidates run without party labels	36	32	34	30
Need one or more parties that could challenge Democrats and Republicans	23	26	26	31
Don't know	3	1	2	*
Total	100%	101%	100%	100%
(*N*)	(1,796)	(1,517)	(1,281)	(838)

Sources: National Election Studies. Data provided by the Inter-university Consortium for Political and Social Research.

* Less than 0.5 percent.

public believes that political parties are necessary to make the political system work. Even fewer people believe that political parties care what ordinary people think.[8] To be sure, partisans have a more positive view of the party they identify with, but political parties in general are not respected.

As shown in Table 3-3, only a little more than one third of the public endorses the two-party system of competition between the Democratic and Republican Parties. Those who prefer an alternative to Republican–Democratic competition are about equally divided between those who want more parties and those who want less partisanship. In recent years there has usually been more support for nonpartisanship than for additional political parties.

Those people who like the idea of more political parties present a difficult problem for political leaders who aspire to form a third party. These potential followers are equally divided into liberals, moderates, and conservatives. Presumably about one third want a party more liberal than the Democrats, one third prefer a party more conservative than the Republicans, and perhaps one third prefer a party more moderate than the existing parties. To make matters worse, these potential third-party supporters are not particularly interested in politics or attentive to public affairs. Independent candidates with some appeal such as Perot or Jesse Ventura may attract new voters to the polls, but it is extremely difficult to convert that casual support into a political party organization. When the focus shifts from a celebrity candidate to building a party, the party activists may discover that their fledgling organization embraces a range of people whose only shared belief is a distaste for both the major parties.

Public financing of presidential candidacies of "official" parties—those that secured at least 5 percent of the nationwide popular vote in the last presidential election—creates a new and unanticipated wrinkle in the development of third parties. The official party organization becomes a "plum" to be taken over by one or another faction to gain access to public financing that can be used with few strings attached. Pat Buchanan's coup in gaining the nomination of the Reform Party netted him $12,600,000 for a presidential campaign that immediately disappeared from view. The failure of either the Buchanan or Nader campaigns to garner 5 percent of the vote nationwide eliminates the possibility of advance public financing of their organizations' campaigns in 2004, a serious disadvantage for any third-party alternative.

Historically, third parties have been the vehicle for voters' transfer of loyalties from one party to another, especially in periods of loosened party ties or dealignments. Despite the low level of enthusiasm for the Democratic and Republican Parties, the structural barriers to third parties, including the winner-take-all feature of the electoral college, the rules surrounding public financing, and limits on participation in presidential debates, make the emergence of a viable third party on the national scene unlikely. In the short-term, if a period of bipartisan unity occasioned by the current national crisis continues, the opportunities for a diverging political movement or a new political party will be lessened.

Notes

1. The most important work on party identification is in Angus Campbell, Philip E. Converse, Warren E. Miller, and Donald E. Stokes, *The American Voter* (New York: Wiley, 1960), 120–167. For a treatment of this subject in comparative perspective, see Ian Budge, Ivor Crewe, and Dennis Farlie, eds., *Party Identification and Beyond* (New York: Wiley, 1976), Part I.

2. For the most important statement of these ideas, see Philip E. Converse, "The Concept of a Normal Vote," in *Elections and the Political Order*, ed. Angus Campbell, Philip E. Converse, Warren E. Miller, and Donald E. Stokes (New York: Wiley, 1966), 9–39.

3. This discussion and data presentation are based on our earlier work in William H. Flanigan and Nancy H. Zingale, "The Measurement of Electoral Change," *Political Methodology* 1 (summer 1974): 49–82.

4. This and most discussions of the classification of elections are based on the work of V. O. Key and Angus Campbell. See V. O. Key, "A Theory of Critical Elections," *Journal of Politics* 17 (1955): 3–18; and Campbell, "A Classification of Presidential Elections," in *Elections and the Political Order*, 63–77.

5. This and the following discussion draw heavily on Jerome M. Clubb, William H. Flanigan, and Nancy H. Zingale, *Partisan Realignment: Voters, Parties and Government in American History* (Boulder: Westview Press, 1990). See especially chaps. 5 and 8.

6. See, for example, William N. Chambers and W. Dean Burnham, eds., *The American Party Systems: Stages of Political Development* (New York: Oxford University Press, 1975).
7. This concept was developed by S. M. Lipset and Stein Rokkan in their discussion of the development of the European party systems in *Party Systems and Voter Alignments* (New York: Free Press, 1967), 1–64.
8. The 1996 National Election Study found that a little more than one third of the public agreed that political parties care what ordinary people think.

Suggested Readings

Beck, Paul Allen. "The Dealignment Era in America." In *Electoral Change in Advanced Industrial Democracies: Realignment or Dealignment?* edited by Russell J. Dalton, Scott C. Flanagan, and Paul Allen Beck. Princeton: Princeton University Press, 1984. A good survey of recent politics as an example of dealignment.

Burnham, W. Dean. *Critical Elections and the Mainsprings of American Politics.* New York: W. W. Norton, 1970. An early, important statement of the electoral realignment perspective.

Campbell, Angus, Philip E. Converse, Warren E. Miller, and Donald E. Stokes. *The American Voter.* New York: Wiley, 1960. This is the classic study of public opinion and voting behavior in the United States.

Clubb, Jerome M., William H. Flanigan, and Nancy H. Zingale. *Partisan Realignment: Voters, Parties, and Government in American History.* Boulder: Westview Press, 1990. A conceptualization of realignments that emphasizes both electoral behavior and political leadership.

Converse, Philip E. "The Concept of a Normal Vote." In *Elections and the Political Order,* edited by Angus Campbell, Philip E. Converse, Warren E. Miller, and Donald E. Stokes. New York: Wiley, 1966. This chapter established the role of party identification as a baseline for the analysis of vote choice.

MacKuen, Michael B., Robert S. Erikson, and James A. Stimson. "Macropartisanship." *American Political Science Review* 83 (December 1989): 1125–1142. A sophisticated analysis of trends in aggregate party identification, arguing that the sizable amount of instability undermines the realignment perspective.

Internet Resources

The Web site of the National Election Studies, www.umich.edu/~nes/, has basic information on partisanship and party identification. Click on "Partisanship and Evaluation of the Political Parties." For information on partisan voting patterns, click on "Vote Choice."

During election years news organizations may have Web sites with election statistics in historical depth. A site with extensive historical data is David Leip's Atlas of U.S. Presidential Elections at www.uselectionatlas.org.

Another source of current information on elections and public opinion is the Elections U.S.A. Web site at www.geocities.com/CapitolHill/6228/. Click on "Elections" for election returns for the states and nation.

Partisans and Partisan Change

AS WE DISCUSSED in Chapter 3, partisanship is a useful concept for tracing the dynamics of American political history. It is also crucial for understanding the political behavior of individuals. We begin this chapter by examining the impact of having—or not having—a party identification on the way people respond to politics. We then turn to the question of partisan change, looking first at change in individuals' partisanship over their lifetimes and then at changes across generations.

Voting Behavior

Recall that the standard party identification question, used in almost all political surveys, asks respondents whether they are Republicans, Democrats, or independents, and also whether they are "strong" or "not very strong" Republicans or Democrats. It is not surprising that the likelihood of voting loyally for one party varies with the strength of individuals' partisanship. The defection rates of strong and weak (not very strong) partisans in each presidential election since 1952 are illustrated in Figure 4-1. Declining party loyalty is apparent with a decrease in the intensity of partisanship. Strong partisans consistently support the candidate of their party at higher rates than do weak partisans. (One should also note that in most years Republicans have been more loyal to their party than Democrats, although this is partly accounted for by southern Democrats who regularly deserted their party in presidential elections. By the end of the century, southern Democrats were no longer distinctive in this regard. Previously defecting Democrats had become independents or Republicans.)

Obviously, differences in candidate appeal affect the propensity to defect. Very few Republicans defected from Dwight Eisenhower in the

FIGURE 4-1   Defection Rates, by Party Identifiers in Presidential Elections, 1952–2000

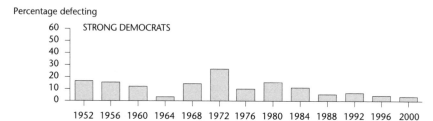

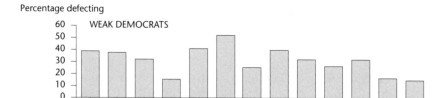

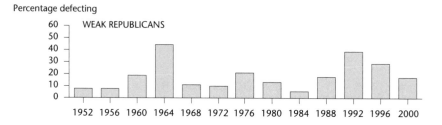

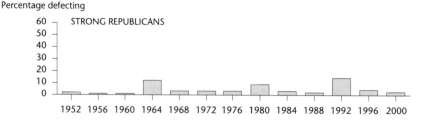

Sources: National Election Studies. Data provided by the Inter-university Consortium for Political and Social Research.

1950s, Richard Nixon in 1972, or Ronald Reagan in 1984; many more deserted Barry Goldwater in 1964. Similarly, Democrats were very loyal to Lyndon Johnson in 1964 but abandoned George McGovern in large numbers in 1972.

Another potential cause of defection is attractive third-party candidates. In 1992 Ross Perot drew defectors from both parties, although more from the Republican side. Ten percent of strong Republicans and 25 percent of weak Republicans defected to Perot. Although few strong Democrats defected to Perot, 17 percent of the weak Democrats did. John Anderson in 1980 and George Wallace in 1968 similarly account for part of the upsurges in defections in those years.

Historically, third-party candidates often have been viewed as "halfway houses" for partisans moving from one party to another. Not quite as dramatic for a partisan as defection to the opposition party, a vote for such a candidate may be a first step away from party loyalty. In any event, support for third parties and an increase in defection rates have generally been symptomatic of the loosening of party ties in a dealignment.

A different pattern—one of high party loyalty on both sides—was exhibited in 2000 as well as 1976, 1988, and 1996. In these elections partisans of both parties remained loyal to candidates who were relatively balanced in their appeal; perhaps partisans were not tempted to defect to the candidate offered by the opposing party. The high degree of loyalty in the 1996 presidential election was all the more unusual in that Perot was available once again as an alternative but attracted many fewer defecting partisans than in 1992. Although there were widespread expectations that defections to Ralph Nader and Pat Buchanan would be large, partisans of both major parties were quite loyal in their presidential voting in 2000.

Although strong partisans vary in their loyalty from year to year depending on the candidates offered by their party, this tendency is much more pronounced among weak partisans. For example, the defection rate of strong Republicans varies from around 2 percent in a "good" Republican year to 10 percent in a "bad" year—a quite narrow range. In contrast, weak Republicans are almost as loyal as strong Republicans when an attractive Republican candidate is on the ticket, but nearly 50 percent defected in the disastrous 1964 election. The behavior of Democrats is similar, although both strong and weak Democrats are more likely to desert their party than are Republicans. Clearly, marked departures from the expected vote of a party are accomplished by wooing away the weaker partisans of the opposite party.

The tendency of both strong and weak partisans to vote according to their party identification becomes even more pronounced as one moves down the ticket to less visible and less publicized offices. This is a product of the dominant two-party system nationwide. Even highly successful third-party or independent candidates down the ticket are merely local disruptions that have virtually no impact on national patterns. The voting behavior of partisans in congressional races since 1952 differs from the presidential data in two significant ways (see Figure 4-2). First, differences between the party loyalty of strong and weak partisans are usually smaller. Second, the defection rate does not fluctuate from year to year nearly as much as in the presidential elections,

FIGURE 4-2   Defection Rates, by Party Identifiers in Congressional Elections, 1952–2000

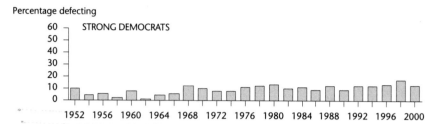

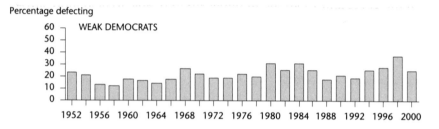

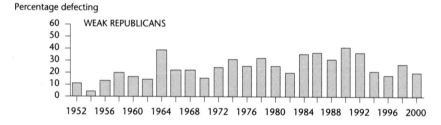

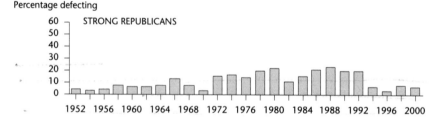

Sources: National Election Studies. Data provided by the Inter-university Consortium for Political and Social Research.

particularly among weak partisans. Both these differences are attributable to the lower visibility of congressional races. In a presidential election, the flood of available information means that a particularly attractive candidate or a stirring issue may touch the consciousness of the weak partisans, causing them to defect from traditional party ties; the firmly attached, strong partisans are more likely to resist. In the less publicized congressional races, the information that might cause weak partisans to defect is less likely to even reach them; in the absence of information about the candidates and issues, weak partisans vote their party identification.

In congressional voting, unlike presidential voting, Democrats were, until 1994, regularly more party loyal than were Republicans (see Figure 4-2). This was both cause and effect of the recent disjuncture of national politics, whereby Republicans were stronger in presidential politics and Democrats dominated in congressional politics. Throughout the 1970s and 1980s the Republicans were able to field more attractive presidential candidates than the Democrats, leading more Democratic partisans to defect in presidential races. In contrast, congressional races saw Republican partisans often defecting to vote for a long-term Democratic incumbent running against token Republican opposition. This changed rather dramatically in 1994, when the Republicans gained control of the House of Representatives in large part by fanning the flames of anti-incumbent, anti-Democratic sentiment. Thereafter, with more Republican incumbents to vote for, Republican partisans were noticeably more party loyal than they had been in previous congressional elections.

The intensity of partisanship affects political behavior beyond its influence on the likelihood of voting for or defecting from a party's candidate. Strong partisans are also more likely to vote in all kinds of elections than are either weak partisans or independents. Indeed, one explanation sometimes offered for the decline in turnout in recent years is the declining partisanship of the American public.[1] The turnout rates of the various categories of partisans and independents for three types of elections—presidential, off-year congressional, and primary—are illustrated in Figure 4-3. Presidential primaries, despite all their accompanying publicity and frenetic campaigning, typically have a lower average turnout than off-year congressional elections. Turnout declines in all categories as the presumed importance of the race decreases, but the rate is much steeper among the less partisan. As a result, the less salient the election, the more the electorate will be dominated by the intense partisans, who are also less likely to defect from party ties in casting their ballots.

These ideas led Angus Campbell to suggest an intriguing theory of electoral change to explain the often observed phenomenon in American politics whereby the party winning the presidency is very likely to lose seats in the legislature in the next congressional election.[2] Because, the argument goes, presidential elections are usually accompanied by a high level of interest, large numbers of weak partisans and independents are drawn to the polls. Because these weak partisans and inde-

FIGURE 4-3　　Turnout by Partisans and Independents in Presidential, Congressional, and Primary Elections

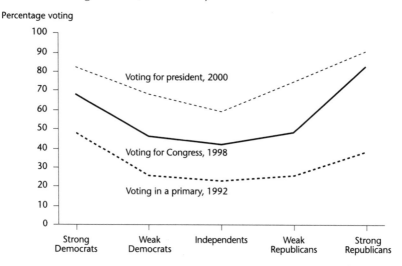

Percentage voting

Sources: 1992, 1998, and 2000 National Election Studies. Data provided by the Interuniversity Consortium for Political and Social Research.

pendents are more easily shifted from one party to another, they add disproportionately to the vote for one presidential candidate, usually the winner. In congressional elections these less committed voters do not turn out, whereas relatively large numbers of intense partisans do. These strong party identifiers are not so likely to shift their vote away from their party. As a consequence, support declines in off-year congressional elections for the party that won the previous presidential election with disproportionately large numbers of less interested voters.

Persuasive as Campbell's argument may be, it rests on some assumptions that may be questionable. First, it assumes that high-stimulus elections will be landslides—that is, it assumes that the short-term forces bringing the less interested voter to the polls will work to the advantage of only one candidate. Even though this has usually been the case, it is not invariable. The extremely close 1960 presidential election, with its emphasis on the religion (Catholicism) of Democratic candidate John F. Kennedy, was a high-turnout election, but different groups of voters were affected in quite different ways. Similarly, the high turnout in 1992 benefited Bill Clinton to a small degree, but Perot much more so.

Second, Campbell's argument suggests that the less interested voters who come to the polls to vote for the attractive presidential candidate will also vote for that party's candidate in congressional elections.

In fact, the evidence shows that in many cases weak partisans who defect in presidential elections return to their own party in congressional elections, or, in the case of Perot voters in 1992 and 1996, have no congressional candidates on the same ticket to vote for. In addition, independents often split their tickets rather than vote for the congressional candidate of the same party as their presidential choice. To some extent, the argument also rests on the assumption that independents are not only less partisan but also less informed, concerned, and interested in politics, a view that is frequently called into question.

Are Independents Apolitical?

Independents, who now account for more than one third of the national electorate, are the most obvious source of additional votes for either party. Although partisans, especially weak partisans, sometimes abandon their party, year after year independents are the largest bloc of uncommitted voters available to both parties. The independent's capacity for shifting back and forth between the major parties is shown in Table 4-1. Each party has, on occasion, successfully appealed to the independents, winning over a large majority to its side. In 1984 the independents voted almost 2 to 1 for Reagan over Walter Mondale, and Johnson held a similar advantage over Goldwater in 1964. The elections of 1976 (Jimmy Carter versus Gerald Ford) and 1960 (Kennedy versus Nixon) demonstrate the situation Republican presidential candidates faced for many years: They had to win a healthy majority of the independent vote even to stay in close contention. The election of George W. Bush in 2000 depended on, among other things, the 50 percent to 43 percent advantage he enjoyed over Al Gore among independents. This represented a strong recovery for the Republican candidate from the weak showings of Bush's father in 1992 and Bob Dole in 1996.

Third-party or independent candidates find these unaffiliated voters a major source of votes. In 1992, 27 percent of the independents voted for Perot. His failure to hold those votes in 1996 turned his earlier, impressive showing into a minor story. In 1968 more than 20 percent of the independents gave their votes to Wallace; and in 1980, 14 percent voted for Anderson. Put another way, more than half of a third-party candidate's votes typically come from independents. Furthermore, independents may shift dramatically in voting for president and remain quite stable in voting for Congress. As Figure 4-4 shows, independent voting for Congress has generally been more volatile in presidential election years than in off-year elections.

On what basis do independents switch their party preferences? Two views of independents have often competed for popularity. The civics

TABLE 4-1   The Distribution of Votes for President by Independents, 1948–2000

	1948	1952	1956	1960	1964	1968	1972	1976	1980	1984	1988	1992	1996	2000
Democratic	57%	33%	27%	46%	66%	32%	33%	45%	26%	34%	46%	42%	49%	43%
Republican	43	67	73	54	34	47	65	55	56	66	53	30	37	50
Wallace[a]						21								
Schmitz[b]							2							
Anderson[c]									14					
Perot[d]												27	14	
Buchanan[e]														1
Nader[f]														6
Other									4		2			
Total	100%	100%	100%	100%	100%	100%	100%	100%	100%	100%	101%	99%	100%	100%
(N)	—	(263)	(309)	(298)	(219)	(228)	(908)	(532)	(306)	(334)	(364)	(573)	(304)	(194)

Sources: National Election Studies. Data provided by the Inter-university Consortium for Political and Social Research.

[a]American Independent Party candidate in 1968.
[b]American Party candidate in 1972.
[c]Independent candidate in 1980.
[d]Independent candidate in 1992, 1996.
[e]Reform Party candidate in 2000.
[f]Green Party candidate in 2000.

FIGURE 4-4   Net Advantage for Republicans or Democrats in Presidential
             and Congressional Voting among Independents, 1952–2000

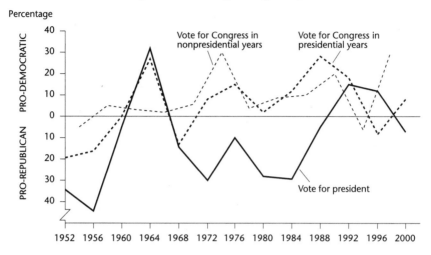

Sources: National Election Studies. Data provided by the Inter-university Consortium for Political and Social Research.

Note: The points in this figure represent the percentage of the vote the independents gave to the Democrats minus the percentage they gave to the Republicans—in other words, the margin of difference between the two parties. For example, in 1978 the independent vote was 52 percent Democratic and 48 percent Republican. This appears as a 4 percent pro-Democratic percentage above the line.

textbook view is of an intelligent, informed, dispassionate evaluator of candidates and issues, who, after careful consideration, votes for "the person, not the party." An alternate view—often attributed to campaign strategists—is of the independent as uninformed and uninterested, on whom intelligent, issue-oriented appeals and reasoned debate would be lost.

To pursue the analysis of independents, we need to make two distinctions that have not intruded on the discussion to this point. We will note these distinctions and then drop them because they complicate the analysis and are usually ignored.

First, there are important differences between nonpartisans who identify themselves as independents and those who lack any political identification. A sizable segment of the electorate answers the party identification question by saying that they identify themselves as nothing or that they do not know what they are. According to the coding conventions used by the National Election Studies, most of these non-identifiers are included with the independents,[3] but there may be important conceptual distinctions between them and self-identified inde-

TABLE 4-2   Party Identifiers, Self-Identified Independents, and People
Claiming No Preference, 1968–2000

	1968	1972	1976	1980	1984	1988	1992	1996	2000
Identify with a party	69%	64%	64%	64%	64%	63%	60%	66%	57%
Identify as independents	27	28	30	24	25	31	32	26	29
Have no preference	3	8	5	12	10	6	7	8	13
Don't know	a	0	a	0	0	0	1	a	1
Not ascertained	a	a	1	a	1	a	a	a	a
Total	99%	100%	100%	100%	100%	100%	100%	100%	100%
(N)	(1,557)	(2,702)	(1,320)	(1,614)	(1,989)	(2,040)	(2,485)	(1,714)	(981)

Sources: National Election Studies. Data provided by the Inter-university Consortium for Political and Social Research.

[a]Less than 0.5 percent.

pendents. These two types of nonpartisans are highlighted in the box in Table 4-2. Those in one set identify themselves as *independents;* the others do not think of themselves in terms of political labels. Since 1972, between one sixth and one third of the nonpartisans failed to identify themselves as independents. It is significant that the electorate is becoming more nonpartisan overall but not invariably more independent because these situations present different implications for the political parties. Self-identified independents think of themselves as having a political identity and are somewhat antiparty in orientation. The nonidentifying nonpartisans have a less clear self-image of themselves as political actors, but they are not particularly hostile to the political parties. They are less self-consciously political in many ways.

Second, within the large group of people who do not identify with a political party there are many people who say they lean toward either the Democratic or Republican Party. These leaners make up more than half of all nonpartisans, and they complicate analysis in a significant way. On crucial attitudes and in important forms of political behavior, the leaning independents appear quite partisan. Independents who lean toward the Democratic Party behave rather like weak Democratic partisans, and independents who lean toward the Republican Party behave like weak Republicans.[4] As can be seen in Figure 4-5, independent leaners are more similar to weak partisans than strong and weak partisans are to each other.

How appropriate, then, is it to include all these "independents" in one category? On some characteristics such as ideological self-

FIGURE 4-5   Percentage of Turnout, High Interest, and Democratic Vote
for President by Partisanship, 2000

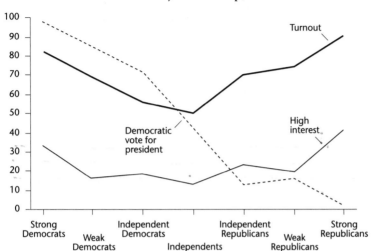

Source: 2000 National Election Study. Data provided by the Inter-university Consortium for Political and Social Research.

identification and interest in public affairs there is much more variation within the three independent categories than between the several partisan categories. The differences between leaners and "pure" independents are often greater than the differences among Republicans or Democrats. Because the concept of "independent" embraces these three dissimilar groups, there is little wonder that some disagreement exists over what the true independent is like.

As a consequence of including these various types of people under the label "independent," it is not surprising that it is difficult to make generalizations about the degree of political interest and information independents possess. Some independents have considerable interest in politics, and others are apathetic. There are more informed, concerned voters among the leaning independents than among other nonpartisans, and the leaning independents are more likely to register and to vote. When we question whether independents are attentive or apathetic toward politics, we must conclude that they are some of both.

To the student of contemporary American politics, these characteristics of the independent remain important because they determine the independent's susceptibility to political appeals. We and others have argued that the American electoral system is presently in a period of increased loosening of political ties, perhaps antecedent to a partisan realignment. The argument is that as larger and larger portions of the electorate either become independent or exhibit more independent behavior, these people form a pool of potential recruits for one of the parties or a new party. Should a new political leader be able to capture the imagination of this pool of available recruits on a lasting basis, it would lead to a significant change in the partisan division in the electorate.

Partisan Change

Partisanship can be thought of as a basic attitude that establishes a normal or expected vote, an estimate about how individuals or populations will vote, other things being equal. However, partisanship itself is not unchangeable. Individuals may change not only their vote but also their long-term party identification from one party to another. More important, over extended periods of time the partisan composition of the electorate may be altered as new voters of one political persuasion replace older voters of another. When the basic partisan division of the electorate changes, a partisan realignment occurs.

In the past the absence of survey data limited analysis of realignments, but during the current period we have the opportunity to study the individual processes of partisan change that underlie aggregate shifts in the partisan division of the electorate. These processes have been a matter of some controversy. One perspective holds that individual partisans are *converted* from one party to the other during a realignment. Other analysts, noting the psychological difficulty in changing long-held and deeply felt attachments, argue that such change probably comes about through *mobilization* rather than conversion. In other words, it is the independents or nonpolitical individuals, perhaps predominantly young voters just entering the electorate without strong partisan attachments, who fuel a realignment by joining the electorate overwhelmingly on the side of one party.

Some evidence on these points comes from the New Deal era. Although survey research was then in its infancy, some scholars have creatively used data from early surveys to try to answer these questions. Research by Kristi Andersen, reported in *The Changing American Voter*,[5] reveals high levels of nonvoting and nonpartisanship among young people and new citizens before the Great Depression. Those uninvolved, uncommitted potential participants entered the electorate in the 1930s disproportionately as Democrats. Andersen's findings on the electorate of the 1920s and 1930s support the view that realignments are based on the mobilization of new, independent voters rather than on the conversion of partisans. In contrast, Robert Erikson and Kent Tedin argue on the basis of early Gallup poll data that much of the increase in the Democratic vote in the 1930s came from voters who had previously voted Republican.[6]

In this section we will examine the processes of partisan change in the contemporary period. Although we are in a better position to do so than we were for earlier eras, efforts are still hampered by a scarcity of panel data—that is, repeated interviews with the same individuals at different points in time. In most cases it will be necessary to infer individual changes from the behavior of similar types of individuals at different times.

Changes in Individuals over a Lifetime

Two types of change in partisan identification can be distinguished, both of which have significant implications for political behavior. First, an individual may change from one party to another or to independent, or from independence to partisanship. Such change is of obvious importance if a large proportion of the electorate shifts in the same direction at about the same time. Second, an individual's partisanship may strengthen or weaken in intensity. A longstanding hypothesis states that the longer individuals identify with a party the stronger their partisanship will become.[7] In the electorate as a whole, these two types of change are not necessarily related to one another, so the occurrence of one form of change does not dictate or prevent the other. The recent increase in the number of independents at the expense of Democrats and Republicans does not necessarily mean that among the remaining partisans there has been no strengthening of loyalty with the lengthening of identification.

Analysts have attempted to explain partisan change by referring to three types of causal effects: (1) *period effects*, or the impact of a particular historical period that briefly affects partisanship across all age groups; (2) a *generation effect*, which affects the partisanship of a particular age group for the remainder of their political lives; and (3) a *life-cycle effect*, which produces changes associated with an individual's age. In current political behavior all three can be illustrated: a period effect that has resulted in an increasing independence in all age groups, a generation effect that keeps Democratic partisan loyalty high in the generation that entered the electorate during the New Deal, and a life-cycle effect that yields greater independence among the young than among their elders.

The difference between 1960, 1980, and 2000 in the proportion of independents in various age groups is shown in Figure 4-6. The solid line represents the percentage of independents in each age group in 1980, and the dotted line represents 2000. The left end of each line reflects a higher rate of independence among the young in 1980 and 2000 when compared with 1960, the broken line.

FIGURE 4-6   Distribution of Independents by Age Cohorts, 1960, 1980, and 2000

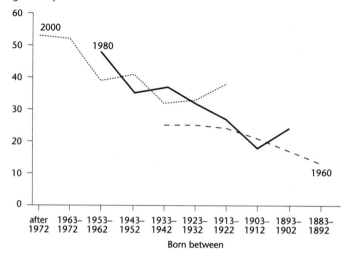

Sources: National Election Studies. Data provided by the Inter-university Consortium for Political and Social Research.

Note: The youngest cohort in each year includes only those old enough to vote.

Each line reveals a downward slope to the right. This indicates that older individuals in each year were less and less likely to be independents compared to younger people in the same year. By looking at the first point on the left of each line, we can compare the youngest respondents in each of the three years; the second point represents the second youngest group; and so on. In general, the cohorts from 1980 and 2000 have higher levels of political independence at each age than the cohorts from 1960.

It is also possible to examine the change in particular age "cohorts" between 1960 and the later years using Figure 4-6.* The youngest co-

_____

*In the absence of repeated observations of the same individuals over time, it is impossible to study many aspects of change. The use of age cohorts is an analytical technique that attempts to assess individual change through the use of surveys of different individuals over the years. Individuals of a certain age are isolated in an early survey—say thirty- to forty-year-olds in 1960—and they are compared with forty- to fifty-year-olds from a 1970 survey. This makes possible the comparison of an age cohort at two different times. This technique has been used in several studies of partisanship. See, for example, Paul R. Abramson, "Generational Change in American

hort in 1960 was more than forty years old in 1980 and reveals a higher level of independence than it did when entering the electorate. By 2000 this cohort was more than sixty years old and had become less independent once again. At each point along the lines, the vertical distance between them represents the changing percentage of independents in that age cohort. Most age cohorts became more independent during the 1980s and somewhat less independent by 2000. To the extent that we can make the comparison, the cohorts were more independent twenty years ago than they were forty years ago.

Contrary to political folklore, there is little evidence that people become Republicans as they grow older—that is, that a life-cycle effect favors Republicans. It is true that older members of the electorate were, for some years, more likely to be Republicans than younger members. The generation of young people who came of age before the Great Depression contained large proportions of Republicans, an understandable situation given the advantage the Republicans enjoyed nationally at that time. Relatively few members of this generation changed partisanship over the years, and these individuals constituted the older, more heavily Republican segment of the electorate. By the same token, the generation that entered the electorate during the New Deal was disproportionately Democratic. Because they also have remained stable in partisanship, older voters now look increasingly Democratic as this generation ages. For the next decade or so it will appear that the older the voters are, the more likely they are to be Democratic.

The tendency of individual partisanship to strengthen with age is the subject of some controversy.[8] During periods of stable party voting, there is likely to be increased partisanship the longer individuals identify with and vote for their party. On the other hand, when party voting is frequently disrupted, this reinforcement of partisanship may not occur. Even when the strength of partisanship does not increase with age, as appears to be the case in recent years, older partisans are less likely to abandon their party for an independent stance. This explains in part why older partisans were less likely to vote for independent candidate Perot than were younger partisans. In 1992, 19 percent of the Republican and Democratic partisans aged twenty-five and younger voted for Perot, but only 11 percent of partisans aged forty-five and older voted for him. In 2000, Nader's vote, although small, was greatest among the young.

Electoral Behavior," *American Political Science Review* 68 (March 1974): 93–105; David Butler and Donald Stokes, *Political Change in Britain: Forces Shaping Electoral Choice* (New York: St. Martin's Press, 1969), especially chaps. 3, 11; and Philip E. Converse, *The Dynamics of Party Support: Cohort-Analyzing Party Identification* (Beverly Hills: Sage Publications, 1976).

Gradual changes in individual partisanship have not been assessed satisfactorily for the entire public because the few election studies based on repeated interviews of the same individuals have covered at most four years. Nevertheless, the possibility that individuals change their partisanship over longer time periods is of considerable interest. In recent years speculation has focused on the possibility that the large number of young independents will become identified with one party or the other, thus creating a substantial shift in the overall partisan balance of the electorate, with or without a realigning crisis.

The best evidence on this point comes from a major study of political socialization conducted by M. Kent Jennings.[9] He surveyed a national sample of high school students and their parents in 1965, with follow-up interviews in 1973 and 1982. This provides a before-and-after picture of young people during the political traumas of the late 1960s and early 1970s, as well as a later snapshot after a more quiescent period. The interviews with the parents allow comparison with an older group experiencing the same political events.

As can be seen in Table 4-3 by looking at the percentages in the highlighted cells, the parental group was highly stable in their partisanship, with approximately three fourths maintaining their party identification and only 3 or 4 percent switching from one party to the other from one interview to the next. About one in five switched into or out of the independent category. Between each time period, about equal numbers switched in each direction, so the aggregate or net change was nonexistent for the parents.

The young people were less stable in their partisanship, especially between 1965 and 1973 when substantial numbers of both Democratic and Republican identifiers shifted to an independent status. During the next interval from 1973 to 1982, these same young people were more stable in their loyalties, with about two thirds maintaining the same party identification. This group, which was made up of individuals roughly thirty-four years of age in 1982, remained much more independent than their parents, but the numbers of independents among them had not increased over this decade. As with their parents, very few young people (about one in twenty) switched parties during either time period.

Changes across Generations

A shift in the partisan composition of the electorate owing to generational change is ordinarily a very gradual one, because political attitudes, including partisanship, tend to be transmitted from parents to their children. Normally, more than two thirds of the electorate identify with their parents' party if both parents had the same party identifica-

TABLE 4-3   Stability and Change of Partisanship in Two Cohorts,
             High School Seniors and Their Parents

Young people

		1973					1982		
		Dem.	Ind.	Rep.			Dem.	Ind.	Rep.
	Dem.	24	14	3		Dem.	23	9	3
1965	Ind.	7	24	5	1973	Ind.	8	32	7
	Rep.	3	9	10		Rep.	2	4	13

Total = 99% N = 952   Total = 101% N = 924

Parents

		1973					1982		
		Dem.	Ind.	Rep.			Dem.	Ind.	Rep.
	Dem.	39	5	3		Dem.	37	6	2
1965	Ind.	5	16	5	1973	Ind.	6	16	3
	Rep.	1	4	23		Rep.	2	4	24

Total = 101% N = 838   Total = 100% N = 822

Source: Adapted from M. Kent Jennings and Gregory B. Markus, "Partisan Orientations over the Long Haul," *American Political Science Review* 78 (December 1984): 1004–1005, Tables 2 and 3.

Note: The highlighted cells (along the diagonal) represent those individuals who remained stable in their partisanship from one time period to the next. The off-diagonal cells represent individuals who changed their partisan identification.

tion. Certainly, the adoption of parents' partisanship by their children is consistent with the notion of family socialization. Children pick up the partisanship of their parents while quite young, but the parents' influence diminishes as the child comes into contact with other political and social influences during the teenage years. For most individuals the political influence of their surroundings will be consistent with their family's political leanings, so the similarity between parents' and offspring's partisanship remains strong. On the other hand, people who remember their parents as having conflicting loyalties are more likely to be independents than either Democrats or Republicans. This is even more true of the children of parents without any partisan attachments. Thus, in each political generation a sizable number of voters lacks an inherited party loyalty.

FIGURE 4-7a   Party Identification of High School Seniors and Their Parents in 1965

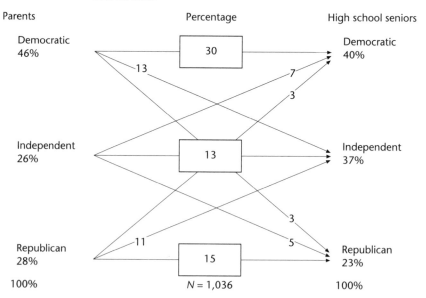

Source: Adapted from Paul A. Beck, Jere W. Bruner, and L. Douglas Dobson, *Political Socialization* (Washington, D.C.: American Political Science Association, 1974), 22.

Note: On the left of the figure is the distribution of the parents' party identification and on the right is their children's. The numbers in the three boxes highlight the percentages of the children who had the same party identification as their parents. The numbers on the remaining arrows show various amounts of change from their parents' partisanship by the children. For example, 7 percent of the total number of children had independent parents but became Democrats.

The Jennings study also permits the examination of the process of generational change because it allows a comparison of party identification for parents and their children. As can be seen in Figure 4-7a, 58 percent of the seventeen-year-olds in 1965 had adopted the party identification of their parents. Of the high school seniors, 30 percent were Democratic and came from Democratic families. Another 10 percent of the seniors were Democratic but came from independent or Republican families. Although not explicitly shown in Figure 4-7a, Democrats had a somewhat higher transmission rate than either Republicans or independents. Despite this higher transmission rate, there were so many more Democratic parents that their children also contributed substantial numbers to the independent ranks.

As we saw before, the parents changed very little between 1965 and 1973, whereas the young people became markedly more independent.

FIGURE 4-7b   Party Identification of Twenty-Five-Year-Olds in 1973 and
Their Parents in 1965

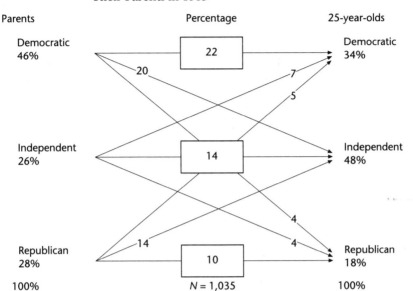

Source: Adapted from Paul A. Beck, Jere W. Bruner, and L. Douglas Dobson, *Political Socialization* (Washington, D.C.: American Political Science Association, 1974).

Thus, by 1973 fewer than half of the children shared their parents' party identification; only half of the children of Democratic parents were still Democrats, and only a little more than one third of the Republican offspring were still Republicans (see Figure 4-7b). The increasing strength of the independents came from both parties. Between 1973 and 1982 (in data not shown) there was no further erosion of the children's loyalty away from their parents' party. If anything, these young people drifted back to the party identification of their childhood.

These data from the Jennings study continue to show substantial transmission of parental political views, although not the high level of durability that earlier findings had suggested. It is reasonable to suppose that in more quiet times there would be greater continuity in the political views of parents and children.

This discussion of partisan change has relevance for understanding the process of electoral realignment. It suggests that changes in the party loyalty of the electorate observed during realignment are less the result of individuals changing from one party to another than of new voters, both young people and the previously uninvolved, who come into the electorate with a different distribution of party loyalties than did previous generations. Of particular interest, then, is the possibility that the youngest members of the electorate differ politically from their elders.

During the late 1960s and 1970s, as we have seen, young people were disproportionately independent. Of those who did adopt a partisanship, the Democrats held a 2 to 1 advantage over Republicans. During the 1980s, however, Republicans began to hold their own against the Democrats in attracting the youngest voters' loyalty. As we would expect, in the wake of Reagan's popularity and the perceived successes of his administration, young people coming of age during that time looked more favorably on the Republicans than they had before. By the end of the Clinton era, with young people coming of age during this time looking more favorably on the Democrats, the balance had shifted once again toward the Democrats. The Democrats again held a 2 to 1 edge among young voters, and the proportion of independents was steady.

As we suggested in Chapter 3, there is ample evidence of dealignment in the electorate. The large number of independents and their shifting vote choices have guaranteed electoral volatility. The weak partisans also have contributed to this instability. As they grow older, however, independents come to identify with one party or the other. Thus, in the midst of dealignment, the political parties continue to attract a following. At the same time, this partisan following is much less loyal than it was decades ago after the New Deal realignment. The unanswered question for the American political parties is whether they can reclaim the level of loyalty from their supporters they once enjoyed. Obviously, the political parties have learned to survive without high levels of loyalty, but if we are approaching an American political system without party loyalty, we are on uncharted ground.

The political parties seem to be as much victims of indifference as they are of hostility. About one fourth of the electorate can think of nothing to say about the Democratic and Republican Parties either positively or negatively. This indifference is even higher among independents. It is possible that if one or the other political party managed to perform well for a period of time, it would easily win over a large following. On the other hand, as the political parties have become more polarized—with the Democrats staking out a liberal position and the Republicans a conservative one on economic and social issues—increasing numbers of citizens find the parties too ideological or too committed to issues with which they disagree.

Notes

1. Paul R. Abramson and John H. Aldrich, "The Decline of Electoral Participation in America," *American Political Science Review* 76 (September 1982): 502–521.
2. Angus Campbell, "Surge and Decline: A Study of Electoral Change," in *Elections*

and the Political Order, ed. Angus Campbell, Philip E. Converse, Warren E. Miller, and Donald E. Stokes (New York: Wiley, 1966), 40–62.

3. Arthur H. Miller and Martin P. Wattenberg, "Measuring Party Identification: Independent or No Partisan Preference?" *American Journal of Political Science* 27 (February 1983): 106–121.
4. John Petrocik, "An Analysis of Intransitivities in the Index of Party Identification," *Political Methodology* 1 (summer 1974): 31–47.
5. Norman H. Nie, Sidney Verba, and John R. Petrocik, *The Changing American Voter* (Cambridge: Harvard University Press, 1976), chap. 5.
6. Robert S. Erikson and Kent L. Tedin, "The 1928–1936 Partisan Realignment: The Case for the Conversion Hypothesis," *American Political Science Review* 75 (December 1981): 951–962.
7. Philip E. Converse, *The Dynamics of Party Support: Cohort-Analyzing Party Identification* (Beverly Hills: Sage Publications, 1976).
8. The main participants in this controversy are Philip Converse and Paul R. Abramson. See Converse, *The Dynamics of Party Support;* and Paul R. Abramson, "Developing Party Identification: A Further Examination of Life-Cycle, Generational, and Period Effects," *American Journal of Political Science* 23 (February 1979): 78–96.
9. The major findings of the first two waves of this study have been reported in M. Kent Jennings and Richard G. Niemi, *The Political Character of Adolescence: The Influence of Families and Schools* (Princeton: Princeton University Press, 1974), and *Generations and Politics* (Princeton: Princeton University Press, 1981); a report on partisanship using all three waves of interviews is contained in M. Kent Jennings and Gregory B. Markus, "Partisan Orientations over the Long Haul: Results from the Three-Wave Political Socialization Panel Study," *American Political Science Review* 78 (December 1984): 1000–1018.

Suggested Readings

Budge, Ian, Ivor Crewe, and Dennis Farlie. *Party Identification and Beyond.* New York: Wiley, 1977. An excellent collection of articles on partisanship and other topics.

Keith, Bruce, David B. Magleby, Candice J. Nelson, Elizabeth Orr, Mark C. Westlye, and Raymond E. Wolfinger. *The Myth of the Independent Voter.* Berkeley: University of California Press, 1992. An effort to reaffirm the importance of party identification in an era of increasing numbers of independents.

Nie, Norman, Sidney Verba, and John Petrocik. *The Changing American Voter.* Cambridge: Harvard University Press, 1976. A major revisionist analysis of public opinion and voting behavior emphasizing the decline of partisanship.

Niemi, Richard G., and Herbert F. Weisberg. *Controversies in Voting Behavior.* Washington, D.C.: CQ Press, 2001. A collection of sophisticated articles on major topics in political behavior and public opinion.

Wattenberg, Martin P. *The Decline of American Political Parties: 1952–1988.* Cambridge: Harvard University Press, 1990. A thorough analysis of the changing patterns of partisanship in recent decades.

Internet Resources

The Web site of the National Election Studies, www.umich.edu/~nes/, has extensive information on partisanship and party identification from 1952 to the present. Click on "Partisanship and Evaluation of the Political Parties." Elaborate data are available separately on Democrats, Republicans, and independents.

Most political parties have Web sites. Any search engine will find them. www.democrats.org and www.rnc.org will reach the respective national committees of the two major parties.

Social Characteristics of Partisans and Independents

To THIS POINT the voting behavior and political partisanship of Americans have been discussed without examining the forces behind these patterns. Attempts to explain American voting behavior have relied on social and economic factors to account for both stability and change in American politics. Research based on the National Election Studies has documented a wide range of relationships in the American electorate between social and economic characteristics and political behavior. Furthermore, many of the descriptions of voting patterns offered by American journalists and party strategists are based on social and economic factors. Analysis regularly attributes political trends to such categories as "soccer moms" or "born-again Christians"; frequently these explanations rely on so-called bloc voting, such as "the black vote," "the senior citizens' vote," or "the union vote," implying that some social factor causes large numbers of people to vote the same way.

These explanations commonly focus on the association between social status and partisan choice. Typically, it is said that lower status people (blue-collar workers), those with less education, those with lower incomes, recently immigrated ethnic groups, racial minorities, and Catholics are more likely to vote Democratic. Higher status people (middle-class individuals, white-collar workers), college-educated individuals, those with high incomes, whites of northern European background, and Protestants are more likely to vote Republican. Although all these relationships exist and are important for understanding and interpreting American political behavior, one must be careful not to overstate the case, because any *single* social or economic characteristic is not likely to be a good predictor of how an individual will behave politically. For example, even though Republicans are much more likely to have white-collar occupations than blue-collar occupations, there are more white-collar Democrats than white-collar Republicans.

The differences are similarly unimpressive for most other socio-economic variables taken alone, mainly because the groups defined by each of these variables are, in the United States, quite heterogeneous with respect to other variables. For example, even though white-collar workers on the average are better off than blue-collar workers, both groups contain individuals of widely varying educational levels, religious affiliations, ethnic group membership, and even income levels. The same can be said about other social and economic variables. One exception is race. Because of the systematic discrimination against blacks in American culture, blacks form a more homogeneous group socioeconomically, as well as a more politically self-conscious one, than most other groups in American society. It is not surprising, then, that their political behavior is also more homogeneous.

The ability to predict the political behavior of whites from their social and economic characteristics is increased if several variables are combined. In effect, more and more homogeneous groups are being created for analysis in this manner, and such groups are increasingly likely to behave in similar ways. The partisanship of selected socio-economic groups in 2000 is displayed in Figure 5-1, using ethnicity, religion, and education as variables. It is clear that blacks are the most Democratic of any group; Hispanics are much more Democratic than Republican. White non-Hispanics with no religious affiliation are the most likely to be independents. Within the various religious groups, the relationship between education and partisanship differs. The most dramatic differences are found among the white Evangelicals, with those with a high school education or less much more likely to be Democrats than Republicans. Among Evangelicals with at least some college, the reverse is found; 51 percent are Republicans and only 13 percent are Democrats. This might be taken to be the expected relationship between social status and partisanship, but notice that among the other white non-Hispanic religious groups there is no tendency for the better educated to be Republican.

One factor that is often important in explaining political behavior and yet complicates simple social and economic interpretations is the nature of the community or the region in which the individual lives. Sometimes the culture and traditions of an area will reverse or reinforce the political tendencies of other social groupings to which the individual belongs; this may result in a pattern of behavior different from that of people with similar characteristics in other parts of the country. Unless the analyst controls for such contextual factors, finding common patterns in the group's behavior may be difficult.

In the past, the most obvious example of such a regional effect was the division between the South and the rest of the nation. Southern vot-

FIGURE 5-1   Party Identification by Race/Ethnicity, Religion, and Education, 2000

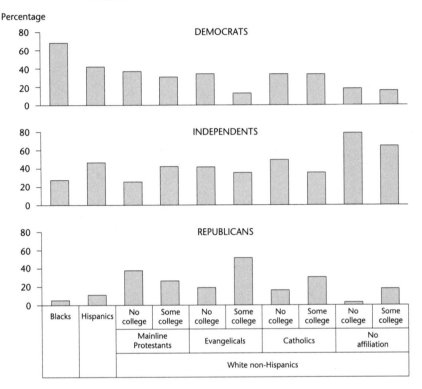

Source: 2000 National Election Study. Data provided by the Inter-university Consortium for Political and Social Research.

ers became overwhelmingly Democratic after the Civil War, and for years this traditional attachment to the Democratic Party virtually wiped out the impact of any other social or economic factor on political behavior. In the 1950s the southern middle-class was about as Democratic as the southern working class, the highly educated about as Democratic as the less well-educated, southern Protestants as Democratic as the relatively few Catholics in that region, and so on. This has changed dramatically in the past forty years. The relationship between education and partisanship is now similar both inside and outside the South, as white southerners, particularly the better educated, have left the Democratic Party. Since 1956 southern whites have gone from 63 percent Democratic to 28 percent. Initially, the corresponding gains appeared primarily in the independent category, but more recently the greatest increase has been among Republicans. The proportion of Republicans among southern whites has increased from 17 percent in 1956 to 28 percent in 2000. During this same period there was little change in partisan support among whites outside the South, although the ranks of independents increased, drawing from both former Republicans and Democrats.

Controlling for region is relatively simple. It is not such an easy matter to take community effects into account, however, because national surveys may contain very little information about community characteristics and very few cases from any one community. Nonetheless, community traditions may have substantial impact. For example, the Cuban population in Miami is strongly Republican; their social group influence is strong, and yet it moves group members in the opposite direction from that taken by similar group influences on Hispanics elsewhere.

The Social Composition of Partisan Groups

Another way of looking at the relationship between socioeconomic characteristics and partisanship is to describe the Democratic and Republican Parties and independents in terms of proportions of different kinds of individuals who make up their ranks. The social composition of Democratic, Republican, and independent identifiers is illustrated in Figure 5-2, using the same social categories used in Figure 5-1 (race/ethnicity, religion, and education). Note, however, that this way of looking at the data gives different results and answers a different set of questions. Instead of asking to what extent particular social groups support the Democratic or Republican Parties, we can ask what proportion of all Democrats are black or Catholic. For example, looking at the partisanship of various social groups in Figure 5-1, we see that blacks are heavily Democratic (68 percent in 2000). If we calculate the proportion of all Democrats who are blacks, as in Figure 5-2, however, we find that blacks make up just 30 percent of the total group of Democrats. Because blacks make up a relatively small proportion of the population, their contribution to the total set of Democrats is not so large, despite their lopsided preference for the Democratic Party.

Studying the partisanship of various social groups has generally been regarded as the more interesting way of looking at the relationship between social characteristics and political behavior, largely because of the causal connection between social characteristics and partisanship. Thus, one is far more inclined to say that race and ethnicity, religion, or education "causes" an individual to select a particular political party than to say that political affiliation "causes" any of the others. Familiarity with the composition of the parties is useful, however, in understanding the campaign strategies and political appeals that the parties make to hold their supporters in line and sway the independents or op-

FIGURE 5-2   Social Composition of Partisans and Independents by
Race/Ethnicity, Religion, and Education, 2000

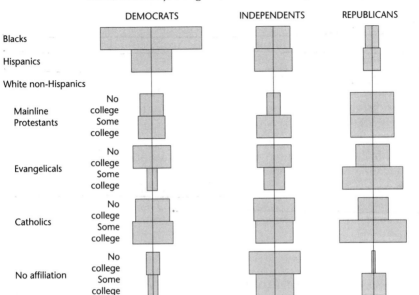

Source: 2000 National Election Study. Data provided by the Inter-university Consortium
for Political and Social Research.

position supporters to their side. For example, the fact that blacks contribute 30 percent of the Democratic partisans but make up just 4 percent of the Republican partisans is a significant factor that both parties take into account.

The composition of the parties affects politics in another way. In a recent book on the evolution of the racial issue in the United States, Edward G. Carmines and James A. Stimson argue persuasively that the composition of the parties, particularly the composition of the party activists, influences the perceptions that less involved citizens hold about the philosophy and issue stands of the parties.[1] The fact that blacks are overwhelmingly Democratic and that vocal racial conservatives—in other words, those with a general predisposition to oppose government actions to correct racial injustices—are increasingly Republican allows the average voter to figure out which party is liberal and which is conservative on racial issues, even if race is never mentioned by candidates during the course of an election campaign.

As can be seen in Figure 5-2, the composition of the partisan identifiers is distinctively different; blacks and Hispanics make a sizable contribution to the Democratic following, yet neither group constitutes a significant share of the Republican following. As a category, Republicans are more homogeneous, consisting of relatively well-educated white non-Hispanic Protestants and Catholics.

Even though the Democrats are considerably more varied in social composition than the Republicans, the main conclusion to be drawn from an analysis of the partisan groupings is that they are basically heterogeneous. Both parties contain substantial proportions of differing religious groups and people with different educational levels; they both draw substantial portions of their votes from blue-collar as well as white-collar workers, from the young, the middle-aged, the old, and so on. This diversity is also true of the independent group, as can be seen in Figure 5-2. As was pointed out in Chapter 4, independent voters hold the balance of power between the major parties and both must appeal to them to win elections. Thus, with few exceptions, neither party can ignore any reasonably large social group. This, perhaps as much as any factor, forces the parties to move toward the center on many social issues.

Social Group Analysis

The impact of social groups on individual behavior is so commonly understood and accepted that it needs little elaboration, and the forms of group influence are too varied to discuss them all. Social analysis of political behavior has examined three main units: primary groups, secondary groups, and social classes. *Primary groups* are the face-to-face groups with which one associates, such as family, friends, and coworkers. *Secondary groups* are those organizations or collections of individuals with which one identifies, or is identified, that have some common interest or goal rather than personal contact as their major basis. *Social classes* are broad groupings based on position in society according to social status.

Primary Groups

Although investigations of the political behavior of primary groups are not numerous, all available evidence indicates that families and groups of friends are likely to be politically homogeneous. Groups of coworkers appear somewhat more mixed politically. Presumably, the social forces in families and friendship groups are more intense and more likely to be based on, or to result in, political unanimity, but in most work situations people are thrown together without an opportunity to form groups based on common political values or any other shared traits. Friendship groups, even casual ones, may be formed so that indi-

TABLE 5-1   Reported Partisan Preferences of Primary Groups
             by Respondent's Party Identification

	Respondent's party identification		
Primary group	Democrat	Independent	Republican
Reported party identification of spouse			
Democrat	75%	18%	14%
Independent	9	57	10
Republican	10	18	70
Don't know	6	8	6
Total	100%	101%	100%
(N)	(176)	(120)	(142)
Reported party identification of friends			
Democrat	66%	27%	19%
Independent	8	33	7
Republican	11	16	53
Don't know	15	23	19
Total	100%	99%	98%
(N)	(542)	(379)	(410)
Reported party identification of coworkers			
Democrat	65%	26%	23%
Independent	8	34	6
Republican	11	11	50
Don't know	16	29	20
Total	100%	100%	99%
(N)	(138)	(107)	(133)

Source: General Social Survey, 1987. Data provided by the Inter-university Consortium for Political and Social Research.

Note: Respondents were asked to name three people with whom they discussed "important matters," after which their relationship with those mentioned was established. Reports only on those people with whom respondents talked about "political matters" on a regular basis.

viduals with much in common, including political views, naturally come together.

Table 5-1 presents findings from the 1987 General Social Survey that illustrate the homogeneity of primary groups. Respondents were asked the political party of those people with whom they regularly discussed politics. The table shows that agreement on partisanship between spouses is highest, with 75 percent of the Democrats and 70 percent of the Republicans reporting that their spouses shared their party preference. Agreement was not quite so high with friends and coworkers but still reflects considerable like-mindedness. Perhaps as important is the relatively low occurrence of mismatches of Democrats and Republicans in primary groups. The fact that significant percentages do not know the partisanship of friends and coworkers may reflect an avoidance of potential conflicts.

This discussion of primary groups has implications for the celebrated "gender gap" in the political preferences of men and women, a favorite topic of political commentators since the early 1980s. Women seem to have been less favorably inclined toward Presidents Ronald Reagan, George Bush, and George W. Bush, and toward Republicans in general, than were men. Conversely, women were more supportive of President Bill Clinton and Vice President Al Gore than were men. Table 5-2 presents the gender gap in partisanship in 2000. If we combine the strong and weak partisans, the gap exists, but it is not large and would be reduced further if we introduced controls for race and socioeconomic variables.[2] Given what we have said about the influence of primary groups, we should not be too surprised by the modest size of the gender gap. Men and women interact with each other in primary groups throughout society. They select friends and spouses from like-minded individuals; they respond, as family units, to similar social and economic forces. In the next chapter we will consider ways in which the views of men and women differ on certain issues, but given the general influence of primary groups, differences in overall political preferences are seldom large.

We have avoided use of the term *conformity* to describe this pattern of primary-group behavior because these group processes are more casual and more a matter of give-and-take than this term implies. Most people care little about politics, and it plays a small part in their personal relationships. In very few primary groups is politics of any consequence, so the things that happen in the group that lead to political homogeneity are of low salience. Individuals gradually create, evaluate, and revise their images of the world under the influence of social processes. Many of these processes are face-to-face exchanges of information or reassurances that others share views or consider them plausible, realistic, and acceptable. Most individuals are not pressured by primary groups to conform or to change politically, at least not nearly as much as they are influenced by casual, impromptu expressions of similar ideas and values. Ordinarily, primary groups do not tolerate high levels of political tension and conflict. Also, very few people are subject to the social forces of only one or two primary groups, so conformity to group pressure would mean conformity to a large number of groups.

TABLE 5-2   Party Identification by Gender, 2000

	Men	Women
Strong Democrat	19%	20%
Weak Democrat	12	21
Independent	45	41
Weak Republican	13	9
Strong Republican	12	9
Total	101%	100%
(*N*)	(426)	(536)

Source: 2000 National Election Study. Data provided by the Inter-university Consortium for Political and Social Research.

In addition to what happens within primary groups, another factor produces political similarity: the likelihood that primary-group members share the same social background and experiences outside the group. Members of any primary group are apt to be socially, economically, ethnically, and racially alike, and being alike in these ways means that the same general social influences are at work on them. Much happens outside the primary group to make it politically homogeneous.

Secondary Groups

Secondary groups form around some common interest and may or may not involve personal contact among members. This covers a range of groups in society, such as labor unions, religious or fraternal organizations, and professional groups. Secondary groups are presumably composed of overlapping primary groups whose pressures toward political homogeneity spill over, tending to make the members of secondary groups alike. In addition, members of secondary groups are likely to be subject to the same social forces outside the group. For example, members of a labor union are likely to be in the same income group, to live in the same type of neighborhood, and to have the same social and educational background, all of which would tend to make them alike politically.

A third factor at work is the role that a secondary group may play as a reference group. A group serves as a reference group for an individual who uses the group as a guide in forming opinions. For example, if union members, identifying with their labor union, perceive that a particular policy is good for the union, perhaps because the union leadership says that it is, and favor the policy because of this, the union is a political reference group for those individuals. In the same way, if a union member believes that other union members support a policy and supports the policy in part for this reason, then the union members serve as a reference group. Also, if a businessperson perceives that unions favor a policy, and he or she opposes it in part for that reason, then unions serve as a negative reference group.

The most sophisticated analysis of social groups and political behavior applied to national survey data appeared in *The American Voter* by Angus Campbell et al.[3] By controlling many outside social influences with matched groups, the authors demonstrated the degree to which an individual's political behavior was influenced by secondary-group membership among union members, blacks, Catholics, and Jews. They were able to show that union members, blacks, and Jews were considerably more Democratic than one would expect from the group members' other social characteristics, such as urban–rural residence, region, and occupational status. Even greater influence was present if the individual identified with the group. To establish the importance of identification with the group and belief in the legitimacy of the group's involvement in politics, the authors analyzed the 1956 presidential votes of union members, blacks, Catholics, and Jews. The increasing impact of identification with the group and of its perceived legitimacy was associated with an increasing Democratic vote. In other words, the stronger the belief in the legitimacy of the group's political involvement and the stronger the group identification, the greater the impact of group standards on vote choice.

Among the groups usually studied, blacks and Jews are the most distinctive politically. Jews have remained strongly Democratic in their partisanship over the years in spite of social and economic characteristics more typical of Republicans. And although Jews have at times not supported the Democratic ticket, Jewish partisanship remains close to what it was in the 1950s—65 percent Democratic, 28 percent independent, and 8 percent Republican. As we saw in Figure 5-1, blacks also are strongly Democratic in partisanship and typically vote more than 90 percent Democratic in presidential contests. The impact of group identification is most dramatically revealed by increased turnout and overwhelming support for black candidates, such as Jesse Jackson in the 1988 presidential primaries.

The behavior of union members in recent years, in contrast, illustrates a decline in group identification. Despite one-sided Democratic partisanship, union members have been quite volatile in voting for president. The election of 1984 represented a major failure of union leaders. They strongly committed themselves and their unions' resources to Walter Mondale but ultimately exercised little influence over the rank and file. Mondale only narrowly outpolled Reagan in union households. In 1992 and 1996 Clinton was much more appealing to union members than his opponents, despite union leaders' general lack of enthusiasm. In 2000 Gore was a clear preference over George W. Bush among union members—57 percent to 40 percent—in spite of Gore's differences with union leadership on world trade issues.

The voting patterns of American religious groups, other than Jews, have not been particularly distinctive, or at least other factors have been considered more important in determining vote choice. In recent years analysts have focused increased attention on religious groups in American society, especially within the highly varied Protestant category. Over recent decades the composition of the Protestant category has changed dramatically. Mainline Protestant denominations like Methodists and Presbyterians have declined from roughly 40 percent to 20 percent of the adult population. Evangelicals and Fundamentalists have grown to one third of the electorate, about the same proportion as Catholics.

In a probing analysis of religious groups spanning 1960 to 1992, David Leege has demonstrated the political distinctiveness of Catholics and evangelical Protestants in comparison with mainline Protestants.[4] Leege shows that for both Catholics and evangelical Protestants there are significant differences in political behavior associated with regularity of church attendance. In general, those who rarely attend church are quite similar to those unaffiliated with any religion. These differences are generally greatest on policy issues and political ideology rather than partisanship. We will return to their consideration in the next chapter. It is important to point out that it is this interaction with like-minded individuals, represented by church attendance, that likely creates and reinforces political distinctiveness.

Social factors, such as religion or union membership, vary in their relative importance from election to election. After years of dormancy a social factor may temporarily become significant during a political campaign and subsequently recede in importance. The 1960 presidential election provides a good example of how secondary groups become relevant in a particular election and temporarily have great influence on voting behavior. John F. Kennedy's Catholicism was a major issue throughout the campaign and of great importance to both Catholics and non-Catholics. Researchers at the University of Michigan showed that Protestant Democrats who were more regular in church attendance were more likely to defect from the Democratic candidate. Among the nominal Protestants who never attended church, Kennedy's Catholicism exerted no such negative effect.[5]

The irregular rising and falling of issues, highlighting particular social groups at a given time, is a partial explanation for the political heterogeneity of American social groups. If the issues that dramatize a given social group become consistently salient, one would expect partisan realignment on the basis of membership or nonmembership in that group. But if the group is politically relevant for only one campaign or so, such major realignment does not occur. As specific issues are raised some partisan movement may occur, but on the whole the changing relevance of particular groups leads to political heterogeneity rather than to pure divisions.

Social Classes

The third major focus of analysis is social class. Some of the leading hypotheses of social and political theory link social classes and political behavior. In general, analysis of social class assumes that differences exist in the economic and social interests of social classes and that these conflicting interests will be translated into political forces. The critical variable in this view appears to be the importance of social class interests. In American society the importance of social class fluctuates but never becomes extremely high. The major political and sociological theories of social class have taken for granted the supreme importance of class interests, an assumption that seems unrealistic in American society. About one third of all American adults say that they never think of themselves as members of a social class.

Given a choice between "middle-class" and "working class," a majority of Americans are able to place themselves in a general social position, even to the point of including themselves in the "upper" or "lower" level of a class. Even though individual self-ratings are not perfectly congruent with the positions that social analysts would assign those individuals on the basis of characteristics like occupation, income, and education, a general social class structure is apparent. The political significance of social class varies from election to election in much the same way as that of secondary groups. In Figure 5-3 the relationship between self-identification as a member of the working- or middle-class and party identification is charted from 1952 through 2000 in the nation as a whole and in the South and non-South. The values shown in the graph represent the strength of the relationship between social class and party, indicated by Somer's d. If all working-class people identified with the Democratic Party and all middle-class people with the Republican Party (with independents split evenly between the two parties), the Somer's d would be +1.0; if the reverse were true, it would be −1.0. If there were no differences in the partisan preferences of middle- and working-class people, the coefficient would be 0.0. Because working-class people have been more likely to be Democratic than have middle-class people in each year since 1952, all the values in Figure 5-3 are positive.

A number of points can be made about the data presented. Although the strength of the relationship between social class and party has varied over the years, the national trend in the relationship is downward. In other words, since 1952 the differences in partisan preference

FIGURE 5-3   The Relationship between Social Class Identification and
               Party Identification, 1952–2000

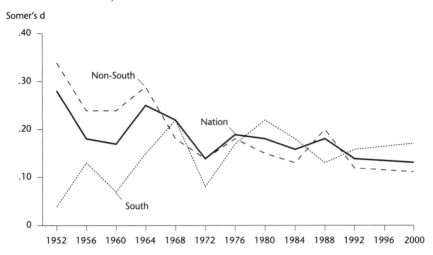

Sources: National Election Studies. Data provided by the Inter-university Consortium for Political and Social Research.

Note: The coefficients represented by points on the graph are Somer's d. The social class identification question was not asked in 1996.

between working- and middle-class people are getting smaller. In this context, 1964, 1976, and 1988 stand out as temporary reversals of this trend. It is also clear from Figure 5-3 that the relationship between class and party has followed quite different patterns in and outside the South. Whereas the relationship has been declining outside the South, it has actually increased in the South. During the early 1950s middle- and working-class southerners were overwhelmingly Democratic; there were virtually no differences between them. Since that time a modest, class-based partisan alignment has emerged in the South. The middle-class has become increasingly Republican, and the working class, particularly the black working class, remains quite solidly Democratic.

Another common expectation about the relationship between social class and partisanship has to do with upward and downward social mobility. To put it simply, the argument has been that upwardly mobile individuals abandon a Democratic identification and become Republicans, whereas the downwardly mobile abandon their Republican identification and become Democrats. Presumably the individual becomes an independent during the period of maximum social and political stress associated with this mobility. It has not been easy to assess mobility at a national level in the United States, so the surprisingly weak relationship usually found may result from inadequate measurement. In broad terms, most members of society are neither upwardly nor downwardly mobile, and the socially mobile seem no more apt to abandon their parents' party loyalty than the socially stable. There is, in fact, very little political difference between the upwardly and downwardly mobile, and this appears to hold for several measures of mobility.

Along with Canada, the United States is usually regarded as an extreme case among developed democracies for the insignificance of social class in political behavior; in most European democracies social class is of greater consequence.[6] This remains true even as the disparity between rich and poor in the United States has reached, since the 1980s, historically high levels. Two factors may depress the apparent relationship between social class and voting behavior in the United States. Aggregating data for the entire population can hide stronger relationships in subgroups and in particular communities. Probably more important are the cultural values of freedom and individualism that exalt the ability and responsibility of the individual to get ahead by talent and hard work. As a result, American political leaders tend not to emphasize or exploit highly divisive social class lines. Social class may serve as a political guide for some citizens on certain issues, but it does not appear to be extremely important in American politics.

Social Cross-Pressures

One of the major ideas developed in the early voting studies by Paul Lazarsfeld, Bernard Berelson, and other researchers at the Bureau of Applied Social Research of Columbia University was the "cross-pressure hypothesis."[7] The cross-pressure hypothesis is simple in outline, but it can be confusing because it takes so many different forms. The hypothesis concerns the situation in which two (or more) forces or tendencies act on the individual, one in a Republican direction and the other in a Democratic direction. Sometimes this is stated as two factors predisposing a voter in a Republican or a Democratic direction. Usually the hypothesis is presented with two social dimensions, like occupation and religion, as in the diagram that follows.

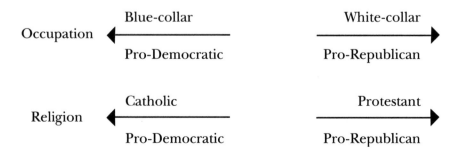

Some individuals are predisposed or pushed in a consistent way, such as white-collar Protestants, whose occupation and religion both predispose them in a Republican direction or blue-collar Catholics predisposed in a Democratic direction.

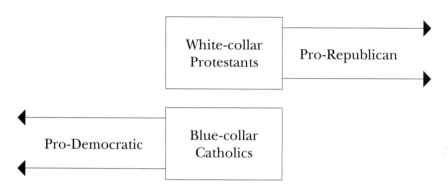

Some individuals are predisposed in both directions, or cross-pressured.

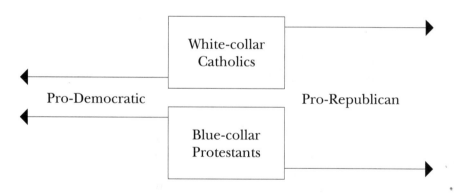

The cross-pressure hypothesis asserts that individuals under consistent pressure behave differently than individuals under cross-pressure. The predictions under the hypothesis are

Consistent Pressure	Cross-Pressure
straight-ticket voting	split-ticket voting
early decision on vote	late decision on vote
high interest in politics	low interest in politics
high level of information	low level of information
consistent attitudes	conflicting attitudes

These expectations about voting behavior under cross-pressure are actually specific applications of more general patterns investigated by sociologists and psychologists in a variety of ways. The responses to cross-pressure predicted by the hypothesis are avoidance reactions—efforts to avoid or to minimize the anxiety produced by conflict.

The cross-pressure hypothesis also has some implications for empirical political theory. According to the cross-pressure hypothesis, many large social groups are expected to be stable politically—that is, they are consistently predisposed to be Republican or Democratic by the social forces working on them. Therefore, these social pressures lead to political stability among both Republicans and Democrats because they have politically consistent social backgrounds.

Between these politically consistent social groups there are cross-pressured groups predisposed toward both parties. According to the cross-pressure hypothesis, these groups are politically unstable, contributing to the voters who switch from one party to another. This means that the available voters—the voters to whom the parties must appeal to win because they hold the balance of power in elections—are in a middle position between Democrats and Republicans. These arguments lead to a reassuring view of the American electorate. There is widespread political stability based on a relatively stable social system. Political flexibility and sensitivity are provided by groups between the partisans who are therefore politically moderate. As long as the stable partisan groups are roughly the same size, stable competitive conditions are guaranteed. As long as social groups overlap somewhat, the necessary cross-pressures will exist to produce the switching political moderates. It appears to be an electoral system that guarantees both competition and stability.

Nevertheless, there are some difficulties with this picture of the electoral system. For one thing, the social cross-pressure hypothesis is merely a tendency and not a perfect description of the impact of social forces on political behavior. The politically stable are more heterogeneous than the previous account implies, and the politically flexible are not under dramatic social cross-pressure, according to the best data available.

Discussion supporting the cross-pressure hypothesis is most extensive in the Elmira study, *Voting*, by Bernard Berelson, Paul Lazarsfeld, and William McPhee, which surveyed residents of Elmira, New York, from June through November 1948. They found that cross-pressures affected the time when individuals decided how to vote. There was a slight tendency for cross-pressures caused by religion and socioeconomic status to be associated with late decisions on voting. There were stronger relationships associated with conflicts in primary groups.

It is possible to conceptualize social cross-pressure as leading to cross-pressure on political attitudes, which in turn leads to the predicted patterns of behavior. Actually, attitudinal cross-pressure is the only form of cross-pressure that is strongly confirmed by national survey data. When attitudes toward the candidates and parties were measured by the National Election Study in 1952 and 1956, conflicting attitudes—those of an individual holding pro-Democratic and pro-Republican opinions—were associated with nonvoting, indecision, and indifference toward the election. These findings linking conflicting political attitudes with patterns of behavior have not always been confirmed in subsequent election studies, depending on exactly which attitudes are examined. Nevertheless, it remains reasonable to expect conflicting political attitudes to be associated with indecisiveness in voting behavior.

The American electoral system appears to operate in a way predicted by the cross-pressure hypothesis. There is partisan stability among both Republicans and Democrats, and the shifting of political fortunes is accomplished without intensity or extreme political appeals. One should, however, be skeptical of explaining these political patterns as a result of the social forces postulated by the cross-pressure hypothesis. Neither short-run partisan stability nor independent flexibility appears strongly associated with social-group predispositions.

Two conclusions can be drawn about social characteristics and voting behavior. Social factors, such as race, religion, and occupation, as well as primary groups, have been shown to be related to partisanship. The long-term social and political patterns in the American electorate appear related. However, the short-term impact of social groups on voting behavior appears uneven and generally insignificant. Occasionally, social factors appear important nationally, as religion did in 1960, and under certain conditions social cross-pressure may operate. Nevertheless, social factors are not expected to show the same consistent, strong relationship with vote choice that was found in the case of partisanship.

Notes

1. Edward G. Carmines and James A. Stimson, *Issue Evolution: Race and the Transformation of American Politics* (Princeton: Princeton University Press, 1989).
2. Richard A. Seltzer, Jody Newman, and Melissa Voorhees Leighton, *Sex as a Political Variable: Women as Candidates and Voters in U.S. Elections* (Boulder: Lynne Rienner, 1997).
3. Angus Campbell, Philip E. Converse, Warren E. Miller, and Donald E. Stokes, *The American Voter* (New York: Wiley, 1960), 295–332.
4. David C. Leege, "The Decomposition of the Religious Vote: A Comparison of White, Non-Hispanic Catholics with Other Ethnoreligious Groups, 1960–1992" (Paper presented at the annual meeting of the American Political Science Association, Washington, D.C., 1993).
5. Philip E. Converse, Angus Campbell, Warren E. Miller, and Donald E. Stokes, "Stability and Change in 1960: A Reinstating Election," in *Elections and the Political Order*, ed. Angus Campbell, Philip E. Converse, Warren E. Miller, and Donald E. Stokes (New York: Wiley, 1966), chap. 5.

6. There are several important works on social class and political behavior. See Campbell et al., *The American Voter,* chap. 13. Students interested in this area of analysis should also see Robert Alford, *Party and Society* (Chicago: Rand McNally, 1963); and Richard Rose, ed., *Electoral Behavior* (New York: Free Press, 1974). Perhaps the most significant work is David Butler and Donald E. Stokes, *Political Change in Britain: Forces Shaping Electoral Choice* (New York: St. Martin's Press, 1969).
7. Paul Lazarsfeld, Bernard Berelson, and Hazel Gaudet, *The People's Choice* (New York: Columbia University Press, 1944); and Bernard Berelson, Paul Lazarsfeld, and William McPhee, *Voting* (Chicago: University of Chicago Press, 1954).

Suggested Readings

Campbell, Angus, Philip E. Converse, Warren E. Miller, and Donald E. Stokes. *The American Voter.* New York: Wiley, 1960. A classic study of the social psychological factors influencing political behavior.

Huckfeldt, Robert, and Carol Weitzel Kohfeld. *Race and the Decline of Class in American Politics.* Urbana: University of Illinois Press, 1989. A study arguing that racial cleavages have become more important than social class divisions in influencing electoral decisions, with serious consequences for the Democratic Party's coalition.

Huckfeldt, Robert, and John Sprague. *Citizens, Politics, and Social Communication.* Cambridge: Cambridge University Press, 1995. An important study examining political attitudes and behavior within their social context.

Lazarsfeld, Paul, Bernard Berelson, and Hazel Gaudet. *The People's Choice.* New York: Columbia University Press, 1944. A classic study of Erie County, Ohio, and the first study of voting to make extensive use of survey research.

Leege, David C., and Lyman A. Kellstedt. *Rediscovering the Religious Factor in American Politics.* New York: M. E. Sharpe, 1993. A collection of articles exploring the impact of religious beliefs on political behavior.

Lipset, Seymour M., and Stein Rokkan. "Cleavage Structures, Party Systems and Voter Alignments: An Introduction." In *Party Systems and Voter Alignments,* edited by Seymour M. Lipset and Stein Rokkan. New York: Free Press, 1967. An important conceptual statement about the role of party and social cleavages in historical perspective.

Petrocik, John. *Party Coalitions: Realignments and the Decline of the New Deal Party System.* Chicago: University of Chicago Press, 1981. An analysis of American politics that emphasizes social and economic characteristics.

Internet Resources

The Web site of the National Election Studies, www.umich.edu/~nes/, has extensive data on social characteristics and party identification from 1952 to the present. Click on "Partisanship and Evaluation of the Political Parties." For every political item there is a breakdow� for each social characteristic in every election year.

For current data on partisans and independents you can find analysis on Web sites such as The Pew Research Center for The People & The Press at www.people-press.org or the Gallup Poll at www.gallup.com.

Public Opinion and Ideology

PUBLIC OPINION—the collective attitudes of the public, or segments of the public, toward the issues of the day—is a significant aspect of American political behavior. Public opinion polls are an ever-present aspect of American journalism. We are constantly informed about what samples of Americans think on all manner of topics. The questions then arise: Are Americans informed, issue-oriented participants in the political process? Do they view problems and issues within a coherent ideological framework? Which issues divide Democrats and Republicans? These questions address the nature and quality of American public opinion.

A *political ideology* is a set of fundamental beliefs or principles about politics and government: what the scope of government should be; how decisions should be made; what values should be pursued. In the United States the most prominent current ideological patterns are those captured by the terms *liberalism* and *conservatism*. Although these words are used in a variety of ways, generally liberalism endorses the idea of social change and advocates the involvement of government in effecting such change, whereas conservatism seeks to defend the status quo and prescribes a more limited role for governmental activity. Another common conception of the terms portrays liberalism as advocating equality and individual freedom and conservatism as endorsing a more structured, ordered society; however, these dimensions are not always joined in the political thinking of Americans. Also, some evidence indicates that since the election campaign of 1964 the terms have become increasingly associated with attitudes on racial integration. To complicate the matter further, public opinion data suggest that a segment of the American electorate uses these terms to signify a set of social attitudes or lifestyles rather than any particular political beliefs.

Despite these ambiguities, most commentators on the American political scene, as well as its active participants, describe much of what happens in terms of liberalism or conservatism. Political history (and current news analysis) portrays situations in terms such as a "trend toward conservatism," "middle-of-the-road policies," and "rejection of liberalism." Furthermore, most political commentary treats the Democratic Party as the liberal party and the Republican Party as the conservative one, even though there is considerable ideological variation in both. Within each party, leaders and platforms are alleged to be relatively liberal or conservative. Candidates of both parties attempt to pin ideological labels on opposing candidates (usually candidates of the other party, but sometimes within their own). In recent years *liberal* has been portrayed more negatively than *conservative*, as illustrated by a nationwide Republican television advertising campaign that labeled several Democratic senators running for reelection as "embarrassingly liberal."

Consideration of the ideological positions of the parties is complicated by the many dimensions of public policy: economic affairs; race relations; international affairs; and a variety of moral, social, and cultural concerns. These issue areas have many facets, and only a few themes dominate public attention at any one time. Not only does public attention to particular issues rise and fall, but the pattern of interrelationships among different sets of issues also changes over time.

Analysts of American political history pay special attention to those rare periods when a single issue dimension dominates the public's views of governmental policy. Periods such as the Civil War or the New Deal revealed deep divisions in the public, paralleled by a distinctiveness in the issue stands of the political parties. Electoral realignments of voters are forged by these unusually strong issue alignments, and during such times we would expect a close correspondence between attitudes on the relevant issues and partisanship.

At other times, highly salient issues may capture the attention of the public, but they are likely to cut across, rather than reinforce, other issue positions and party loyalties. If the parties do not take clearly differentiated stands on such issues and if party supporters are divided in their feelings toward the issues, party loyalty and the existing partisan alignment are undermined. In a complex political system like that of the United States, new, dissimilar issue divisions accumulate until a crisis causes one dimension to dominate and obscure other issues.

The most consistent and the most distinctive ideological difference between the parties emerged during the New Deal realignment. It focused on domestic economic issues, specifically on the question of what role the government should take in regulating the economy and providing social welfare benefits. These issues still underlie the division between the parties. Since the 1930s, the Democratic Party has advocated more government activity, and the Republicans have preferred less. Historically, American political parties have not been viewed as particularly ideological, in part because other issues, such as racial or social issues, have cut across the economic dimension and blurred distinctions between the parties. For example, in the 1940s and 1950s, the Republican Party was at least as liberal on race (i.e., supportive of civil rights legislation) as was the Democratic Party with its strong southern base. Similarly, in the 1970s the two parties were both divided internally on the issue of abortion. Today, however, the two parties have become more ideologically polarized over a broader range of issues. The parties' supporters seem to have sorted themselves out, and now the Democratic Party takes liberal positions and the Republican Party conservative positions on racial and social issues as well as economic ones.

In this chapter we will consider public opinion on several important issues and explore the relationship of social characteristics and partisanship to these opinions. We will look at the extent to which Americans have a political ideology representing a coherent set of fundamental beliefs or principles about politics that serves as a guide to current political issues, much as partisanship does. Finally, we will briefly consider the impact of public opinion on political leaders.

The Measurement of Public Opinion

The commercial opinion-polling organizations have spent more than sixty years asking Americans about their views on matters of public policy. Most of this investigation has taken one of two forms: (1) asking individuals whether they "approve or disapprove of" or "agree or disagree with" a statement of policy or (2) asking individuals to pick their preference among two or more alternative statements of policy. This form of questioning seriously exaggerates the number of people who hold views on political issues. People can easily say "agree" or "disapprove" in response to a question, even if they know nothing at all about the topic. If given the opportunity, many people will volunteer the information that they hold no views on specific items of public policy. In 1964, for example, more than one third of the American electorate had no opinion on U.S. involvement in Vietnam. In contrast, on issues like abortion or the death penalty in the past several decades, fewer than 5 percent of all adults were without an opinion. More typically, in recent years approximately 10 percent of the electorate has had no opinion on major issues of public policy. Philip Converse has shown, in addition, that a number of those individuals who appear to have an opinion may be regarded as responding to policy questions at random.[1]

There are several ways to explain this lack of opinion and information on topics of public policy. In general, the same factors that explain nonvoting also account for the absence of opinions. Individuals with little interest in or concern with politics are least likely to have opinions on matters of public policy. Beyond this basic relationship, low socioeconomic status is associated with no opinion on issues; low income and little education create social circumstances in which individuals are less likely to have views and information on public policies.

Some issues of public policy, such as abortion or the death penalty, are relatively easy to understand; other issues may be much more difficult, requiring individuals to face complex considerations. Edward G. Carmines and James A. Stimson have argued that different segments of the public respond to "hard" issues that involve calculation of policy benefits and "easy" issues that call for symbolic, "gut responses." Relatively unsophisticated, uninterested members of the electorate respond to "easy" issues; the more sophisticated, most interested citizens take positions on "hard" issues.[2]

It is no simple matter to describe the distribution of opinions in the American electorate because no obvious, widely accepted method has been established to measure these opinions. Asking different questions in public opinion polls will elicit different answers. Even on the issue of abortion, on which most people have views, the distribution of opinions can be substantially altered by asking respondents whether they approve of "killing unborn children" as opposed to "letting women have control over their own bodies." Furthermore, there is no direct means to validate measures of opinions as there is with reports of voting behavior. As a consequence, descriptions of public opinion must be taken as more uncertain, more tentative than conclusions drawn from the discussion of partisanship because independent indicators of opinions on public issues are rare.

Domestic Economic Issues

The Republican victory in Congress in 1994 was widely heralded as a "conservative revolution." Speaker Newt Gingrich called it an endorsement of the Contract with America, which was a blueprint for, among other things, reducing government involvement in the economy and cutting support for various social programs. Similarly, Ronald Reagan's victory in 1980 and his administration's subsequent slashing of taxes and social programs had been portrayed as a reversal of fifty years of economic liberalism. In policy terms, these have certainly been consequences of the Republican victories of the 1980s and 1994. In terms of public opinion, however, there remains broad public support for many governmental initiatives, especially where longstanding programs that appear to benefit "deserving" segments of the population are concerned.

The responses to public opinion questions, and public opinion itself, can be affected by political rhetoric and election slogans. For example, the General Social Survey asks a long series of questions on whether spending on various programs is "too much, not enough, or about right." Over the years, sizable proportions of the public have said that too much is being spent on "welfare." At the same time, similarly large proportions have said not enough is being spent on "assistance to the poor."[3] Clearly, years of anecdotes about "welfare queens" and promises to "end welfare as we know it" have had their effect on the way particular programs are perceived, if not on the public's general willingness to use government as an instrument for social purposes.

The distribution of attitudes toward spending for different governmental purposes is shown in Figure 6-1. These data were collected by the General Social Survey from 1973 to 2000. The form of these questions—whether too much or too little is being spent on a problem—elicits answers that reflect the attitude of the respondents, the wording of the question as noted previously, and also the current state of public policy. Thus, a period of cutbacks in public spending, such as in the 1980s, would be expected to produce more responses of "too little" even if public attitudes about the ideal level of such spending had not changed. In Figure 6-1, we see a drop in negative attitudes toward welfare spending after the Reagan administration had slashed these programs, as well as a rise in proportions saying "too much" is spent in the

FIGURE 6-1   Attitudes toward Domestic Policies, 1973–2000

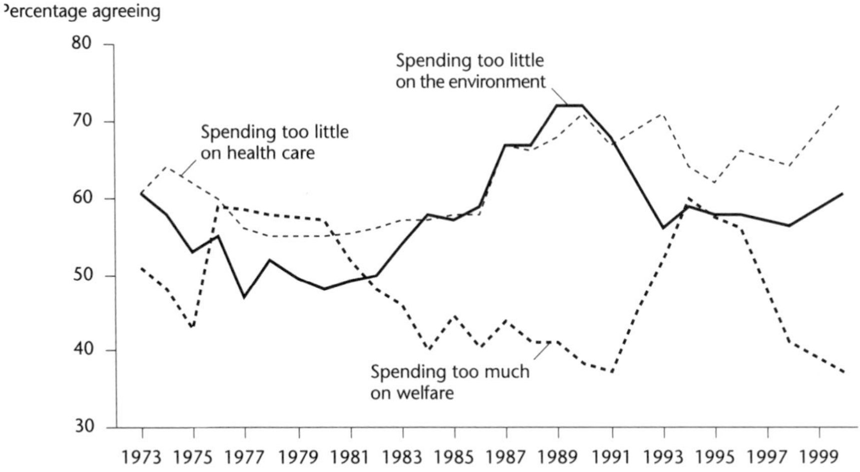

Sources: National Opinion Research Center, *General Social Surveys, 1972–2000 Cumulative File.* Data provided by the Inter-university Consortium for Political and Social Research.

1990s as both political parties promised welfare reform. The implementation of those reforms, in turn, led to a sharp drop, in 1998 and 2000, in the proportion believing too much is being spent. Attitudes favorable toward spending on the environment show a steady increase during the 1980s. Support for more spending on health care has been high for several decades. Overall, Figure 6-1 shows fairly widespread willingness to support government spending on domestic social programs.

When one examines the relationship between social characteristics and issue stands on traditional economic issues, one can expect to find dramatic differences among social groups. Figure 6-2 is based on a question in the National Election Study that offers respondents a choice between "cutting spending and decreasing services" and "increasing services and increasing spending." The pattern in the figure is not difficult to describe: The least economically secure—blacks, Hispanics, and less well-educated whites—support government services most strongly. The most support for cutting spending and reducing services is found among better-educated whites, except for those with no religious affiliation.

Men and women do not respond to domestic economic issues in quite the same way. In general the distribution of men's attitudes runs in

FIGURE 6-2   Attitudes toward Cutting Spending versus Increasing Government Services by Race/Ethnicity, Religion, and Education, 2000

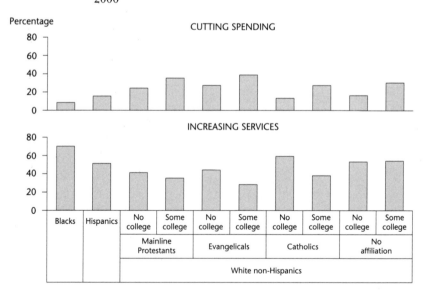

Source: 2000 National Election Study. Data provided by the Inter-university Consortium for Political and Social Research.

a conservative direction and women's attitudes in a liberal direction. In the 2000 National Election Study, 46 percent of the men surveyed supported decreasing government services and reducing spending, whereas only 31 percent of the women polled agreed with that position. Controls for socioeconomic circumstances do not significantly alter these results, so we can conclude that men and women from the same social backgrounds have somewhat different views on certain domestic economic policies.

Favoring services over spending cuts represents the type of choice in governmental policy that characterized the New Deal. Thus, it would be reasonable to expect a dramatic difference between Democrats and Republicans on such an issue. Economic issues have divided Democrats and Republicans since the 1930s. During the past sixty years, partisans have supported or opposed economic policies quite consistently, whereas other issues have been of only temporary significance for the parties. As a consequence, the relationship in Table 6-1 showing that Democrats disproportionately favor increased government services and Republicans favor cuts is no surprise. Strong Democrats favor increased services over a reduction in spending by a margin of 70 percent to 5 percent; strong Republicans are just the opposite, favoring a reduction in spending over increased services by a margin of 46 percent to 16 percent. This basic pattern has existed for decades, but it is also important to observe that noticeable proportions of Democrats and Republicans hold opinions opposed by a majority of their fellow partisans. In recent years the relationship between party identification and this issue has strengthened.

The biggest policy conflict during the first Clinton administration was the debate over a national health care program. After stressing this issue during the 1992 presidential election, Clinton appointed a task

TABLE 6-1   Attitudes toward Cutting Spending versus Increasing Government Services by Party Identification, 2000

	Strong Democrats	Weak Democrats	Independents	Weak Republicans	Strong Republicans
Favor cutting spending	5%	10%	25%	38%	46%
Neutral	25	24	31	36	38
Favor increasing government services	70	66	44	26	16
Total	100%	100%	100%	100%	100%
(*N*)	(149)	(128)	(386)	(85)	(93)

Source: 2000 National Election Study. Data provided by the Inter-university Consortium for Political and Social Research.

TABLE 6-2   Attitudes on Health Care by Party Identification, 2000

	Strong Demo- crats	Weak Demo- crats	Indepen- dents	Weak Repub- licans	Strong Repub- licans
Favor governmental health insurance	54%	52%	47%	31%	19%
Neutral	23	14	24	16	18
Favor private health insurance	23	34	29	53	62
Total	100%	100%	100%	100%	99%
(*N*)	(174)	(146)	(367)	(92)	(98)

Source: 2000 National Election Study. Data provided by the Inter-university Consortium for Political and Social Research.

force, headed by First Lady Hillary Rodham Clinton, to study alternatives and devise a program that would cover all Americans. The "managed competition" program eventually proposed was not the national health care program favored by the most liberal advocates, but the ensuing debate was cast in terms of governmentally mandated and regulated programs versus private insurance companies with individual choice in health care providers. Ultimately, the Clinton administration lost the battle in Congress and in the arena of public opinion. By 1996, 40 percent of the National Election Study sample said they thought medical expenses should be paid by private insurance plans whereas 34 percent opted for a governmental plan. This was a rather sharp change from 1992 when a governmental insurance plan was preferred 44 to 24 percent over private plans. In 2000 the public remained evenly divided on the health care issue, with about one third favoring a government program and one third favoring private health insurance. Like most other issues of government involvement in social programs and regulation of the economy, clear differences between Democratic and Republican partisans appear on the issue of health care, as can be seen in Table 6-2.

Racial Issues

Race and attitudes associated with race hold a prominent place in American political history. For many years after Reconstruction, there was little overt public attention to racial issues. The South was allowed to impose its system of segregation on its black population by law, while informal, *de facto* methods created much the same system of separate neighborhoods leading to segregated schools in the North. After integration became a major national and international focal point of attention in the 1940s and 1950s, a number of significant developments in the political attitudes of the public occurred. First, during the past fifty years southern blacks have become increasingly concerned with public policies affecting them and have changed from a largely apathetic, uninterested group to a concerned, involved, politically motivated group. As chronicled in Chapter 2, removing the legal barriers to voting in the South has enabled the black population in southern states to command the attention of politicians at the ballot box and in state legislatures and governors' mansions.

Second, large numbers of southern whites have adjusted their opinions to accept the realities of the new legal and political position of blacks. The public, as a whole, has come to support the general principle of racial equality. Figure 6-3 shows the evolution of public opinion on support for school integration from the 1940s to 2000. The recent near unanimity on this point means that Americans no longer support policies and practices that discriminate against racial groups, and it is no longer consistent with the dominant political culture to make political appeals based on blatant racism.

At the same time the public has not moved significantly closer to supporting government programs designed to improve the economic and social position of racial groups. Northern, as well as southern,

FIGURE 6-3   Public Attitudes toward School Integration, 1942–2000

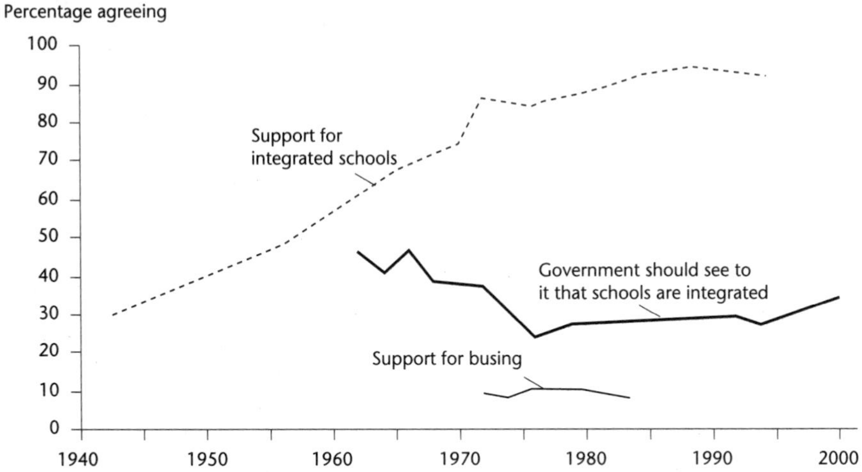

Sources: Hadley Cantril, *Public Opinion, 1935–1946* (Princeton: Princeton University Press, 1951), 508; National Opinion Research Center, 1956–1985, NBC News, 1989, Princeton Survey Research Associates, 1995, all from the Roper Center for Public Opinion Research; National Election Studies. Data provided by the Inter-university Consortium for Political and Social Research.

whites have consistently opposed busing for the purposes of integration; more than two thirds of whites oppose affirmative action on behalf of racial minorities. The proportion of the public supporting various forms of governmental action to aid blacks is shown in Table 6-3. In contrast to the near unanimity of support for "letting black and white children go to school together," less than half the public supports positive actions on the part of government to improve the social and economic position of blacks.

This lack of connection between broad principle and policy implementation has been the focus of both political debate and scholarly disagreement. One side argues that opposition to programs to aid blacks is based on opposition to government activities in general and, in particular, programs that benefit a subgroup of society.[4]

This position, often referred to as "racial conservatism," is seen as stemming from a general philosophical commitment to limited government and a belief in individualism. The attitudes, it is argued, are based on principles rather than racism.

The other view argues that opposition to policy proposals to use governmental programs to aid the social and economic circumstances of blacks and other minorities stems from racial hostility, even though so-called racial conservatives may have learned to cloak their racism in acceptable philosophical language. To complicate the matter further, scholars take quite different views of how racial hostility expresses itself in political attitudes. Various scholars have used these dimensions of racial hostility to explain white support for or opposition to government policies regarding race:

1. Racial resentment (the feeling that blacks are getting more than they deserve)[5] or racial disapproval (the feeling that blacks do not live up to certain value expectations like working hard, etc.)[6] These contentions are often referred to as "symbolic racism."
2. Group conflict (zero-sum conflicts over scarce resources).[7]
3. Social dominance (protection of the status quo by a dominant group).[8]

Obviously dimensions of this type can be interrelated and may reinforce one another. It is very difficult to separate them or to be confident in measuring them or evaluating which dimension contributes the most to racial attitudes.*

---

*Although these dimensions are often labeled as if they were positive or negative in content, we must keep in mind that the dimensions have both pro-black and anti-black extremes. In other words, if a black person believes strongly that black people are not getting what they deserve, this may involve "racial resentment" just as much as a white person believing that blacks are getting more than they deserve.

TABLE 6-3   Public Attitudes on School Integration and Employment Practices

		White	
	Black	South	Non-South
Do you think the government in Washington should see to it that white and black children go to the same schools or stay out of this area as it is not the government's business? (2000)			
Government should see to it	78%	39%	50%
Not government's business	17	54	45
Other, don't know	5	7	5
Total	100%	100%	100%
(N)	(137)	(255)	(604)
There is much discussion about the best way to deal with racial problems. Some people think achieving racial integration of schools is so important that it justifies busing children to schools out of their own neighborhoods. Others think letting children go to their neighborhood schools is so important that they oppose busing. Where would you place yourself on this scale, or haven't you thought much about this? (1984)			
Bus to achieve integration	29%	4%	7%
Neutral	15	4	8
Keep children in neighborhood schools	56	92	85
Total	100%	100%	100%
(N)	(84)	(197)	(585)
Should the government in Washington see to it that black people get fair treatment in jobs or is this not the federal government's business? (2000)			
Government should see to it	89%	40%	50%
Not government's business	10	55	46
Other, don't know	2	5	4
Total	101%	100%	100%
(N)	(137)	(255)	(604)
Some people say that because of past discrimination, blacks should be given preference in hiring and promotion. Others say that such preference in hiring and promotion of blacks is wrong because it gives blacks advantages they haven't earned. What about your opinion—are you for or against preferential hiring and promotion of blacks? (2000)			
For preferential treatment of blacks	60%	13%	10%
Against preferential treatment	26	81	84
Other, don't know, refused to say	14	7	7
Total	100%	101%	101%
(N)	(137)	(255)	(604)

Sources: National Election Studies. Data provided by the Inter-university Consortium for Political and Social Research.

To connect these dimensions with attitudes about policies designed to provide governmental aid to minorities, it seems reasonable to assume that people must view potential beneficiaries of government aid as "deserving." How deserving blacks and other minorities are viewed by white Americans may depend on whether blacks are seen as individually responsible for their position or whether they are seen as victims of social and economic forces beyond their control. Presumably whites who believe that blacks can improve their situation through their own efforts will not view them as deserving of special government programs on their behalf. This basis of opposition would fit the "symbolic racism" perspective. Whites who see social structures and conditions imposing special hardships on blacks regardless of their individual efforts will view blacks as deserving of special assistance.

Even if blacks are viewed as deserving, special programs may be opposed if whites see these programs as coming at the expense of whites. Another, similar basis for opposition to programs for blacks would be the expectation that the status quo, which favors whites, would be disrupted and that is undesirable from the point of view of whites. In general these objections would fit into the "group conflict" perspective.

To bring the "racial conservative" back into the discussion, the argument might be that there once was a time when all the relevant Democratic principles were on the side of helping blacks but that more recently such principles work both ways. Blacks should have an equal chance to get an education, find a job, and so forth, but they should not be given advantages over other deserving people. There are, of course, great differences in the perceptions of blacks and whites about whether or not blacks have an equal chance in American society.

These racial attitudes have had a profound effect on the American political landscape. In their book, *Issue Evolution*, Carmines and Stimson argue that an evolution of the racial issue since the early 1960s has led increasingly to the Democratic Party being perceived as the liberal party on civil rights issues and the Republican Party being perceived as the conservative party.[9] They see this distinction as the dominant perception of the parties in the eyes of the public. If this is so, it represents a fundamental redefinition of the issue alignment that has characterized the parties since the New Deal.

Before the 1960s, the Republican Party was seen as more progressive on civil rights than the Democrats, particularly in light of the strongly segregationist cast to the southern wing of the Democratic Party. Carmines and Stimson show that a change occurred during the 1960s and 1970s, when the elites of the two parties—members of Congress, presidential candidates—as well as party activists became quite distinctive in their racial views. The Democratic Party became dominated by northern liberals advocating stronger governmental action to ensure equal rights. At the same time the leadership of the Republican Party became "racially conservative," that is, opposed to government intervention to ensure equal rights for minorities. As the elites and activists sorted themselves into distinct groups on the basis of their attitudes toward racial issues, the perceptions that the mass public held of the parties followed suit. Increasingly through the late 1960s and 1970s, Carmines and Stimson argue, the partisan choices of individual citizens fell in line with their attitudes on racial questions.

The role of race and racial issues in American politics is not always easy to trace, however. Because certain issues that are not explicitly stated in terms of race are nevertheless symbols of race in the minds of some people, candidates can make appeals based on racist attitudes without using racial language. For example, "law and order" may mean "keeping blacks in their place" to some, "welfare" may carry racial overtones, and so on.

Furthermore, the lack of support among whites for policies that target assistance to blacks, discussed previously, gives both parties an incentive to avoid embracing such policies, according to Kinder and Sanders. Republican leaders can oppose these policies and win support from their overwhelmingly white constituency, particularly southern whites. But Democratic leaders also have an incentive to avoid endorsing policies that would help blacks in order to garner white support. Leaders of both parties thus have incentives to avoid racial issues.

If race is not an issue to be openly discussed in political campaigns, it makes it hard to uncover the political significance of race in people's attitudes and perceptions of the political parties. On the whole, straightforward efforts to capture distinctive party images along racial lines do not succeed. Although more than half of the public in 2000 believed there were differences in what the parties stand for, only a small percentage characterized the differences in racial terms. Overwhelmingly, when people articulate differences between the parties it is in terms of symbols and issues associated with the New Deal realignment. This in all likelihood reflects the lack of overt discussion of racial issues by the political leadership of either party.

Social Issues

When presidential candidate Pat Buchanan issued a call for a "cultural war" at the Republican national convention in 1992, he reflected an emphasis on so-called traditional values that increasingly divide the two political parties. Issues such as abortion, pornography, gay rights, and sex education and prayer in the public schools have become prominent in recent years. Although common wisdom positions Democrats

on the liberal side and Republicans on the conservative side of these issues, significant numbers of political activists and leaders in both parties
are not so easily placed. Indeed, E. J. Dionne has argued that a major
reason why Americans are disenchanted with politics is that the parties
insist on defining *liberal* and *conservative* in terms of the New Deal policy
dimension, whereas the public is more interested in the traditional
value dimension.[10] Certainly one of the most potent of these social
issues is abortion. The 1973 Supreme Court decision in *Roe v. Wade*
immediately generated a polarized response, turning election races in
some areas into one-issue campaigns. Sixteen years later, *Webster v. Re-
productive Health Services* had a similar effect when the Court appeared to
invite state restrictions on the availability of abortion.

One of the difficulties in examining public opinion on the issue of
abortion lies in the responses that different question wording elicits. Although responses to the same question are quite similar over time, different phrasing of questions will produce differing proportions of "pro-
choice" or "pro-life" answers. In the following analysis, we use data from
the National Election Studies (NES), which has used the same question
in each biennial survey since 1980.

The public's views on abortion are associated with several personal
characteristics, most notably age, education, and religion. No matter
what combination of characteristics is examined in the general public,
invariably more than half of the people in the NES surveys support the
right to abortion under at least some circumstances.** In simple terms,
young people generally favor the right to abortion, the elderly are much
more likely to oppose it, and the less educated are less supportive of legal abortion than are the better educated. Given the frequent labeling
of abortion as a "women's issue," it is worth noting that there is virtually
no difference in the views of women and men.

Perhaps surprisingly, given the Roman Catholic Church's clear position in opposition to abortion, Catholics are no more inclined than
Protestants to oppose abortion. The real impact of religious differ-

---

**These figures undoubtedly underestimate the proportion taking the pro-life po-
sition. The two response choices at the pro-life end of the continuum are that abortion should never be permitted and that abortion should be permitted only to save
the life or health of the mother. The first is a more extreme position than many pro-
life advocates would take; on the other hand, the second includes circumstances
(health reasons) that have been explicitly rejected by pro-life advocates in and out
of Congress. Thus, neither category is an entirely satisfactory indicator of pro-life
sentiment. The most extreme pro-choice alternative offered is that by law a woman
should always be able to obtain an abortion as a matter of personal choice. We have
used the most extreme category at either end of the continuum to indicate pro-life
and pro-choice positions.

FIGURE 6-4   Attitudes toward Abortion among Catholics and Protestants by
              Frequency of Church Attendance, 2000

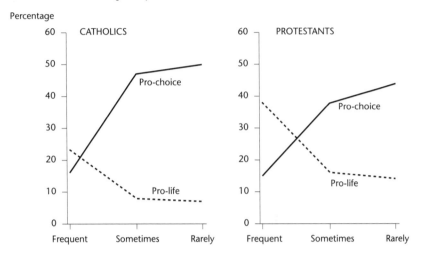

Source: 2000 National Election Study. Data provided by the Inter-university Consortium for Political and Social Research.

ences is seen when the frequency of church attendance is taken into account. Figure 6-4 shows the percentages taking the most extreme pro-life position and the most extreme pro-choice position for Catholics and Protestants with different frequencies of church attendance. Among both Catholics and Protestants, opposition to abortion increases with frequency of church attendance, but the percentages expressing pro-choice and pro-life sentiments are quite similar for the Catholic and Protestant groups. If anything, Protestants are slightly more pro-life and less pro-choice than Catholics at similar levels of church attendance.

The data in Figure 6-4 mask the different attitudes on abortion among Protestant groups, especially among whites. Table 6-4 divides mainline Protestants from Evangelicals and compares them with Catholics and those with no religious affiliation, again controlling for frequency of church attendance. The evangelical Protestants who regularly attend church are more pro-life than the Catholics who regularly attend. However, the mainline Protestants who regularly attend church are considerably more pro-choice than the frequent attenders of other faiths. Because most mainline Protestant churches take a position of individual moral responsibility on the question of abortion, the prochoice stance of many of their adherents is not surprising.

TABLE 6-4 Views on Abortion by Religion and Frequency of Church Attendance, 2000

	Mainline Protestants			Evangelical Protestants			Catholics			No affiliation
	Frequent	Sometimes	Rarely	Frequent	Sometimes	Rarely	Frequent	Sometimes	Rarely	
Pro-life	14%	3%	4%	45%	24%	18%	23%	8%	7%	8%
Pro-life, with exceptions	37	23	15	32	32	37	50	27	35	19
Pro-choice, with limitations	21	19	24	9	8	11	11	15	8	13
Pro-choice	27	52	53	14	34	35	16	46	49	57
Other, don't know	2	3	3	0	1	0	0	3	1	4
Total	101%	100%	99%	100%	99%	101%	100%	99%	100%	101%
(N)	(40)	(49)	(64)	(85)	(83)	(84)	(66)	(82)	(105)	(143)

Source: 2000 National Election Study. Data provided by the Inter-university Consortium for Political and Social Research.

Foreign Affairs

During the cold war years, foreign policy—and the study of public opinion about foreign policy—focused on relations between the United States and the Soviet Union. Questions centered on the relative strength of the two countries, the likelihood of nuclear conflict between them, and the preference for negotiation or military strength as a strategy for keeping the peace. With the breakup of the Soviet Union, the focus of foreign policy has shifted away from superpower military relations toward involvement, or noninvolvement, in trouble spots around the world. Although the American public has kept abreast of these developments, most attitudes on international affairs have remained quite stable. As Figure 6-5 shows, public opinion on two items of expenditure, foreign aid and the military, reacted very little to dramatic events abroad. The brief increase in the view that too little was being spent on the military corresponds to Reagan's campaigning on this theme in 1980. We would anticipate that the terrorist attacks on New York and Washington, D.C., bringing foreign policy into the domestic arena, will increase support for military expenditures dramatically, at least in the short run.

Some common patterns appear in many attitudes toward foreign affairs. There is almost always a notable gender gap, with women being

FIGURE 6-5   Attitudes toward Foreign Aid and Increased Spending for the Military, 1973–2000

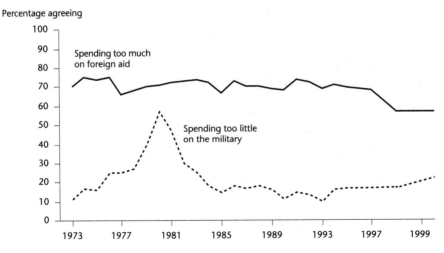

Sources: National Opinion Research Center, *General Social Surveys, 1972–2000 Cumulative File.* Data provided by the Inter-university Consortium for Political and Social Research.

less in favor of the use of military power than are men. Partisan differences also appear, with partisans of the president in office more supportive of whatever actions are taken than are partisans of the party out of power. This was seen most clearly during the war in Vietnam. Republicans were more likely to think getting involved in Vietnam was a mistake before 1969, when Democratic President Lyndon Johnson was in charge; thereafter, with Republican Richard Nixon in the White House, Democrats were more likely to view the war as a mistake.

Issues of foreign affairs vary greatly in salience, particularly in response to involvement of the nation in a military conflict. In analyzing the public's attitudes toward international events, we need to distinguish between brief conflicts and longer lasting wars. There is a truism now in American politics that says the American public will support—usually enthusiastically—brief military involvement in a foreign conflict that seems to be successful (and they will forget it quickly if it is not successful). If, however, combat drags on, support will diminish, especially if there are significant U.S. casualties. In the case of Vietnam, opposition to the war developed at a sluggish pace over a considerable period of time, as did recognition of the seriousness of U.S. involvement. In the early years, opposition to the war (as measured by support for a prompt withdrawal) was low—less than 10 percent. By 1968, it had grown to 20 percent and increased more rapidly after that. By 1970, support for withdrawal was more than 30 percent; by 1972 it was more than 40 percent. Clearly, as the war dragged on, support for military involvement declined dramatically. The Korean War more than fifty years ago offers similar evidence of the failure of public support for prolonged conflicts.

In contrast, military episodes that develop rapidly command great public attention and almost always garner public support. In the Persian Gulf War in the early 1990s, deployment of American military forces to Saudi Arabia began in the late summer of 1990, in response to Iraq's invasion of Kuwait. In the late fall, as deployment of U.S. troops continued, the public was somewhat divided in its support of this policy (Table 6-5). Fifty-nine percent of the public polled said they believed this was the correct policy to pursue, and 39 percent said they believed it was not. These views shifted fairly dramatically after the brief and well-televised war with Iraq in early 1991. When the same people were interviewed again in June 1991 following the war, 81 percent felt the war had been the right thing to do, and only 18 percent thought the United States should have stayed out.

Political analysts have long noted a "rally-round-the-flag" phenomenon that occurs at times of international crisis.[11] Presidents invariably get a boost in popularity ratings in the polls in the midst of an international incident, even when the actions of the administration are not particularly successful. John F. Kennedy got such a boost after the disastrous

TABLE 6-5   Public Opinion before and after the Persian Gulf War (Percentage Agreeing)

	Fall 1990, before the Persian Gulf War	June 1991, after the Persian Gulf War	Fall 1992, a year and a half after the Persian Gulf War
The United States did the right thing to send the military to the Persian Gulf	59	81	74
The United States should have stayed out of the Gulf	39	18	20
The United States has become stronger in the world	26	61	27
It was worth it to fight the Persian Gulf War		65	52
Approval of President Bush's handling of the Persian Gulf War	59	85	67

Sources: National Election Studies, 1990, 1991, 1992. Data provided by the Inter-university Consortium for Political and Social Research.

Bay of Pigs invasion of Cuba in 1961, as did Jimmy Carter—temporarily—when hostages were taken at the American Embassy in Iran in 1979. And as Table 6-5 shows, public approval of the senior President George Bush's handling of the Gulf War was extremely high during and immediately following the conflict, representing a substantial increase over his earlier ratings.

Not all of this enthusiasm survives the passage of time. By the fall of 1992 when the same respondents were interviewed for a third time, approval of the president's handling of the war had fallen almost 20 percent, although it was still quite high. Only a little more than half of the public thought anything good had come from the Gulf War. It would be a mistake to view these reservations as opposition to the war. Most of the people who were disenchanted with the outcome believed the fighting should have continued until Saddam Hussein was driven from power.

We can use this distinction between quick military episodes and more drawn out conflicts in our thinking about the impact of the September 11 terrorist attacks on the United States. As has been found in past crises, there was an immediate gain in presidential job approval. ABC News and the *Washington Post* completed a national survey the weekend before the attacks in which President George W. Bush's job approval was at 55 percent, about average for modern presidents in the first year of their first term. Immediately after the disaster, his job approval climbed to 86 percent. The change in "strong" approval was from 26 to 63 percent.[12]

The administration of George W. Bush faced a difficult dilemma. Swift and massive retaliation on the terrorist networks involved in the attacks would certainly be popular, but logistically difficult. The long, patient, and largely invisible campaign that most likely would have the greatest success might make it difficult for the president to sustain continued and unified public support. As this book goes to press, the military successes in Afghanistan have been sufficient to keep the president's popularity high, along with public support for the war.

Issues and Partisanship

A leading assumption is that partisan identification provides guidance for the public on policy matters—that is, most Americans adopt opinions consistent with their partisanship. Of course, it also is likely that policy positions developed independently of one's partisanship but consistent with it will reinforce feelings of party loyalty or that attitudes on issues will lead to a preference for the party most in agreement with them. Furthermore, issue preferences inconsistent with party loyalty can erode or change it. For any particular individual it would be extremely difficult to untangle the effects of partisanship and policy preferences over a long period of time. Common sense suggests that many other elements of personality and circumstances contribute to the development of issue positions, so it is no surprise to find many political views existing quite independently of partisanship.

The relationship between attitudes on public policy and partisanship is not particularly strong in any event. Even though on many issues most partisans of one party will hold a position different from that held by the majority of the other party, large numbers of people with issue positions "inconsistent" with their party identification remain loyal to that party. To account for this, it is variously suggested that (1) issues are unimportant to many voters; (2) only the issues most important to individuals need be congruent with their partisanship; (3) individuals regularly misperceive the positions of the parties to remain comfortable with both their party loyalty and their policy preferences; or (4) the positions of each party are so ambiguous or so dissimilar in different areas of the country that no clear distinction exists between the parties and thus it is not surprising that partisans of different parties appear so similar. Undoubtedly, all these explanations have some degree of truth. A long time has elapsed since there has been a crisis that would realign issues along party lines, so it is understandable that many issues are relatively independent of partisan ties. It is an indication of the recent increased polarization of the parties that racial issues and so-called moral issues have joined traditional domestic economic issues that quite clearly differentiate Democrats from Republicans.

Political Ideology

A *political ideology* is a set of interrelated attitudes that fit together into some coherent and consistent view of or orientation toward the political world. Americans have opinions on a wide range of issues, and political analysts and commentators characterize these positions as "liberal" or "conservative." Does this mean, then, that the typical American voter has an ideology that serves as a guide to political thought and action, much the same way partisanship does?

When Americans are asked to identify themselves as liberal or conservative, most are able to do so. The categories have some meaning for most Americans, although the identifications are not of overriding importance. Table 6-6 presents the ideological identification of Americans over the past two decades. A consistently larger proportion of respondents call themselves conservative rather than liberal. At the same time, about a quarter of the population regards itself as middle-of-the-road ideologically. The question wording provides respondents with the op-

TABLE 6-6   Distribution of Ideological Identification, 1972–2000

	1972	1974	1976	1978	1980	1982	1984	1986	1988	1990	1992	1994	1996	2000
Liberal	9%	13%	8%	10%	8%	7%	9%	7%	7%	9%	10%	8%	9%	11%
Somewhat liberal	10	8	8	10	9	8	9	11	9	8	10	8	11	9
Middle-of-the-road	27	26	25	27	20	22	23	28	22	25	23	27	24	25
Somewhat conservative	15	12	12	14	14	13	14	15	15	14	15	14	16	13
Conservative	12	14	13	14	15	14	15	15	17	12	15	21	19	16
Haven't thought about it	28	27	33	27	36	36	30	25	30	33	27	22	21	27
Total	101%	100%	99%	102%	102%	100%	100%	101%	100%	101%	100%	100%	100%	101%
(N)	(2,155)	(2,478)	(2,839)	(2,284)	(1,565)	(1,400)	(2,229)	(2,170)	(2,035)	(1,987)	(2,481)	(1,795)	(1,714)	(838)

Sources: National Election Studies. Data provided by the Inter-university Consortium for Political and Social Research.

portunity to say they "haven't thought much about this," and fully a quarter to a third typically respond in this way. The series of liberal and conservative responses has been remarkably stable over the years. Ideological identification, in the aggregate, is even more stable than party identification. The slight drop in the percentages saying they "haven't thought about" themselves in these terms, and the corresponding increase in the proportion of those calling themselves conservatives in 1994 and 1996, may be a response to the heightened ideological rhetoric of the 1994 campaign and the increased polarization of the political parties. The overall stability of these numbers, however, should make us cautious of commentary that finds big shifts in liberalism or conservatism in the American electorate.

Table 6-7 shows the relationship between ideological self-identification and party self-identification. Democrats are more liberal than conservative, Republicans are disproportionately conservative, and independents are rather evenly balanced. But conservatives are four times as likely to be Republicans as Democrats, and liberals are far more likely to be Democrats. The relationship between ideology and partisanship is shown in the low coincidence of liberal Republicans and conservative Democrats. Also, the electorate tends to perceive the Democratic Party as liberal and the Republican Party as conservative. Those who see an ideological difference between the parties believe the Republicans are more conservative than Democrats by a ratio of more than four to one.

Figure 6-6 presents the relationship between various social characteristics and ideological self-identification. Self-identified liberals are most frequent among blacks and college-educated whites who claim no religious affiliation. Self-identified conservatives are most common among educated white Evangelicals and Catholics. As is apparent in Figure 6-6, less well-educated evangelical Protestants are much more likely to call themselves middle-of-the-road. The major impact of education is

TABLE 6-7   Relationship between Ideological Self-Identification and Party Identification, 2000

	Democrats	Independents	Republicans	Total
Liberal	15%	10	2	27%
Middle-of-the-road	12	16	4	32
Conservative	5	12	23	40
Total[a]	32%	38	29	99%

Source: 2000 National Election Study. Data provided by the Inter-university Consortium for Political and Social Research.

[a]$N = 1,163$. "No opinion" and "haven't thought about it" responses are omitted.

FIGURE 6-6   Ideological Identification by Race/Ethnicity, Religion, and
               Education, 2000

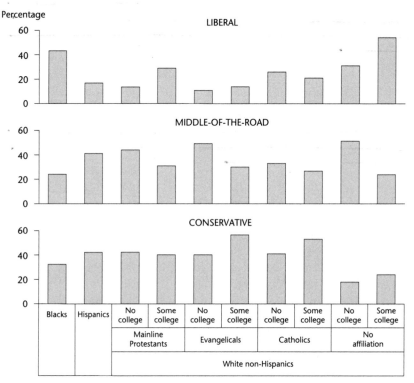

Source: 2000 National Election Study. Data provided by the Inter-university Consortium
for Political and Social Research.

to reduce the proportion of respondents who opt for the middle category. The college educated are more likely to call themselves either liberal or conservative than the high school educated. This tendency
would be even greater if those who offered no self-identification were
included.

Approximately half the public identifies itself as liberal or conservative. Do these individuals use this ideological orientation to organize
political information and attitudes? Does political ideology play a role
for Americans similar to the role of partisanship as a basic determinant
of their specific political views? Analysis has usually centered on two
kinds of evidence to assess the extent of ideological thinking in the
American electorate: the use of ideological concepts in discussing politics and the consistency of attitudes on related issues, suggesting an underlying perspective in the individual's approach to politics.

Data reported in Angus Campbell et al.'s *The American Voter* showed

TABLE 6-8   Distribution of the Levels of Conceptualization, 1956–1988

Levels of conceptualization	1956	1960	1964	1968	1972	1976	1980	1984	1988
Ideologues	12%	19%	27%	26%	22%	21%	21%	19%	18%
Group benefit	42	31	27	24	27	26	31	26	36
Nature of the times	24	26	20	29	34	30	30	35	25
No issue content	22	23	26	21	17	24	19	19	21
Total	100%	99%	100%	100%	100%	101%	101%	99%	100%
(N)	(1,740)	(1,741)	(1,431)	(1,319)	(1,372)	(2,870)	(1,612)	(2,257)	(2,040)

Source: Richard G. Niemi and Herbert F. Weisberg, eds., *Controversies in Voting Behavior,* 3d ed. (Washington, D.C.: CQ Press, 1993), 89.

that very few members of the electorate discussed their evaluations of the parties and the candidates in ideological language; only 12 percent did so in 1956.[13] The work of John Pierce and others has contributed to similar analysis of subsequent years.[14] As shown in Table 6-8, a change occurred in 1964. In fact, the proportions of "ideologues" doubled in 1964 over 1956 but still constituted only about one quarter of the electorate. This does not mean that most voters have no notions about what the parties stand for or what they are likely to do when in office. Large proportions of the electorate evaluate the parties with group symbols: "The Democrats help the working man" and "Republicans are good for business." Still, there is a general lack of commitment to some set of abstract principles about the role of government in society on the basis of which the parties are evaluated.

Of course, individuals may simply be unsophisticated in the verbal descriptions of their feelings about politics and political parties. Their ideology may guide their political decisions, but they may be unable to articulate it. In that case, the individuals' attitudes toward public issues might be expected to show a degree of coherence and consistency, because those positions would be arrived at through the application of a common underlying set of political ideals. If individuals are liberal on one issue, one would expect them to be liberal on other related issues; if they are conservative on one, they would be conservative on others. The most sophisticated analysis of ideological perspectives and consistency in issue positions, usually called *issue constraint,* was carried out by Philip Converse using data from 1956, 1958, and 1960.[15] He found that the strength of relationship among domestic issues and among foreign policy issues was about twice as strong as the relationship between domestic and foreign issues. By normal standards even the strongest relationship among domestic issues did not suggest particularly impressive issue consistency. In 1974 Norman Nie and Kristi Andersen augmented this analysis with the addition of another decade of coverage.[16] As with several other patterns, a change occurred during the campaign of 1964.

The degree of issue constraint on various policy matters increased in 1964 and remains relatively high to the present.

As might be expected, the degree of consistency among attitudes on different issues varies with the level of education of the individual; the more educated are substantially more consistent in their views than the less educated. However, increasing levels of education do not appear to account for the increase in issue constraint. The work of Nie and Andersen shows convincingly that interest in politics is more critical. In other words, as the public becomes more concerned with issues and more attentive to political leaders, the public perceives a higher degree of issue coherence. Almost certainly the electorate generally has the capacity for greater issue constraint than it has shown; however, the exercise of the capacity depends much more on political leaders and events than on the characteristics of the electorate. When political leaders use ideological terms to describe themselves and the clusters of issues that they support, the electorate is quite capable of following suit.

The degree of issue constraint will, of course, depend on the range of issues considered. *The American Voter* documented a rather coherent set of attitudes on welfare policies and governmental activity, even in the 1950s. When the analysis moves to more disparate issues, such as support for welfare policies and civil liberties, the relationship weakens substantially. It can be argued, of course, that little relationship should be expected between positions in these different issue areas because they tap different ideological dimensions with no logical or necessary connections among them. For example, there is nothing logically inconsistent in a person's opposing government regulation of business and believing in racial equality. In the past, internationalist views in foreign policy were considered the liberal position and isolationist attitudes conservative; however, the cold war and Vietnam did much to rearrange these notions as liberals argued against American involvement and conservatives became more aggressive internationalists. In considering the question of issue constraint, two points should be kept in mind: (1) the meaning of the terms *liberal* and *conservative* change with time, as do the connections between these ideologies and specific historical events; and (2) analysts, in studying issue constraint, invariably impose on the analysis their own version of ideological consistency, which, in light of the ambiguities surrounding the terms, is likely to be somewhat artificial.

A less strenuous criterion than issue constraint for assessing the impact of ideology on political attitudes is simply to look at the relationship between individuals' ideological identification and their positions on various issues taken one at a time. Here we find substantial relationships. The relationship between ideological identification and liberal views on various policy matters over the past twenty-eight years is shown in Table 6-9. About one fourth of the people sampled did not have an ideological position or did not profess attitudes on these issues and are,

TABLE 6-9   Relationship between Ideological Identification and Liberal Positions on Issues, 1972–2000

	Liberal	Somewhat liberal	Middle-of-the-road	Somewhat conservative	Conservative
Increase government services (2000)	63	61	39	29	24
Favor government health insurance (2000)	49	42	35	29	20
Pro-choice on abortion (2000)	67	52	47	27	20
Government help for blacks (2000)	34	18	19	14	9
Protect the environment (2000)	56	53	47	56	28
Oppose school vouchers (2000)	44	48	52	46	28
Protect homosexuals from job discrimination (1996)	87	79	68	63	39
Not worth it to fight in Persian Gulf (1992)	66	45	41	30	24
Cut defense spending (1988)	60	50	36	26	18
Support for the Equal Rights Amendment (1980)	91	78	64	48	38
Legalize marijuana (1976)	60	49	24	24	10
Oppose the Vietnam War (1972)	76	61	39	33	27

Sources: National Election Studies. Data provided by the Inter-university Consortium for Political and Social Research.

Note: The numbers in the table are the percentages taking the liberal position on each issue.

therefore, missing in this analysis. Nevertheless, the data in Table 6-9 document strong, consistent relationships between ideological identification and many issue positions. The data do not, however, demonstrate that ideology determines issue positions.

If everyone had a strong ideology, attitudes would be determined by that ideology. To a considerable extent, this appears to happen to the most politically alert and concerned in our society, but this group is only a small minority of the total adult population. To the extent that the major American political parties are ideologically oriented, then by following the parties or political leaders in these parties, Americans have their opinions determined indirectly by ideology. American political parties are often characterized as nonideological, and there have been substantial historical periods when the parties have seemed bent on obscuring the differences between them. At other times, such as 1964 and the early 1990s, political leaders were more intent on drawing distinctions between themselves and the opposing party in ideological terms. At these times, the public responds by appearing more ideological, too.

Public Opinion and Political Leadership

The study of public opinion is of obvious relevance to public officials and political journalists who wish to assess the mood of the people on various topics, but the extent to which decision makers are influenced by public opinion on any particular policy is almost impossible to determine. Although policy makers must have some sense of the public mood, no one supposes that they measure precisely the attitudes of the public or are influenced by public opinion alone.

Political analysts and public officials both have difficulty assessing the likely impact of public opinion as measured by public opinion polls because the intensity of feelings will influence the willingness of the public to act on their views. Public officials who value their careers must be conscious of the issues that raise feelings intense enough to cause people to contribute money, to campaign, and to cast their ballots solely on the basis of that issue. As a result, public officials may be more responsive to the desires of small, intense groups than to larger, but basically indifferent, segments of the public.

In American society public attitudes toward policies usually can be described in one of two ways: as *permissive* opinion, whereby a wide range of possible government activities are acceptable to the public, or, in contrast, as *directive* opinion, either supportive or negative, whereby specific alternatives are definitely demanded or opposed. Ordinarily, policy alternatives advocated by both political parties are within the range of permissive opinion, a situation that does not create highly salient issues or sharp cleavages in the public even though political leaders may present their various positions dramatically. Only when many people hold directive opinions will the level of issue salience rise or issue clashes appear among the public. For example, undoubtedly there is widespread directive support for public education in this country; most individuals demand a system of public education or would demand it were it threatened. At the same time there is permissive support for a wide range of policies and programs in public education. Governments at several levels may engage in a variety of programs without arousing the public to opposition or support. Within this permissive range the public is indifferent.

On occasion, out-and-out opposition to programs develops, and directive opinion is formed that imposes a limit on how far government can go. For example, the widespread opposition to busing children out of their neighborhoods for purposes of integration has perhaps become a directive, negative opinion. It is no easy matter for political analysts or politicians to discover the boundaries between permissive and directive opinions. Political leaders are likely to argue that there are supportive, directive opinions for their own positions and negative, directive opinions for their opponents' views. One should be skeptical of these claims because it is much more likely that there are permissive opinions and casual indifference toward the alternative views. Indifference is widespread and, of course, does not create political pressure. It frees political leaders of restrictions on issue positions but, on balance, is probably more frustrating than welcome.

Notes

1. Philip Converse, "The Nature of Belief Systems in Mass Publics," in *Ideology and Discontent*, ed. David Apter (New York: Free Press, 1964), 206–261.
2. Edward G. Carmines and James A. Stimson, "The Two Faces of Issue Voting," *American Political Science Review* 74 (1980): 78–91.
3. In the 1993 General Social Survey, for example, 57 percent said "too much" was being spent on "welfare"; however, 65 percent said "too little" was being spent on "assistance to the poor."
4. This view is most prominently associated with Paul M. Sniderman and Edward G. Carmines, *Reaching Beyond Race* (Cambridge: Harvard University Press, 1997). See also Paul M. Sniderman, Philip E. Tetlock, and Edward G. Carmines, *Prejudice, Politics, and the American Dilemma* (Stanford: Stanford University Press, 1993).
5. A strong, recent statement of this "symbolic racism" position is in Donald R. Kinder and Lynn M. Sanders, *Divided by Color* (Chicago: University of Chicago Press, 1996).
6. This is closely linked to the "symbolic racism" contention that a belief in individualism combines with racial hostility to produce racial resentment as a position based on a nonracial principle.

7. This position is most commonly associated with Lawrence Bobo. See his "Race and Beliefs about Affirmative Action," in *Racialized Politics*, ed. David Sears, Jim Sidanius, and Lawrence Bobo (Chicago: University of Chicago Press, 2000), chap. 5.

8. This position is represented by Jim Sidanius in *Social Dominance: An Intergroup Theory of Social Dominance and Oppression* (Cambridge: Cambridge University Press, 1999).

9. Edward G. Carmines and James A. Stimson, *Issue Evolution: Race and the Transformation of American Politics* (Princeton: Princeton University Press, 1989).

10. E. J. Dionne, *Why Americans Hate Politics* (New York: Simon & Schuster, 1991).

11. John E. Mueller, *War, Presidents, and Public Opinion* (New York: Wiley, 1973), 208–213.

12. These data were available at www.pollingreport.com on September 14, 2001.

13. Angus Campbell, Philip E. Converse, Warren E. Miller, and Donald E. Stokes, *The American Voter* (New York: Wiley, 1960), 249.

14. John C. Pierce, "Ideology, Attitudes and Voting Behavior of the American Electorate: 1956, 1960, 1964" (Ph.D. diss., University of Minnesota, 1969), Table 3.1, 63; and Paul R. Hagner and John C. Pierce, "Conceptualization and Consistency in Political Beliefs: 1956–1976" (Paper presented at the annual meeting of the Midwest Political Science Association, Chicago, 1981). See also Norman H. Nie, Sidney Verba, and John R. Petrocik, *The Changing American Voter* (Cambridge: Harvard University Press, 1976), chap. 7.

15. Converse, "The Nature of Belief Systems in Mass Publics," 206–261.

16. Norman H. Nie and Kristi Andersen, "Mass Belief Systems Revisited: Political Change and Attitude Structure," *Journal of Politics* 36 (September 1974): 541–591.

Suggested Readings

Carmines, Edward G., and James A. Stimson. *Issue Evolution: Race and the Transformation of American Politics*. Princeton: Princeton University Press, 1989. A fascinating account of the role of racial issues and policies in American politics in recent decades.

Converse, Philip E. "The Nature of Belief Systems in Mass Publics." In *Ideology and Discontent*, edited by David Apter. New York: Free Press, 1964. A classic analysis of the levels of sophistication in the American public.

Hochschild, Jennifer L. *What's Fair*. Cambridge: Harvard University Press, 1981. An intensive, in-depth study of the beliefs and attitudes of a few people that deals with traditional topics from a different perspective.

Mayer, William G. *The Changing American Mind*. Ann Arbor: University of Michigan Press, 1992. Analysis of changes in issue positions between 1960 and 1988.

Page, Benjamin J., and Robert Y. Shapiro. *The Rational Public*. Chicago: University of Chicago Press, 1992. Analysis of the American public's views on policy issues over the past fifty years.

Sniderman, Paul M., Richard A. Brody, and Philip E. Tetlock. *Reasoning and Choice*. Cambridge: Cambridge University Press, 1991. A political, psychological approach to the study of issues and ideology.

Internet Resources

The Web site of the National Election Studies, www.umich.edu/~nes/, has extensive data on the topics covered in this chapter. Click on "Ideological Self-Identification" for a variety of ideological items in a number of election years. Click on "Public Opinion on Public Policy Issues" for a wide range of attitudes from 1952 to the present. Each political item is broken down by an extensive set of social characteristics.

Political Communication and the Mass Media

MUCH ATTENTION has been focused on the process of change in political opinions, both in terms of the conditions for such change and the possibilities of instigating widespread changes in political beliefs through the mass media. At the extremes, the process of influencing political opinions is labeled *brainwashing* or *propaganda;* in reality, only a matter of degree separates these forms of influence from political persuasion, campaigning, or even education. All the efforts covered by these terms are directed toward changing individuals' political ideas, values, and opinions or toward fostering some political action. Enormous amounts of time and money are expended in American society to change political views. The very diversity of these efforts to influence the public mind, along with the diversity and complexity of the society itself, makes highly unlikely a quick or uniform public response to any one of these attempts. Only dramatic events or crises can quickly change the public's views. Although news of these events comes through the media, the impact results from the events themselves, not simply the media imagery.

Political persuasion probably is most effective in casual personal relationships. The impact of the mass media is probably important in shaping the contours of political discourse but only gradually and over fairly long periods of time. At the same time, the role that the media have in making information widely available is extremely important in creating the conditions under which attitude change occurs. In this chapter we will consider the basic processes of opinion change and the impact of the mass media and election campaigns on individual political behavior.

Functions of Opinions
for Individuals

Social psychology suggests that an individual's opinions can serve various purposes: cognitive, social, and psychological. Cognitive functions of opinions cover the efforts to give meaning to our social environment and to relate elements of belief and knowledge to one another. Opinions generally relate directly or indirectly to an individual's most significant goals or values. Somehow the policy supported by a political opinion is expected to be consistent with one's most important political values.

Opinions serve a social function if they aid the individual in adjusting to others or in becoming part of a group. In some cases individuals may use opinions to set themselves apart from others. Political and social issues may be too unimportant in general to serve social purposes for most people, and there is little evidence to indicate that strong social conformity pressures affect their views on most political issues. Nevertheless, for highly salient issues an individual is apt to find that holding a socially unacceptable view is both uncomfortable and costly.

An opinion also may serve purposes for an individual that are not dependent on its social, economic, or political meaning but on its special psychological significance for the individual. For example, an individual might hold strongly prejudicial opinions against some group because it enhances self-esteem to feel superior to others, or an individual might project undesirable qualities onto a certain group and thereby disassociate him- or herself from those qualities. The problem with psychological attachments of this kind is that the opinions so based are not responsive to ordinary influence because of their psychological importance to the individual. Most Americans do not appear to attach strong psychological meaning to their political opinions. Furthermore, in a modern pluralistic society with its open political processes, opinions on significant political subjects are unlikely to remain privatized and solely of psychological relevance to the individual; opinions also take on social and cognitive functions.

Most discussions of political opinions imply a more or less reasoned handling of opinions by individuals. They imply that individuals intelligently relate their opinions to one another and that a logical relationship exists between a goal and a preference for policies leading to that goal. The implication of this perspective, as we shall see in the next section, is that opinions can be changed if the cognitive content of the attitude is changed—that is, if new information is brought to the attention of the individual. However, if individuals hold their opinions for the social or psychological purposes they serve, rather than for the cognitive, providing these individuals with more information or altering the policy implications of the opinion will not necessarily lead to opinion change.

Opinion Consistency and Dissonance

The analysis of inconsistency in opinions has much in common with the cross-pressure hypothesis considered in Chapter 5. In psychology this analysis of opinions has taken the form of identifying elements of several opinions as consistent with one another or as being in conflict (dissonant). Because dissonance is assumed to be disturbing, an individual presumably will try to avoid or reduce dissonance. An example of dissonance should clarify these concepts.[1]

Suppose a Republican believes that all Democratic administrations are corrupt and that Republicans stand for honest government, and the individual's party loyalty is justified on this basis. If the individual hears that a Republican governor is taking bribes, this information conflicts with the person's earlier views and may create dissonance among them. The dissonance could be reduced by justifying his or her loyalty on a new basis or by denying or discrediting the new information. A denial might take the form of deciding that the governor is being framed by opponents.

Individuals have many psychological defenses against the potential dissonance represented by new information that conflicts with their existing attitudes: *selective exposure*, or not paying attention to conflicting information; *selective perception*, misinterpreting such information, or rejecting the sources of the information as lacking credibility; *compartmentalization*, not making the connections between dissonant attitudes; and *rationalization*, developing an unwarranted interpretation of a situation to avoid confronting the real one. Should the meaning of the information be unavoidable, attitude change to restore harmony may result. Typically, individuals will change dissonant patterns in the easiest way; the opinions or beliefs that are least important to the individual will be changed rather than important ideas or values.

Political opinions are probably most often changed simply by providing individuals with more information. This additional information may be no more than some new facts about the environment or indications that many political leaders whom an individual respects hold a particular view. The low salience of most political issues, plus the widespread emphasis on debate and discussion, leads to circumstances that improve the opportunities for changing opinions with information.

Political Communication
and Attitude Change

Individuals in the public receive ideas and information intended to alter their political opinions from a variety of sources. Some sources are political leaders and commentators whose views arrive impersonally through the mass media; others are friends, coworkers, and family members who influence opinions through personal contact. Much remains to be learned about political persuasion and communication, but at least occasionally many Americans engage in attempts to influence others, and almost everyone is regularly the recipient of large quantities of political communication.

A somewhat oversimplified view of the transmission of political information would have the media beaming a uniform message to a mass audience made up of isolated individuals. The audience would receive all or most of its information from the media; thus, public opinion would be a direct product of the information and perspective provided through the media. A more complex view suggests that information is transmitted in what is called a "two-step flow of communication."[2] Information is transmitted from "opinion elites" (leaders in the society, such as politicians, organizational leaders, news commentators) to a minority of the public—the "opinion leaders"—and from them to the remainder of the public:

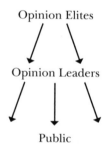

Opinion Elites

Opinion Leaders

Public

The information from opinion elites usually is sent through the mass media, but this view implies that only a portion of the audience, the opinion leaders, is attentive to any particular type of information such as political news. These opinion leaders, as intermediaries, then interpret, modify, and explain facts and events to those friends and neighbors who are less interested in or concerned with these happenings. In the process, the original message conveyed through the media becomes many somewhat different messages as it reaches the public.

The two-step flow model may not be literally true in most cases, and public opinion research has generally failed to turn up many people who recognize themselves as opinion leaders. Even so, most members of the public probably do receive information from the mass media in the context of their social groups. Thus, they filter the information and interpretations of the media through not only their own perceptions, experiences, and existing attitudes but also those of people around them. Only when the media have the attention of most members of the audience and a virtual monopoly over the kinds of information received by a public that has few existing attitudes about the subject can the media produce anything like a uniform change in public attitudes.

A somewhat different argument, also based on the role of social influences on the development of public opinion, has been made by Elisabeth Noelle-Neumann in *The Spiral of Silence*.[3] She argues that members of society sense that some views are increasing in popularity, even if these ascending viewpoints are held only by a minority. Under such circumstances people become reluctant to express opinions contrary to the presumed ascending view, whereas individuals holding that view are emboldened and express themselves more freely. This furthers the illusion that one viewpoint is widely shared. People then adopt the viewpoint because of this largely imaginary public pressure. Although intriguing, the attractiveness of this argument is diminished somewhat by the almost total lack of evidence in support of it.

In the remainder of this chapter we will consider the impact of the mass media on political attitudes in the context of political campaigns. Because the media can be influential only if people are paying attention, we will look at the question of the overall attentiveness of the public to political news. Because the impact of the media varies depending on the existing attitudes and information of the audience, we will examine the impact of the media on different kinds of people and in different campaign contexts. To begin, however, we need to draw some distinctions among the various types of media. First, the impact of information may be different depending on the type of media through which it is received. Precisely the same information received through television, radio, or a newspaper may impress the recipient quite differently. For example, viewing a speech on television may be more dramatic than hearing it on radio or reading the text in a newspaper. Something like this occurred in 1960 when television viewers of the first of three presidential debates between John Kennedy and Richard Nixon had a less favorable impression of Nixon than did radio listeners. A difficult topic, however, may be more easily absorbed by reading and rereading a newspaper article rather than having a story flash by once on television.

Second, the media differ in what they offer. Simple elements of information are more quickly and dramatically presented to a large audience on television than they can be through the print media. Television, however, may systematically underinform its audience by rarely offering more than a "headline service" of a minute or two on any one story. The more the public wants information and is motivated to seek it, the more important newspapers, magazines, and the Internet become. It is easy to search for items of information in print media, and quite difficult with radio and television. The characteristics of the media give them different roles in the formation of public opinion. In general, television alerts the public to a variety of topics; newspapers inform a smaller segment of the public in greater depth.

Third, there exists an increasing diversity of news sources available through television, especially over the past ten years. CNN, MSNBC, and Fox News are genuine alternatives to the broadcast networks, especially when it comes to fast-breaking news. Surveys done by The Pew Research Center for The People & The Press in 2000 estimate that more than half the public watches CNN "sometimes" and 21 percent do so "regularly."[4] The CSPAN channels provide extensive coverage of both the U.S. House of Representatives and the Senate, as well as other political events, without the intermediary of network editing and commentary. Call-in television and radio provide lengthy discussions of public issues and, since 1992, offer a mechanism whereby candidates can bypass the normal news channels and receive unmediated coverage.

The Internet as a news source is a recent development with intriguing characteristics. Providing almost unlimited access to information, it requires the consumer actively to seek it out. It also offers opportunities to "talk back" or comment on the news and to be put in touch with other like-minded people. There are few obvious "gatekeepers" on the Internet, and the issues of the reliability and credibility of information are largely left to the user to determine. The opportunities for "whispering campaigns" of rumor and misinformation are awesome.

Fourth, the impact of editorial endorsements by newspapers (television and radio stations rarely make endorsements) should be assessed independently of news coverage, although editorial preferences may bias news stories. Newspaper endorsements seemingly have a minimal impact in presidential elections where many other sources of influence exist.[5] In less visible, local races, a newspaper editorial may influence many voters.[6] Some concern exists that major newspaper chains could wield significant power nationally by lining up their papers behind one candidate. However, in recent years the large chains have generally left their papers free to make decisions locally.

Fifth, throughout our discussion we need to make the distinction between the impact of news coverage by the media and political advertising carried by the media. This is not easy to do, especially because the news media often cover political advertising as if it were news and consciously or unconsciously pick up themes from political ads and weave them into their own coverage.[7] The placing of political advertising in news programs increases the difficulty in separating news from ads. Even the "ad watches" that news organizations use to critique the advertising of candidates may contribute to confusion over what is news and what is paid advertising.

Attention to the Media

Obviously, for the media to have an impact on an individual's political attitudes and behavior, the individual must give some degree of attention to the media when political information is being conveyed. Almost all Americans have access to television and watch political news at least some of the time. In 2000, a majority of Americans (63 percent) reported reading a daily newspaper; somewhat fewer read a newspaper for political news. This represents something of a decline in daily newspaper readership from more than 70 percent earlier in the 1990s.[8] Occasional newspaper reading is, of course, higher.

There is much discussion in the scholarly literature on mass media of the capacity to bring matters to the attention of the public or to conceal them.[9] This is usually referred to as *agenda setting*. The literature suggests that the media have great influence over what the public is aware of and concerned with. Television news and front-page stories in newspapers focus the public's attention on a few major stories each day. This function, sometimes called "headline service," tells the public: Here are important developments you should be aware of. Major events, such as the September 11 terrorist attacks, or scandalous happenings, such as the Monica Lewinsky affair, push other stories off the agenda. The media made it almost impossible for an ordinary American to be unaware of these events. That is agenda setting.

Television often plays a critical role in bringing events and issues to the attention of the American public. Television presents certain types of information in an exceptionally dramatic or impressive way. The Persian Gulf War was televised to an unprecedented extent. The American public watched a real-life video arcade of modern warfare. Sixty-seven percent of a national sample reported following the war "very closely."[10] In the short run, this coverage created the impression of an overwhelming military victory and great satisfaction with the performance of the president, George Bush. In just ten days, from January 7 to January 17, 1991, approval of the senior President Bush's handling of the crisis jumped from 57 percent to 85 percent, and those supporting military action increased from 47 percent to 78 percent.[11] With the passage of time, evaluations became more mixed.

Perhaps nothing in television history compares with the coverage of the attacks on the World Trade Center and the Pentagon. The major news channels abandoned regular programming and focused on the attacks and their aftermath for days. Virtually everyone in the country was attentive to this coverage, and most people had a strong emotional reaction to what they saw.

The news media, particularly television, can rivet public attention on certain issues and, in doing so, limit the policy-making options of political leaders. The range of subjects on which this can be done is rather narrow, however. Death, destruction, intrigue, or pathos is generally an essential ingredient. More abstract or mundane political issues are easily ignored by most of the public.

It is also true, however, that many potential news items are never reported, either in the print media or on television. This is the result of a process often referred to as *gatekeeping*,[12] which has been alluded to earlier. The media are more selective than a phrase such as "all the news that's fit to print" suggests. Bias in gatekeeping and agenda setting can occur when items are kept from the public that would have been of considerable interest or when items the public otherwise would have ignored are made to seem important. Neither of these effects is easily demonstrated with political information and opinions. It is fairly easy to show that a particular newspaper or a given television station may ignore certain topics or exaggerate others, but it is extremely difficult to find evidence of any impact of selective coverage on the public.

Although the media may focus on certain news items, the public has an enormous capacity for ignoring the coverage and being highly selective about what to take an interest in. First the *Los Angeles Times Mirror* and later The Pew Research Center for The People & The Press have engaged in an extensive project to explore the public's awareness of and interest in news stories.[13] Its analysis shows that some news stories, like the explosion of the space shuttle *Challenger* or the 1989 San Francisco earthquake, were followed with great interest by most of the public. As shown in Table 7-1, almost all the news stories from January 1986 to November 2001 that were followed "very closely" by large percentages of the public were military operations or disasters of one sort or another. In contrast, fewer than 25 percent of the public paid close attention to news stories about the mapping of the human genetic code, charges that Speaker Newt Gingrich violated House ethics rules, or the Helsinki summit between President Clinton and Boris Yeltsin.

As would be expected, a large percentage of the public followed news about the terrorist attacks on September 11, 2001, very closely. Some of the people who did not follow the story said they were so distraught they avoided the news on terrorism. Public attention to the military activities in Afghanistan, shown in Table 7-1 at 51 percent, is noticeably below the level of attention to the Persian Gulf War in 1991 at

TABLE 7-1   Most Closely Followed News Stories and Other Selected News
Items, 1986–2001

News stories	Percentage following very closely
Ten most closely followed news stories	
Explosion of the space shuttle *Challenger* (January 1986)	80
Terrorism attacks on the United States (September 2001)	74
San Francisco earthquake (November 1989)	73
Verdict in Rodney King case and subsequent violence (May 1992)	70
TWA 800 crash (July 1996)	69
Rescue of little girl in Texas who fell into a well (October 1987)	69
Columbine High School shooting (April 1999)	68
Persian Gulf War (January 1991)	67
Hurricane Andrew (September 1992)	66
Iraq's invasion of Kuwait and deployment of U.S. forces (August 1990)	66
Other news stories	
Increases in the price of gasoline (October 1990)	62
Increases in the price of gasoline (June 2000)	61
Increases in the price of gasoline (May 2001)	61
Outcome of 1996 presidential election (November 1996)	55
Release of U.S. air crew held in China (April 2001)	55
Crash of John F. Kennedy Jr.'s plane (July 1999)	54
Death of Princess Diana (September 1997)	54
U.S. military effort in Afghanistan (October 2001)	51
Waco, Texas, incident (May 1993)	50
Breakup of the Soviet Union (October 1991)	47
Clinton health care reform proposals (December 1993)	45
Debate over Elian Gonzalez (January 2000)	39
Outcome of the presidential election (November 2000)	38
Reports about the condition of the U.S. economy (April 2001)	36
Debate in Congress over George W. Bush's budget and tax cut plan (February 2001)	31
Charges that Newt Gingrich violated House ethics rules (January 1997)	23
Election of Jesse Ventura as governor of Minnesota (November 1998)	20
Mapping the human genetic code (July 2000)	16
Helsinki summit between President Bill Clinton and Boris Yeltsin (April 1997)	6

Source: The Pew Research Center for The People & The Press, www.people-press.org.

67 percent. In data not shown, the Pew Research Center found that attention to the war in Afghanistan dropped in November 2001. The Afghanistan war and the anthrax stories were followed very closely by slightly less than half the public.[14]

The combination of television, newspapers, radio, and magazines represents an extraordinary capacity to inform the public rapidly and in considerable depth about major political news items. Add to this the informal communication about the news of the day that most people engage in and it is easy to see that the American public is in a position to be well informed. That as many people persist in *not* informing themselves about most political news is not a failure of the mass media to make the news available in a variety of forms.

A number of scholars have pointed out that it may be quite rational for voters to ignore a lot of the political information around them. Rational choice theorists, following the lead of economist Anthony Downs,[15] argue that the benefits derived from reaching a "correct" decision on a candidate or policy may not be worth the costs the voter incurs in finding out the information. It is rational, therefore, for the voter to take a number of information shortcuts, such as relying on someone else's judgment or voting according to one's established party identification. Samuel Popkin[16] uses the analogy of "fire alarms" versus "police patrols" to explain how most people view political information. Rather than patrolling the political "neighborhood" constantly to make sure there is nothing there that requires their attention, most citizens rely on others to raise the alarm when something really important happens. Television news and newspaper headlines may be enough to tell average citizens whether they need to delve deeper into a particular story.

A minority of people are motivated to follow political news and inform themselves broadly about public affairs. Some people need to be informed about government and politics—or some aspects of it—to do their jobs. Others are simply interested in politics, so searching out information is less burdensome to them. It is not surprising that scholars studying media behavior have consistently found a strong relationship between interest in politics and attention to political news. In his study of the media behavior of voters in Erie, Pennsylvania, and Los Angeles during the 1976 presidential election, Thomas Patterson found that the most interested voters not only paid the most attention to the media, they also were able to recall political news heard on television or read in the newspaper better than the less interested.[17] Interested individuals are better equipped than the uninterested and inattentive to retain and use new elements of information that come their way.

Because the most interested voters are also the most partisan, there is also a relationship between attention to the media and partisanship. The fact that strong partisans and politically interested people are most

FIGURE 7-1   Hypothetical Relationship between Mass Media Attention and Stability of Voting Behavior

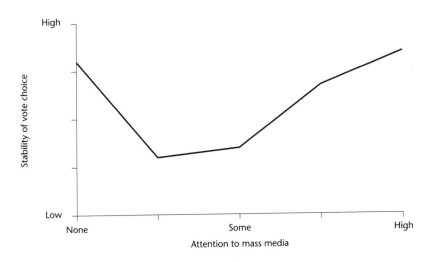

attentive to the media accounts for the somewhat paradoxical finding that those with the most exposure to the media are among the least affected by it. The impact of mass media exposure on voting behavior in elections in the 1950s was studied by Philip Converse, who drew several conclusions based on findings similar to those represented in Figure 7-1.[18] The voters most stable in their preferences (whether stability is measured during a campaign or between elections) would be those who are highly attentive to mass media but firmly committed. Those who pay no attention to media communication remain stable in their vote choices because no new information is introduced to change their votes. The shifting, unstable voters are more likely to be those with moderate exposure to mass media. Unfortunately, efforts at replicating Converse's findings for other election years have failed to uncover similar patterns. One difficulty may be the virtual disappearance of voters with no exposure to the mass media in recent years. Nevertheless, the reasoning behind this expected relationship is quite compelling: The impact of the media is likely to be greatest when the recipients of the message have little information and few existing attitudes.

The Media and Presidential Approval Ratings

Presidential approval ratings, regularly measured by public opinion polling organizations, reflect both the effect media coverage can have on political attitudes and its limitations. Media polls regularly ask about and report on the public's views on how the president is handling his job.

The various polling organizations ask the question in different ways, but basically what they report, and what we report here, is the percentage of the public that approves of the way the president is doing his job—not the degree of enthusiasm people feel. The approval measure sometimes behaves oddly. For example, President Ronald Reagan's approval rating jumped 10 percent after he was shot, presumably an expression of sympathy and not an assessment of the job he was doing.

In one sense, the ratings are a function of media content, because media coverage is the only source of information about the president for most people. The most precipitous changes in approval ratings, though, result from dramatic and important events. Although the media coverage colors the recipient's perception of these events, the media are usually not free to ignore them; it is the events themselves, not just the coverage, that makes them compelling.

Most presidents begin a term with high ratings, a phenomenon referred to as a "honeymoon effect." Presidents usually suffer a decline in approval ratings the longer they are in office. We not only expect the ratings to decline over time, but as the public becomes more knowledgeable about a president, the approval ratings should become more stable and more retrospective. In other words, the more people know about the president, the less impact some new element of information has and the more their approval or disapproval represents a summary judgment. As this happens, the day-to-day events covered by the media, and the coverage itself, have less impact in shaping the attitudes of the public.

Extraordinary events can boost a president's popularity while in office. As noted in the previous chapter, international crises usually produce an increase in approval ratings as the public rallies round the flag and its representative, the president. Winning a second term (or even campaigning for one), with the accompanying election fanfare, also lifts presidential approval scores. These boosts usually prove to be temporary, and popularity ratings usually drift downward again as time in office passes.

The senior president Bush's approval ratings illustrate the transitory nature of the increase in popularity associated with international crises. Bush's approval ratings improved dramatically during the 1991 Persian Gulf War, far into his term as president. Poll results varied, but generally he was getting approval ratings as high as any president had ever received. A year later, by the fall of 1992, his ratings had dropped to half of that, and he was receiving ratings about as low as any past president.

What happened to Bush's ratings also illustrates the public's shifting focus on what matters in the assessment of the president. Before and after the Persian Gulf War, the public's attention was on the economy. Throughout 1990, 1991, and 1992, President Bush received low ratings for his handling of the economy, so when the economy mattered most to people, his overall approval ratings were low. During the Persian Gulf War, attention shifted to foreign affairs, an area in which Bush had always enjoyed high ratings, and this translated, for a while, into high overall approval ratings.

The trend of President Clinton's approval is somewhat unusual in that he managed to reverse a rather precipitous decline in popularity on the basis of a confrontation in domestic politics, rather than an international one. As with so many attitudes, approval ratings are colored by partisanship. In a domestic political conflict, the enhanced approval a president gains from his own partisans might be expected to be offset by increased hostility of partisans of the other party. But, in fact, in Clinton's confrontation with congressional Republicans over shutting down the government in 1995, his approval ratings moved up and down in similar ways across all partisan categories.

Clinton ended his term in office in January 2001 with approval ratings of 61 percent, unprecedented for a modern president at the end of his second term. Commentators and politicians have asked repeatedly how Clinton could maintain such high approval ratings when the public was thoroughly aware of his personal misbehavior. To put it differently, if the public disapproved of Clinton's personal behavior, why did the public not disapprove of the job he was doing as president? One possibility is that the personal behavior of a public official does not matter to most people—but clearly that is not the case. An overwhelming majority of Americans thought Clinton lacked the ability to provide moral leadership for the country and that providing moral leadership was important for a president to do. The explanation, to the extent that we have one, appears to be partisanship. Republicans made the connection between personal misbehavior and the job Clinton was doing as president and reported their disapproval. Democrats did not link the two views. One supposes that with a Republican president the patterns would be reversed. In Clinton's case independents behaved more like Democrats than like Republicans—they did not link personal behavior with the job of president. In July of 1998 a CBS News poll asked people whether they thought of "this whole situation more as a private matter having to do with Bill Clinton's personal life, or more as a public matter having to do with Bill Clinton's job as president."[19] The results shown in Table 7-2 follow partisan divisions.

At the beginning of his first term as president, George W. Bush had job approval ratings in the 50 percent range—exactly the same ratings his father and Clinton had at the beginning of their presidencies. As

TABLE 7-2   Attitudes toward President Clinton and the Monica Lewinsky
Scandal According to Partisanship, 1998

	Democrats	Independents	Republicans
Private matter having to do with Bill Clinton's personal life	80%	68%	37%
Public matter having to do with Bill Clinton's job as president	16	22	53
Both equally	1	2	6
Don't know, no answer	3	8	4
Total	100%	100%	100%

Source: CBS News Poll, July 30, 1998, at www.pollingreport.com/scandal.htm.

dramatic a change in approval ratings as has been seen in the past sixty years occurred after September 11, 2001, when George W. Bush's approval ratings rose 30 percentage points following the terrorist attacks.

Campaigns

Political campaigns are efforts to persuade voters to support candidates or issues by providing them with information, rationales, characterizations, and images to convince them that one candidate or position is better than the alternatives and to get them to act on that preference. Massive amounts of money are spent in modern campaigns to saturate the airwaves in an effort to influence the voter. A perennial question for politicians, political commentators, and scholars is, "How much difference does a campaign make?"

Although most professional politicians take for granted the efficacy of political campaigns, scholarly analysis has often questioned their impact. In most elections the majority of voters decide how they will vote before the campaign begins. Beyond this, the general low level of political information in the American electorate throws doubt on the ability of undecided voters to absorb ideas during a campaign. Andrew Gelman and Gary King have offered an especially interesting form of this argument.[20] They contend that a voter's eventual choice can be predicted quite satisfactorily at the start of a campaign, well before the candidates are even known. Furthermore, because a voter may move away from this ultimate choice during the course of a campaign, intermediate predictions, so popular in media coverage and campaign organizations, are misleading.

Other analysts, based on economic forecasting models, argue that the outcome of the election—indeed, the margin of victory—can be predicted well before the election campaign from such variables as the rate of economic growth, the inflation rate, or the unemployment rate.[21] That an individual voter's choice is determined at the start of a campaign may be difficult to believe. Yet evidence indicates that in most years the vote choices of most voters are not affected by political campaigns. The National Election Study regularly asks voters when, during the presidential campaign, they made their voting decisions. Table 7-3 shows the time of decision for voters in the presidential elections of 1948 to 2000. In most years about two thirds of the electorate decided before or during the conventions, with the final one third deciding during the campaign. Over the years, fewer people report deciding during the conventions, presumably because, in recent decades, the candidates have essentially been chosen by the end of the presidential primaries in late spring.

The decision times of partisans and independents vary because the loyal party votes line up early behind the party's candidate. In all recent presidential elections, the independents and weak partisans were more likely to make up their minds during the campaign, whereas strong partisans characteristically made their decisions by the end of the conventions. To put it differently, the less committed partisans are still undecided at the start of the general election campaign. In fairly close elections, this relatively uncommitted group can swing the election either way with 10 to 15 percent of the voters making a decision in the last days of the election campaign. In 1992, for example, almost one in five voters reported deciding for whom to vote in the last few days of the campaign. Perot voters were especially likely to report a last-minute decision.

The possibility clearly exists that campaigning can influence a small but crucial proportion of the electorate, and many elections are close enough that the winning margin could be a result of campaigning. Clearly, professional politicians drive themselves and their organizations toward influencing undecided voters in the expectation that they are the key to providing, or maintaining, the winning margin. One can easily think of examples of elections in which the only explanation for the outcome was the aggressive campaign of one of the candidates. Multimillionaire publisher Steve Forbes could never have won the 1996 Republican presidential primaries in Arizona and Delaware without the expensive media advertising campaign he waged in those states. One can, however, just as easily think of examples of well-financed campaigns that failed. In early 1996 Sen. Phil Gramm of Texas raised more money and won fewer delegates than any other Republican presidential candidate. The simple, if unsatisfying, answer to the question, "Do campaigns work?" seems to be "Sometimes."

TABLE 7-3   Distribution of Time of Decision on Vote Choice for President, 1948–2000

Time of Decision	1948	1952	1956	1960	1964	1968	1972	1976	1980	1984	1988	1992	1996	2000
Before conventions	37%	34%	57%	30%	40%	33%	43%	33%	42%	49%	32%	39%	49%	51%
During conventions	28	31	18	30	25	22	17	20	17	16	28	14	13	10
During campaign	25	31	21	36	33	38	35	45	40	29	37	45	34	39
Don't remember, not ascertained	10	4	4	4	3	7	4	2	1	5	3	2	3	0
Total	100%	100%	100%	100%	101%	100%	99%	100%	100%	99%	100%	100%	99%	100%
(N)	(424)	(1,251)	(1,285)	(1,445)	(1,126)	(1,039)	(1,119)	(1,667)	(958)	(1,376)	(1,209)	(1,684)	(1,171)	(566)

Sources: National Election Studies. Data provided by the Inter-university Consortium for Political and Social Research.

In this section we will explore the conditions under which campaigns, and the information they seek to convey, are likely to have the most impact. In general, the impact of information provided in a campaign will depend on (1) the amount already known about the candidate (or issue); (2) the extent to which the information is countered by competing claims; and (3) the extent to which the information is in a form that resonates with the concerns and life experiences of the voter.

New information has the greatest impact in situations in which little is known about the candidate or issue and in which the voters have few existing attitudes. We can see the application of this generalization in many areas. For example, the candidate who is less well known has the most to gain (or lose) from joint appearances, such as debates. The 1960 debates between Kennedy and Nixon, the first-ever series of televised presidential debates, appear to have had substantial impact on the election outcome, in large part because Kennedy was, at the time, not well known to the public. According to several different public opinion polls in 1960, about half of the voters reported that they were influenced by the debates in their evaluation of the candidates, with Kennedy holding an advantage of three to one over Nixon.[22] Although Nixon's poor showing is often blamed on his five o'clock shadow, it is unlikely that his appearance caused many to turn against him, because he had been in the public eye as vice president for eight years. Rather, Kennedy's advantage came from undecided Democrats who had little existing information about Kennedy (but were favorably disposed toward him because he was the Democratic candidate) who were given a reason to vote for him by his attractive appearance and good performance. The immediate effect of this 1960 experience was the abandonment of presidential debates until 1976. Incumbent presidents or campaign front-runners were unwilling to offer such an opportunity to their lesser-known challengers.

Because new information has the greatest impact when little is known, voter preferences or opinions will be more volatile when candidates or public figures are not well known. Public opinion "trial heats" that are intended to gauge the preferences of the electorate during the course of the election campaign can be highly unstable when one or all of the candidates are not well known. In the spring and summer of 1992, Clinton was a virtual unknown to most voters, although he had already clinched the Democratic nomination for president. Perceptions of independent candidate Ross Perot were similarly vague, although he was recognizable as an eccentric billionaire. George Bush was, in contrast, well known to the public as the incumbent president and former vice president. Figure 7-2 shows the trial-heat preferences of voters in Gallup polls during this period. The preferences for Clinton and Perot were quite volatile and made additionally so by Perot's sudden exit from the race in July and equally sudden re-entry in September. Although pref-

FIGURE 7-2   Trial Heats for the Presidential Elections of 1992 and 2000

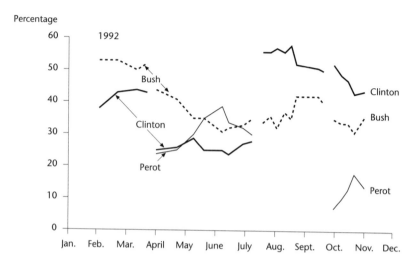

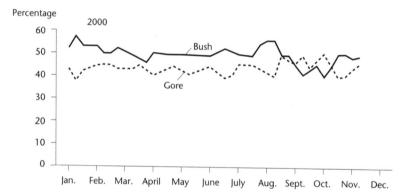

Source: George Gallup Jr., *The Gallup Poll Public Opinion 1992.* Wilmington, Del.: Scholarly Resources, 1993. Gallup Web page, www.gallup.com.

erences for Bush were more stable, the changing set of alternatives with which he was compared made his support fluctuate as well. In contrast, with two familiar candidates in the presidential race in 2000, the trial heat preferences for Al Gore and George W. Bush from January to November were quite stable. Almost from the beginning the contest was too close to call.

The second condition under which campaigns and the information they provide is most effective in influencing attitudes is when counter-information is not available. The obvious example is when one candidate has substantial resources for campaigning and the opponents do not. The well-endowed candidate can present a favorable image of him- or herself—or an unflattering image of the opponent—without having those images contradicted. This situation is more likely to occur in primaries, where candidates must rely on their own funds and whatever they can raise from others, than in general elections where both candidates can tap party resources.

In presidential elections, the national nominating conventions offer each party the opportunity, at least temporarily, to get its message to the public without the annoyance of sharing the stage with the other party. The televised acceptance speech of the nominee, the ability to showcase rising stars and celebrate past heroes, all before a prime-time audience, offer unique opportunities for the political parties to present themselves and their campaign themes as they wish the public to see them. Although the news media interject commentary and analysis, the media's view of what is interesting generally leads them to emphasize strategy and motives rather than outright contradiction of a party's claims. The result of this nationwide opportunity for favorable publicity is the convention "bounce" that presidential nominees typically receive in their approval ratings and trial-heat results immediately after their party's convention.[23] In Figure 7-2, one can see George W. Bush's mid-August convention bounce, which was almost immediately wiped out by Gore's convention bounce.

The political parties have not always been able to use the nominating convention to their advantage. The battle-marred Democratic convention in 1968 and George McGovern's acceptance speech long after midnight in 1972 represent dramatic failures to use this opportunity to benefit the party's nominee. Opponents within one's party may present the case against a nominee as effectively as the opposing party could. In recent years, when the nomination has been a foregone conclusion months before the nominating convention, both parties have tried to control their conventions as tightly as possible, keeping controversial issues and personalities under wraps. However, as the conventions become more staged in an effort to promote the most favorable image of the candidate, the audience and the news coverage for them has shrunk, making it less likely that those images will be conveyed to the public.

Another, less obvious, situation in which unchallenged information has an impact is when the characterizations of a candidate or issue are agreed on by all parties. If, for example, both candidates agree on which of them is liberal and which is conservative (although not on which position is "good" and which is "bad"), this information will be effectively conveyed to voters during the course of a campaign. An intriguing finding from a study by Thomas Patterson and Robert McClure in the Syracuse, New York, area in 1972 suggests that a major impact of television advertising may be on increasing voters' awareness of the issue stands of the candidates.[24] They concluded that television advertising contained more explicit information about the candidates' stands on issues than did news stories and had a correspondingly greater impact on voters' awareness of the issue positions of candidates. Television news stories were too brief and focused too much on campaign action to convey much issue information to the viewer.

In studying the 1976 election, Patterson found that the association between voters' issue positions and their candidate choices increased over the course of the campaign.[25] Voters in his sample did not appear to be persuaded to change their attitudes on issues by candidate appeals or to switch their vote choices; rather, as they learned which positions the candidates took, voters discovered (in many instances) that they were closer to their preferred candidate. This finding might be used to argue that the campaign is a process of clarification, an articulation of issue linkages that were potential all along.

A third factor affecting whether information in a campaign will have an impact on voter attitudes is the extent to which the voters accept the information as having relevance to their own concerns. In *The Reasoning Voter*, Samuel Popkin offers "Gresham's law of information," which states that small amounts of personal information drive out large amounts of impersonal information.[26] In other words, because personal information has more meaning to average voters—they use similar kinds of data every day in assessing friends and colleagues—they use such information about a candidate to make inferences about the kind of person that candidate is and how he or she will perform in office.

Information will also be more or less effective depending on the context in which the recipient receives or understands it. Cognitive psychologists use the concept of "framing" to study how people's preferences or decisions depend on the context or frame in which the alternatives are presented. For example, in the summer of 1979, in public opinion polls, Democrats preferred Sen. Edward Kennedy over President Jimmy Carter by a margin of three to one as their party's nominee for president.[27] By March 1980 Carter was ahead of Kennedy by two to one among Democrats.[28] Although a number of things had intervened between these times, an important element seems to have been reminding the voters of Senator Kennedy's involvement in the accidental death of Mary Jo Kopechne a decade earlier. When the voters' frame of reference was an unpopular president viewed as responsible for high inflation, Kennedy was an attractive alternative. Later, when Kennedy was framed as a fatally irresponsible playboy, Carter was preferred.

The fact that voters respond differently to information depending on its presentation obviously offers opportunities for campaign managers to use sophisticated techniques to create favorable images of their candidates. There is no question that highly paid political consultants use an arsenal of social science knowledge and techniques in an attempt to do just that. Although some of these attempts have been notably successful, serious limitations also exist.

To successfully "sell" a candidate with advertising techniques, image makers must be able to control the information available about their candidate, thereby controlling the perceptions the voters hold about him or her. Reagan was more successfully handled in this way than most other presidential candidates. Perhaps his training as an actor made him more susceptible to management by his advisers. However, to a considerable degree, maintaining his public image depended on protecting him from the press and public exposure rather than manipulating the content of publicity about him. This approach was especially effective in the campaign of 1980 when the focus of attention and public dissatisfaction rested on President Carter rather than on the challenger Reagan.

For most candidates, however, manipulating a public image by controlling information is either impossible or self-defeating. For a relatively unknown challenger, such as McGovern in 1972 or Carter in 1976, this type of strategy would appear self-defeating because few candidates have had the resources to become well-known nationwide through advertising and staged appearances alone. (Perot in 1992 is an exception.) Instead, unknowns must scramble for exposure in any forum they can find, and this prevents the careful manipulation of an image. Conversely, well-known candidates or incumbents, who can afford to sit back and let the public relations people campaign for them, probably already have images that are impossible to improve in any significant way over the relatively short period of time available in an election campaign. The most famous alleged attempt to "repackage" a candidate was the effort of the Nixon campaign staff in the 1968 presidential election.[29] However, the evidence suggests that more voters decided to vote for other candidates during the course of the campaign than decided to vote for Nixon. After about twenty years of nationwide public exposure, a "new Nixon" reinforced existing images, both negative and positive; he simply could not create a new, more favorable image.

Campaign organizations also attempt to affect the public image of their candidate by supplying the news media with information favorable to their candidates. If successful, this can be particularly effective, because the information arrives through the more credible medium of news coverage, rather than paid advertising. One way to do this is to stage media events that provide the media, particularly television, with an attention-grabbing headline, sound bite, or photo opportunity. The campaigns of Nixon in 1968 and Bush in 1988 were particularly successful in manipulating news coverage favorable to their candidates by staging media events and otherwise limiting access to the candidates. In recent years campaign organizations have had difficulty in getting news stories aired or printed about their issue positions and policy stands, but they have had more success with negative stories and attacks on other candidates.

Another tactic is to seduce the media into covering paid political advertising as if it were news. In her book, *Dirty Politics*, Kathleen Hall Jamieson details how, in 1988, the news media continually reinforced the premise behind the infamous Willie Horton ads that attacked Democratic candidate Michael Dukakis's position on crime.[30] In 1992 and 1996, television and newspapers regularly featured "ad watches" that attempted to dissect the claims made in candidates' paid advertising, but in the course of doing so provided the ads with a wider audience.

Although it may be difficult to sell a candidate by manipulating an image in a positive way, there appears to be a far greater opportunity to hurt an opponent's image through negative campaigning and advertising. In recent years candidates' campaigns and independent organizations have attacked the images of candidates in personal and political terms. The volume of this particular form of negative advertising, sometimes called "attack ads," has increased greatly. Many of these ads are paid for by committees, interest groups, and organizations not connected directly to a candidate or a campaign. The Supreme Court has ruled that such attack ads are issue advocacy and therefore cannot be limited because of the First Amendment. As a result, a candidate can be hit with a massive campaign that the opposing candidate need take no responsibility for and that is basically outside the regulations and agreements governing the candidates and their campaign organizations. Two generalizations about negative campaigning can be made: (1) The public disapproves of negative campaigning; and (2) even so, it sometimes works. Because the public disapproves of negative advertising, some candidates have managed to be positive in their own ads while allowing independent organizations to trash their opponents for them.

If negative campaigning illustrates the capacity to use the mass media to accomplish political purposes, the difficulty candidates have in using the media to respond to these attacks reveals its limitations. Victims of negative campaigning have tried to ignore the attacks, attempted to answer the charges, or counterattacked with their own negative campaign. None of these responses appears to be notably successful—a fact that encourages the continued use of negative campaigning. Attacks in the form of ridicule or humor may be particularly difficult to answer. Some strategists have urged the victims of negative campaigning to respond immediately and defend themselves aggressively. This may be good advice, but it requires a lot of the victim. To respond promptly with advertising requires a great deal of money (perhaps near the end of a campaign when resources are limited) and a skilled staff. Moreover, victims of negative campaigning need to have a strong, effective answer to such attacks.

In their study of the 1992 presidential campaign, Just et al.[31] offer a useful way to look at the "construction" of a candidate's persona over the course of an election campaign. Rather than the candidate's image being the creation of a campaign staff or the product of straight news coverage, it will evolve through the three-way interaction of the candidate's campaign, the news media, and the public. The candidates' initial attempts at establishing themselves face a range of reaction from press and public—encouragement, incredulity, boredom—and the candidates adjust accordingly. Likewise, the news reporters assess and react to the response of colleagues and the public to their coverage of candidates. Finally, the public's judgments in public opinion polls, radio call-in programs, live interviews, and e-mail indicate displeasure or support about the behavior of both candidates and news media. The final "picture" that emerges may not be a faithful reflection of the candidate's inner being, but neither is it likely to be an artificial creation of campaign technicians nor the distortion of an overbearing press.

Presidential Primary Campaigns

Because the impact of new information is greatest when there are few existing attitudes, we should expect the impact of campaigns to be potentially greatest in primary elections, especially with little-known candidates. In primaries, where all the candidates are of the same party, the voter does not even have partisanship to help in the evaluation of candidates. In such situations, whenever new information is provided it can have a substantial impact.

After 1968 various reforms in the presidential nominating process led to an increased use of presidential primaries as a means of selecting delegates to the Democratic and Republican nominating conventions. The purpose of these reforms was to make the choice of the presidential candidates more reflective of the preferences of the party's supporters in the electorate. In fact, this increased use of presidential primaries opened the door, at least initially, to the nomination of candidates little known to the general public. Political newcomers, such as Carter in 1976, Gary Hart in 1984, or Steve Forbes in 1996, have an opportunity to focus their energy and campaign resources on a few early primaries or caucuses, gain national media attention by winning or doing surprisingly well in those early contests, and generate momentum to allow them to challenge more established and well-known potential nominees. Such candidates often do not have long-term viability; their early appeal, based on little information, dissipates as more, often less flattering, information becomes available. Nevertheless, by the time this happens, the candidate may already have secured the nomination (Carter in 1976) or severely damaged the front-runner, as Hart damaged Walter Mondale in 1984. Primaries can do considerable damage to candidates' images under some circumstances. Well-known front-runners such as Bush Sr. in 1992 and Bob Dole in 1996 suffered a loss of popularity that they never recovered under the campaign attacks of fellow Republicans. Intraparty fighting is typically destructive for established candidates. Ever since 1972, segments of the Democratic party expressed concern that the new reliance on presidential primaries was preventing the party from nominating its best or most electable candidates.

Before the 1988 election season, southern Democratic leaders decided that concentrating their states' primaries early in the election year would focus media and candidates' attention on the southern states as well as give a head start to more conservative candidates who could pick up a large bloc of delegate votes from these states. Although this strategy did not work in the short run—the Democrats nominated the liberal northeastern governor Dukakis in 1988—the creation of Super Tuesday considerably shortened the primary season by allowing candidates to amass enough delegates to secure the nomination months before the summer convention.

In 1992 and 1996, additional states moved their primaries forward, in hopes of capturing some media attention or, at least, to hold their primaries before the nominations had been decided. This "front-loading" of primaries seems to have had the effect of favoring the front-runner and decreasing the opportunity for less well-known candidates to ride favorable media coverage to the nomination. Because the primaries are so close together in time, candidates cannot concentrate their resources in a few states and use victories there to generate favorable coverage in other states. Instead, beginning in early March, candidates must campaign all across the country in many states. The unknown candidate has almost no time to capitalize on early success by raising money and creating state campaign organizations. Suddenly all the advantages are back with the established, well-known candidates.

In the presidential primaries of 2000, Republican John McCain, and to a lesser extent Democrat Bill Bradley, challenged their parties' front-runners with some success in a few early primaries. But very quickly, the front-loading of the primaries took its toll. On March 7 alone, George W. Bush won 433 delegates to McCain's 113. With the next week's primaries mainly in the South where Governor Bush and Vice President Gore were expected to do well, both McCain and Bradley abandoned their challenges. In 2000, about two thirds of the convention delegates had been chosen by the end of March. Not too many years ago, only one third of the delegates were selected by then. Without intending to, state party leaders have moved the country close to a version of a national primary, in which candidates must campaign nationwide from the beginning.

The role of the news media in influencing presidential primaries with their coverage has changed as the format of the primaries has changed. In the 1970s and 1980s, the media had considerable potential to enhance one candidate's campaign momentum and to consign others to obscurity. Patterson's study of the role of the media in 1976 shows that during the primaries, Carter benefited from the tendency of the press to cover only the winner of a primary, regardless of the narrowness of the victory or the number of convention delegates won.[32] Even the accident of winning primaries in the eastern time zone gave Carter disproportionately large, prime-time coverage on evenings when other candidates enjoyed bigger victories farther West.[33] This was possible because few voters were well-informed about or committed to any of the many Democratic candidates. During the same period the media exaggerated the significance of President Gerald Ford's early primary victories without noticeably influencing the public's feelings about him or his challenger, then-governor of California Reagan.[34] It is much more difficult to influence voters who have well-informed preferences.

The "winner-take-all" commentary on the presidential primaries has been replaced in recent years by commentary on "unexpected" winners and losers. Attention focuses on who does much better or much worse than expected, regardless of the number of votes they receive. The most favorable coverage may be given to a second- or third-place finisher, and the real winner in terms of numbers of votes is treated as a loser. The irony of this type of commentary is that it essentially converts the errors in the media's pre-election coverage into newsworthy political change. With the front-loading of the primaries, however, media coverage becomes irrelevant after the first few primaries.

Inequality in the resources available to candidates in presidential primary campaigns has an effect, and is likely to be greater than in the presidential general election where an equal amount of public financing is available to both major-party candidates. As mentioned previously, Forbes's ability to pour massive amounts of personal funds into a few early primaries allowed him to win victories over Dole in South Carolina and Arizona in 1996. Forbes's similar strategy in 2000 failed, no doubt because the voters were more familiar with him after four years and thus less able to be impressed by an expensive television advertising campaign.

In the 2000 election campaign, George W. Bush raised more than $100 million, more money by far than any of the other candidates and more than twice as much as any previous candidates for president. He also raised his money early. Six months before the first primary, he had raised more than half his eventual total. Although his challenger for the Republican nomination, Senator McCain, had adequate funding for the early primaries, it was not sufficient to withstand George W. Bush's huge war chest plus the attacks on McCain by independent groups working on Bush's behalf. Vice President Gore and his challenger, Bradley, were quite even in financial resources because both accepted public funding with its spending limits. However, a challenger would undoubtedly need far more resources than simple parity to be successful against a sitting vice president.

Campaign Strategy

Those attempting to communicate with the American public on political matters face an awkward dilemma. The attentive members of the public, the individuals most likely to receive political messages, are least likely to be influenced by one or a few items of information. On the other hand, the individuals who are open to persuasion are uninterested in politics and not likely to pay attention to politics in the media.

In conclusion, we can use material from this chapter as a basis for generalizing about political communication and campaign effects from the perspective of a candidate. In political campaigns, candidates stand little chance of altering the electorate's issue preferences on policies that are sufficiently prominent to affect their vote choices. In the short run, to change individuals' preferences on issues that they care about is difficult by any means, and it is particularly difficult through the impersonal content of mass media. To change an individual's preferences or pattern of behavior, personal contact is more effective than the media; therefore, vote choice or turnout is likely to be influenced, if at all, by an acquaintance of the individual.

To a limited degree, candidates can alter the prominence of a few issues for some segments of the public, but their capacity to increase or decrease the importance of issues is slight compared with what will happen in the ordinary course of events. For example, a candidate cannot make corruption in government a salient issue solely through his or her campaign, but a major scandal can make it an issue whether the candidates want it to be or not. Nevertheless, it is worth some effort to increase the visibility of issues that are expected to benefit the candidate, even though that effort will probably fail. It is also worth some effort to attempt to reduce the salience of issues that hurt a candidate, though, again, this strategy is not likely to succeed.

The public's perceptions of candidates' positions on issues are much more susceptible to change. News and advertising through the mass media can convey a lot of information on issue stands and dramatize the differences between candidates. The more factual this information and the more the candidates agree on the respective characterizations, the more fully this information is absorbed by the public. This is the area of attitude change and public awareness in which candidates can accomplish the most.

In the final analysis, candidates are most interested in winning votes, regardless of how strong a preference each vote represents. But there are grounds for wanting large numbers of supporters with very strong preferences. Individuals with an overwhelming preference, holding no significant conflicting views, form the base of support for a candidate that yields campaign contributions and workers. These are the individuals all through society who casually influence the people around them to hold views favorable to a candidate. These are the opinion leaders who interpret and misinterpret the news on behalf of their candidate.

The more obviously partisan or one-sided the content of either media message or personal contact, the less likely it is to influence the uncommitted, not to mention the hostile. This poses a problem for the campaigner. Even though extreme messages are most likely to attract the attention of the relatively apathetic uncommitted voter, those same messages are least likely to get results. For this reason, in part, events dramatizing an issue can be valuable or damaging to a candidate. Events that affect a candidate's personal image are especially important because these perceptions are the most difficult to change through direct appeals in campaign advertising.

The overall implications of this discussion are several. It takes a long time and probably noncampaign periods of low intensity to switch individual issue stands or party loyalties. The media presentation and personal discussion of political and social conditions or events have a greater impact on attitudes than advertising or party contacts.

To a considerable degree, these generalizations about political influence and communication imply that by the time a candidate wins nomination, he or she faces a constituency whose basic values and preferences can be changed only by events over which the candidate probably has little or no control. The only impact the candidate can have through campaigning is to make issue positions known as dramatically as possible and to contrast those positions with the opponents'. No candidate will know in advance what the net effect of these efforts will be, and most will never know. But most elections are contested under conditions that give one candidate a great initial advantage in the partisan loyalty and issue preferences of the constituency. The best chance for candidates is to exploit what they believe are their advantages, but in most cases the stable party loyalties and unchanging issue preferences of a constituency impose significant constraints on how much difference campaign strategies can make.

Speculation on the nature of political communication has ranged from alarm over the vulnerability of the mass public to manipulation through the media, to annoyance at the difficulty of reaching the public. The American people make use of the mass media to inform themselves on matters of interest, but this does not mean that the public pays attention to everything in the media. Individuals have a remarkable ability to ignore information—a capacity as fully developed as the ability to absorb information. Influencing individuals on a subject about which they feel strongly is extremely difficult because they reject the media content, and influencing individuals on a subject about which they are indifferent offers problems because they ignore the media content.

Also, the media are difficult to use for manipulation because so many different points of view are found within the media. An extremely wide range of political perspectives is available to some degree in the mass media, although some perspectives are much more frequently available and more persuasively presented than others. The media in American society allow all views to enjoy some expression, although media coverage of many topics may be expressed in a manner favorable to some viewpoints and unfavorable to others. It would be difficult to disentangle the bias associated with the news and commentary in the media from the distortion found in the individual's reception of political information. The public has a considerable capacity for ignoring media content or misinterpreting that content. Either of these conditions would be adequate to account for considerable discrepancy between political reality and the public image of that reality. No analyst of public opinion would contend that the American people are extremely well informed politically or hold views that are free of systematic bias. There is, however, quite a difference between this recognition and the contention that the mass media cause particular misperceptions. In any case, the long-term impact of the biases and style of the mass communication channels on public attitudes has not received adequate attention. Universal exposure to the prevailing political culture as offered through the mass media in news reporting, popular commentary, and the arts will certainly make subcultural variations more difficult to establish and maintain.

Notes

1. The classic statement on cognitive dissonance was Leon Festinger, *A Theory of Cognitive Dissonance* (Evanston, Ill.: Row, Peterson, 1957). For some of the most interesting experimental work in this field, see Milton J. Rosenberg, Carl I. Hovland, William J. McQuire, Robert P. Abelson, and Jack W. Brehm, *Attitude Organization and Change* (New Haven: Yale University Press, 1960).
2. Elihu Katz and Paul F. Lazarsfeld, *Personal Influence: The Part Played by People in the Flow of Mass Communications* (New York: Free Press, 1964).

3. Elisabeth Noelle-Neumann, *The Spiral of Silence* (Chicago: University of Chicago Press, 1984).

4. The Pew Research Center for The People & The Press, "2000 Media Report: Questionnaires," taken from the center's Web site at www.people-press.org.

5. Everette E. Dennis, *The Media Society* (Dubuque, Iowa: Wm. C. Brown, 1978), 37–41.

6. Michael B. MacKuen and Steven L. Coombs, *More than News* (Beverly Hills: Sage Publications, 1981).

7. Kathleen Hall Jamieson, *Dirty Politics: Deception, Distraction, and Democracy* (New York: Oxford University Press, 1992).

8. The Pew Research Center for The People & The Press, "2000 Media Report: Questionnaires."

9. For an early statement of this point, see Bernard C. Cohen, *The Press and Foreign Policy* (Princeton: Princeton University Press, 1963).

10. Times Mirror Center for The People & The Press, *Times Mirror News Interest Index*, October 15, 1991, 16–21.

11. CBS News/*New York Times* Poll press release, January 17, 1991.

12. See Dennis, *The Media Society*, chaps. 5, 7.

13. A variety of publications, including monthly reports, are available on the Web site of The Pew Research Center for The People & The Press at www.people-press.org.

14. The Pew Research Center for The People & The Press, News Interest Index at www.people-press.org.

15. Anthony Downs, *An Economic Theory of Democracy* (New York: Harper and Brothers, 1957).

16. Samuel Popkin, *The Reasoning Voter* (Chicago: University of Chicago Press, 1991), 47–49.

17. Thomas E. Patterson, *The Mass Media Election* (New York: Praeger, 1980), 14–15.

18. Philip Converse, "Information Flow and the Stability of Partisan Attitudes," *Public Opinion Quarterly* 26 (winter 1962): 578–599.

19. CBS News Poll, July 30, 1998. Data provided by the Inter-university Consortium for Political and Social Research.

20. Andrew Gelman and Gary King, *Why Do Presidential Election Campaign Polls Vary So Much When the Vote Is So Predictable?* (Cambridge: Littauer Center, 1992).

21. Michael S. Lewis-Beck and Tom W. Rice, *Forecasting Elections* (Washington, D.C.: CQ Press, 1992). These economic forecasts limit themselves to two-party races and cannot accommodate third-party candidates such as Perot.

22. Recomputed from Elihu Katz and Jacob J. Feldman, "The Debates in the Light of Research: A Survey of Surveys," in *The Great Debates: Background, Perspective, Effects,* ed. Sidney Kraus (Bloomington: Indiana University Press, 1962), 212.

23. James E. Campbell, Lynna L. Cherry, and Kenneth A. Wink, "The Convention Bump," *American Politics Quarterly* 20 (July 1992): 287–307.

24. Thomas E. Patterson and Robert D. McClure, "Television News and Televised Political Advertising: Their Impact on the Voter" (Paper presented at the National Conference on Money and Politics, Washington, D.C., 1974); and Thomas E. Patterson and Robert D. McClure, *Political Advertising: Voter Reaction to Televised Political Commercials* (Princeton: Citizens' Research Foundation, 1973).

25. Thomas E. Patterson, "Vote Choice in the 1976 Presidential Primary Elections" (Paper presented at the annual meeting of the Southern Political Science Association, New Orleans, 1977).

26. Popkin, *The Reasoning Voter*, 73.

27. *Gallup Opinion Index* 183 (December 1980): 51.

28. "Opinion Roundup," *Public Opinion* 3 (April/May 1980): 38.

29. Joe McGinniss, *The Selling of the President* (New York: Trident Press, 1969).
30. Jamieson, *Dirty Politics*, chap. 1.
31. Marion R. Just, Ann N. Crigler, Dean E. Alger, Timothy E. Cook, Montague Kern, and Darrell M. West, *Crosstalk: Citizens, Candidates, and the Media in a Presidential Campaign* (Chicago: University of Chicago Press, 1996).
32. Thomas E. Patterson, "Press Coverage and Candidate Success in Presidential Primaries: The 1976 Democratic Race" (Paper presented at the annual meeting of the American Political Science Association, Washington, D.C., 1977).
33. James D. Barber, ed., *Race for the Presidency* (Englewood Cliffs, N.J.: Prentice-Hall, 1978), chap. 2.
34. Patterson, *The Mass Media Election*, 130–132.

Suggested Readings

Graber, Doris. *Processing the News*. New York: Longman, 1988. An in-depth study of a few respondents on the handling of political information from the media.

Jamieson, Kathleen Hall. *Dirty Politics: Deception, Distraction, and Democracy*. New York: Oxford University Press, 1992. A blistering commentary on political advertising strategies and the interaction between advertising and news coverage.

Just, Marion R., Ann N. Crigler, Dean E. Alger, Timothy E. Cook, Montague Kern, and Darrell M. West. *Crosstalk: Citizens, Candidates, and the Media in a Presidential Campaign*. Chicago: University of Chicago Press, 1996. A multimethod study of the 1992 presidential election campaign.

Neuman, W. Russell, Marion R. Just, and Ann N. Crigler. *Common Knowledge*. Chicago: University of Chicago Press, 1992. An interesting analysis of mass media and political attitudes.

Patterson, Thomas E. *The Mass Media Election*. New York: Praeger, 1980. A major study of the impact of mass media on public opinion and voting behavior.

Popkin, Samuel L. *The Reasoning Voter*. Chicago: University of Chicago Press, 1991. A wide-ranging discussion of campaigning and presidential vote choice.

West, Darrell M. *Airwars: Television Advertising in Election Campaigns, 1952–2000*, 3d ed. Washington, D.C.: CQ Press, 2001. An interesting survey of political advertising over the years.

Internet Resources

The Web site for The Pew Research Center for The People & The Press, www.people-press.org, has both data and analysis of many topics covered in this chapter. For various information, click on "PollWatch," "Recent Survey Results," and "News Interest Index." For the most important items there are data from many surveys during the past decade.

During election years most major news organizations have Web sites with survey data on many political items.

Vote Choice and Electoral Decisions

THE CENTRAL FOCUS of research on American political behavior is vote choice, especially presidential vote choice. No other single form of mass political activity has the popular interest or analytic significance that surrounds the selection of a president every four years. Most Americans follow presidential campaigns with greater attention than they give other elections, and eventually about 50 percent of the electorate expresses a preference by voting. The results of presidential balloting are reported and analyzed far more extensively than any others. This chapter will explore the main determinants of vote choice and the interpretation of election outcomes in light of these determinants. We will attempt to generalize the discussion beyond presidential choice, but inevitably most of the illustrations are drawn from recent presidential election studies.

Earlier chapters have emphasized party loyalty as a basic characteristic that influences many aspects of an individual's political behavior. In regard to vote choice, an individual's partisanship can be construed as a long-term predisposition to vote for one party or another, other things being equal. In other words, in the absence of any information about candidates and issues or other short-term forces in an election, individuals can be expected to vote according to their partisanship. On the other hand, to the extent that such short-term forces have an impact on them, they may be deflected away from their usual party loyalty toward some other action. Clearly, the more short-term forces there are in an election—or the more a voter is aware of them—the less will be the impact of partisanship. This idea is crucial for understanding the relative impact of partisanship in different types of elections. In highly visible presidential elections, when information about candidates and at least some issues is widely available, partisanship will typically be less important to the voter's decision than in less visible races down the ticket. Clearly, too, more potent short-term forces would be required to cause a very strong partisan to vote for another party than would be necessary to prompt a weak partisan to defect. An individual's vote in an election can be viewed as the product of the strength of partisanship and the impact of the short-term forces on the individual.

In most elections, both candidates and political commentators give their attention to short-term forces, such as the personalities of the candidates, issues, and the parties' records, because these are the variable elements that the actions of candidates and campaign strategies seek to modify. Although in many respects partisanship is the most important element, it is taken as a constant because, in the short run, it is not likely to change. This chapter will consider the impact of the short-term forces of candidate image, current party images, and issues within a setting of stable party loyalties.

Candidate Image

The appeal of candidates has been given more attention in recent elections than any other short-term influence. During the past fifty years national samples have been extensively questioned about likes and dislikes concerning the presidential candidates. During this period there have been several very popular candidates with extremely favorable images, as well as several who were rejected by the electorate largely on the basis of their personal attributes.

The specific content of candidates' images has varied greatly, and, as can be seen in Figure 8-1, no single pattern appears associated with either party. Perhaps the most prominent feature of this series is its downward trend. Presidential candidates of both parties are viewed far less favorably now than in the past. The disenchantment with government and politics, catalogued in Chapter 1, clearly extends to the personal images of the presidential candidates.

The form of analysis shown in Figure 8-1, which simply counts the number of positive and negative comments about the candidates in response to open-ended questions in the NES surveys, should be viewed cautiously because the relative seriousness of the complaints—for example, being too old versus being unprincipled—is not taken into account. In addition, the comments about the candidates are in response to a question about what the respondent likes and dislikes about the candidate. They range from comments on personal traits ("He's dishonest") to those quite removed from the personality of the candidate ("I like what he's saying about health care"). Although both are counted

FIGURE 8-1   Images of Presidential Candidates, 1952–2000

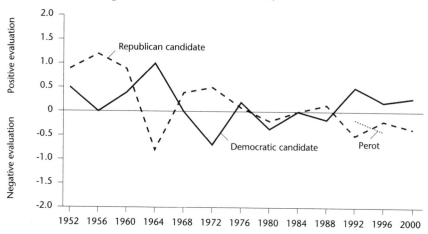

Sources: Warren E. Miller and Santa Traugott, *American National Election Studies Data Sourcebook, 1952–1986* (Cambridge: Harvard University Press, 1989), 113, 115; National Election Studies. Data provided by the Inter-university Consortium for Political and Social Research.

as reflecting feelings about the candidate's image, they are quite different in tone. Given the unusually high number of issue-related comments about the Democratic candidates in recent elections, we need to be careful not to interpret candidate image as reflecting only personality traits.

Dwight D. Eisenhower in 1952 and 1956 and Lyndon Johnson in 1964 had very positive images. Richard Nixon enjoyed a more favorable image than his various opponents in 1960, 1968, and 1972. Although most American voters would ultimately revise their evaluations, in 1960 Nixon was more favorably perceived in personal terms than John Kennedy; his personal image rivaled Eisenhower's. Kennedy's image improved during his presidency, but his extraordinary popularity came after his assassination. Sometimes a candidate enjoys an advantage because the opponent is extremely unpopular. Johnson had such an advantage over Barry Goldwater, as did Nixon over George McGovern.

It is interesting, given his presumed personal popularity, that Ronald Reagan received more negative than positive comments in both 1980 and 1984. In both years a large share of the negative comments referred to his age; although many people mentioned this point, it does not seem to have been an intensely unfavorable evaluation. Fortunately for Reagan, his opponents were viewed even more negatively.

In 1988, the images of George Bush and Michael Dukakis were quite evenly balanced, with Bush holding a slight advantage. By 1992 Bush's image had deteriorated to one of the worst in forty years; only Goldwater and McGovern had been viewed more unfavorably. Bush's reneging on his campaign promise of "read my lips, no new taxes" and his perceived responsibility for the bad state of the economy were the most damaging contributors to his image problem.

By contrast, Bill Clinton had, on balance, a quite positive image in 1992. He was not viewed so favorably in personality terms (for example, on traits such as honesty and experience or for his avoidance of military service during Vietnam), but this perception was more than offset by positive comments about his views on a wide range of issues. Respondents mentioned Clinton's positions on health care or the deficit as things they liked about him. By any standards, Clinton's image in 1992 was unusually issue-based.

In 1996 Clinton still enjoyed a favorable image, although not as favorable as in 1992. Positive comments about Clinton continued to focus on issues. His integrity was still questioned by significant numbers of respondents, and negative comments about First Lady Hillary Rodham Clinton increased rather dramatically between 1992 and 1996. Bob Dole, Clinton's challenger in 1996, had a better image than Bush in 1992, but Dole was still seen more negatively than positively. Dole was seen as honest and experienced, but like Reagan, received many negative comments about his age.

Ross Perot was a significant factor in the election of 1992, less so in 1996, but he did not have a positive image in either election. In 1992 he was not particularly well known. He received positive comments about being a successful businessperson, but these were offset by negative comments about his lack of governmental experience. In 1996, he received almost no positive issue or governmental policy references, and comments about his personal characteristics were strongly negative. His temporary withdrawal from the race in 1992 still drew unfavorable comment in 1996.

In 2000 the public's overall evaluation of George W. Bush was quite balanced between positive and negative mentions of both personal qualities and issue positions. The slight negative balance overall resulted from the criticism that he favored big business and the rich. As his campaign undoubtedly intended, the positive issue responses were focused on taxes, abortion, and gun control. Al Gore's image with the public was different. He was viewed more negatively than positively in personal terms. On issues, however, he was viewed much more positively than negatively. The favorable response to his issue stands on social security, health, and education more than offset his unfavorable personal image.

A good deal of nonsense has been written in recent years about winning elections by manipulating the images of the candidates, mainly through the mass media. The implication has been that the images of candidates are easily created and altered, but as we saw in Chapter 7, to do either is difficult, particularly with well-established candidates about whom voters are reasonably well informed. Campaigns do have some choices about raising particular issues, as, for example, the Kennedy campaign in 1960 had the choice of raising or not raising the issue of Kennedy's Catholicism—a factor that they knew would generate both positive and negative reactions. But once such a decision is made, there is less leeway in controlling the impact of the issue.

In most other cases, candidates have little control in deciding whether to raise certain topics, for often the opponent or the media will do so anyway. In 2000 there was little George W. Bush could do to create the impression that he was well versed in foreign affairs. He had to hope, rather, that foreign policy did not loom large during the campaign. Had international events intervened in a dramatic way, his campaign would have been hard-pressed to avoid talking about them.

An incumbent candidate or a former vice president benefits from a perception of being experienced, which is not purely a result of campaign advertising. Neither can negative reactions aroused by being involved in an unpopular administration be avoided. Gore benefited some from the years of prosperity during the Clinton/Gore administration. However, at the same time he was closely tied to the negative aura surrounding Clinton and had a difficult time distancing himself from it.

The public's impressions of candidates for major office seem to be realistic, gained primarily through ordinary news coverage. This is not to say that these images are completely accurate or fair or sophisticated, but neither are they fictitious pictures created by public relations personnel. The Gore campaign's attempt to redesign his personality throughout the campaign and especially before each debate failed utterly—but not disastrously. After eight years in the public eye, Gore's image as "wooden" and a bore could not be changed, but neither could the perception that he was smart and issue-oriented.

Unlike incumbents and established candidates, presidential candidates who are less well known have a greater opportunity to create a favorable image during the relatively brief period of the campaign. Conversely, such candidates are also more vulnerable to an attempt by an opponent to pin an unattractive image on them. In 1988 the Bush campaign was remarkably successful in creating an image of Dukakis as weak on crime and incompetent on military issues. Skillful manipulation of images was part of this success, but this was only possible because Dukakis was not particularly well known.

Very few candidates for other offices are as well known or as well publicized as candidates for the presidency. Most candidates in most elections are unknown quantities for the average voter. Typically, voters will be aware of the candidate's party affiliation and whether he or she is an incumbent, but not much more. In fact, these pieces of information may come to the attention of the voter only if they are indicated on the ballot.

Normally, the impact of candidate image on vote choice declines as one goes farther down the ticket to less visible and less well-known offices. This does not mean that the candidate's personal qualities are unimportant in winning election to these offices. They may be of paramount importance in obtaining the nomination or endorsement of the party organization, in raising financial support, in putting together a campaign staff, and in gaining backing from the leadership of influential organizations. But these personal attributes are unlikely to influence the decisions of the average voter simply because the voter is unlikely to be aware of them.

Party Image

The images of the parties are another factor that can influence the voting decisions of the electorate. Even though party images are strongly colored by longstanding party loyalties, the focus of this analysis is a set of potentially variable attitudes toward the parties that can be viewed as short-run forces at work in an election. These attitudes usually have to do with the relative ability of the parties to manage government, to keep the economy healthy, and to keep the country out of war. Party images also affect and are affected by the images of the candidates running under the party label and by the attitudes toward issues espoused by the candidates or the party platforms. These factors can be kept distinct conceptually, though it may be impossible to disentangle the various effects in any actual situation.

Traditionally, the Republican Party has been viewed as the party best able to keep the country out of war; the Democratic Party held a similar advantage as the party of prosperity. Figure 8-2 shows the trends in these party images in recent years. In 2000 the Republicans lost their traditional advantage as the party better able to handle the nation's foreign affairs. Perceptions of which party is best able to handle the economy have fluctuated rapidly. The Democratic Party had a considerable advantage in 1992, but the Republicans had a comparable edge in 1994. By 2000 the Democrats had regained the advantage. Of course, a large proportion of the electorate does not perceive a difference between the parties on these items.

The role of party images in vote choice has been labeled "retrospective voting" by Morris Fiorina, who argued that voters continuously evaluate the performance of the political parties, especially the president's party.[1] Voters use this evaluation of past performance as an indi-

FIGURE 8-2   Party Better Able to Handle the Nation's Economy and
Foreign Affairs, 1988–2000

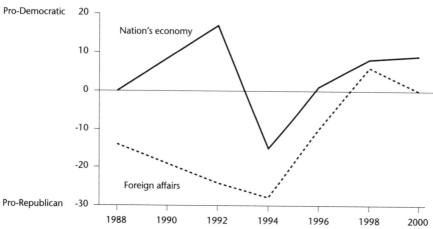

Sources: National Election Studies. Data provided by the Inter-university Consortium for Political and Social Research.

Note: The data points in the figure represent the percentage of respondents answering "Democrats" minus the percentage answering "Republicans."

cator of future performance, and they take this retrospective assessment into account in making their vote choices. Because these assessments are likely to involve the performance of the current administration, questions about the incumbent president's handling of various policy areas have been used as indicators of the extent of retrospective voting. In a sophisticated analysis of presidential voting in 1988, Merrill Shanks and Warren Miller demonstrated that voters' approval or disapproval of Reagan's performance as president had a noticeable impact on the choice between Bush and Dukakis.[2] In both 1992 and 1996 there was an incumbent president to be evaluated as he ran for reelection. President Bush had very low evaluations in 1992 and this had a disastrous impact on his reelection prospects. It was just the opposite in 1996 for President Clinton, who came into the race with fairly positive evaluations. Once again in 2000 two nonincumbents faced each other. President Clinton's high job approval rating undoubtedly helped Gore. There was a strong relationship between job approval or disapproval of Clinton and vote choice between Gore and Bush. The impact of Clinton's approval rating on the vote (see Table 8-6 later in the chapter) was actually greater in 2000 than on Clinton's own candidacy in 1996. This pattern was quite comparable to the help President Reagan's approval rating gave the elder Bush in 1988.

Party images and presidential evaluations are strongly related to partisanship, with partisans more likely to embrace positive images of their party and to reject negative ones than independents or partisans of the opposition. Partisanship and party image, however, are not synonymous, because individuals often hold unfavorable perceptions of their party without changing party identification. Yet, at some point, negative images of one's own party or positive perceptions of the other party undoubtedly lead to partisan change.

The images of local or state parties may be considerably different from and independent of those of their national counterpart. A state or local party organization may be perceived in different terms from the national party, and many a local or state party has gained a reputation for ineptitude or corruption that did not influence voting decisions for national offices. At the same time, these local images may become increasingly important in voting for offices at lower levels because party labels become a more important identifying characteristic in those races.

Issue Impact

Obviously, candidate images and party images may be closely related to issues, and under some circumstances they are indistinguishable. The perception of the stands of candidates and parties on issues is a basis for making vote choices, a basis usually distinct from either personality characteristics or longstanding symbolism. Most significantly, candidates can establish issue positions or alter their appeals through their presentation of issues in ways that are not applicable to personal images or party characteristics. In the short run, candidates cannot change their job experience or religion or party, but they can take new stands on issues or attempt to change the salience of issues. It is feasible, then, for candidates to attempt to appeal for votes on the basis of issues.

Over the years, considerable commentary has focused on the rise of single-issue voting. Collections of voters, caring intensely about a particular issue, vote for whichever candidate is closest to their views on that issue, regardless of the candidate's party, personal characteristics, or positions on other issues. There is nothing new about this phenomenon. The classic example of single-issue voting in American politics was abolition, an issue of such intensity that it destroyed the Whig Party, launched several new parties including the Republican Party, and was a major contributing factor to the Civil War. Abortion is currently an issue that determines the way many people will vote.

Although organizational sophistication and increased opportunities for dissemination of information make single-issue groups a potent force in American politics today, politically ambitious candidates have always searched for issues of this type to help them gain a following. At the same time, incumbent candidates and the broadly based political parties have seen advantages in avoiding or glossing over such issues. Intense concentration on a single issue is potentially divisive and damaging to parties that must appeal to a broad range of voters or to those in office who must cast votes on a wide range of issues. Nevertheless, the political opportunity for the candidate who can capture a group of voters willing to vote on the basis of a single issue or cluster of issues is so great that it is unlikely that any intense concern in the electorate will be long ignored.

Several characteristics of electoral behavior conflict with this description of the role of issues in influencing vote choice. For one thing, in most elections many voters are unaware of the stands taken by candidates on issues. Voters commonly believe that the candidates they support agree with them on issues. This suggests that voters may project their issue positions onto their favorite candidate more often than they decide to vote for candidates on the basis of their position on issues. Furthermore, when voters agree on issues with the candidate they support, they may have adopted this position merely to agree with their candidate. Actually, candidates and other political leaders frequently perform this function for members of the electorate; they provide issue leadership for their following. Within the enormous range of possible issues at any given time, complete indifference to many is quite common. Most issues important to political leaders remain in this category for the general public.

The extent to which voters are concerned with issues in making vote choices is a subject of considerable debate. Several prominent scholarly efforts were designed to rescue the voter from an undeserved reputation for not being issue-oriented.[3] *The Changing American Voter,* by Norman Nie, Sidney Verba, and John Petrocik, documents a rise in issue voting associated with the election of 1964.[4] According to their data, the correlation between attitudes on issues and vote choice peaked in the ideological Johnson-Goldwater campaign but remained through 1972 at a considerably higher level than in the "issueless" 1950s. More recently, in a thorough assessment of the impact of issues in the elections of 1988 and 1992, Merrill Shanks and Warren Miller found relatively low levels of issue impact.[5]

In 2000, as in most years, there is a fairly strong relationship between a domestic issue like increasing or decreasing government services and the vote for president. As can be seen in Table 8-1, those who favored decreasing governmental services and spending voted overwhelmingly for George W. Bush and very few voted for Gore. (Although they do not represent a large percentage of the voters, it is at this conservative end of the scale where both the Nader and Buchanan voters are most fre-

TABLE 8-1   Presidential Vote and Attitude toward Government
Services, 2000

	Decrease government services		Neutral		Increase government services
Al Gore	11%	17%	48%	72%	70%
George W. Bush	82	80	49	24	27
Pat Buchanan	2	a	a	a	a
Ralph Nader	5	4	3	3	3
Total	100%	101%	100%	99%	100%
(*N*)	(60)	(60)	(160)	(97)	(122)

Source: 2000 National Election Study. Data provided by the Inter-university Consortium
for Political and Social Research.

ªLess than 0.5 percent.

TABLE 8-2   Presidential Vote and Attitude toward Government Help for
Blacks, 2000

	Government help for blacks		Neutral		Let blacks help themselves
Al Gore	70%	65%	60%	40%	43%
George W. Bush	26	30	37	55	55
Pat Buchanan	a	a	a	a	1
Ralph Nader	4	5	2	5	2
Total	100%	100%	99%	100%	101%
(*N*)	(42)	(51)	(144)	(90)	(196)

Source: 2000 National Election Study. Data provided by the Inter-university Consortium
for Political and Social Research.

ªLess than 0.5 percent.

quent.) Those voters who favored increasing services and spending preferred Gore over George W. Bush by a sizable margin.

On another domestic issue—whether the government should help
blacks versus letting blacks help themselves, shown in Table 8-2—a similar liberal-conservative relationship exists. Those people who favor government programs to help blacks voted for Gore over George W. Bush
70 to 26 percent. The voters who said blacks should help themselves
were more evenly divided but favored George W. Bush 55 to 43 percent.

TABLE 8-3   Presidential Vote and Attitude toward Defense Spending, 2000

	Cut defense spending	←	Neutral	→	Increase defense spending
Al Gore	58%	73%	62%	46%	35%
George W. Bush	26	19	33	54	65
Pat Buchanan	a	a	1	a	a
Ralph Nader	16	8	4	a	a
Total	100%	100%	100%	100%	100%
(*N*)	(36)	(42)	(128)	(141)	(137)

Source: 2000 National Election Study. Data provided by the Inter-university Consortium for Political and Social Research.

a Less than 0.5 percent.

TABLE 8-4   Presidential Vote and Attitude toward Abortion, 2000

	Pro-life ←			→ Pro-choice
Al Gore	46%	40%	50%	66%
George W. Bush	54	56	46	31
Pat Buchanan	a	a	2	a
Ralph Nader	a	3	2	3
Total	100%	99%	100%	100%
(*N*)	(84)	(161)	(85)	(223)

Source: 2000 National Election Study. Data provided by the Inter-university Consortium for Political and Social Research.

a Less than 0.5 percent.

Because both these issues deal with themes that have long divided the parties, it is not surprising that we find substantial relationships between holding a certain view and supporting a particular candidate. The next two issues, defense spending and abortion, have not always been so closely related to vote choice. The strong relationship found in 2000, shown in Tables 8-3 and 8-4, suggests increasing polarization between the major parties.

The relationship between defense spending and vote choice in Table 8-3 shows that those voters who wanted to cut defense spending favored Gore over George W. Bush more than two to one. George W. Bush's support was greatest among those who would increase defense spending. Table 8-4 shows a fairly strong pattern of relationship between

FIGURE 8-3   Vote for President According to Voters' Ideological
              Identification and Perceptions of Candidates' Ideology,
              2000

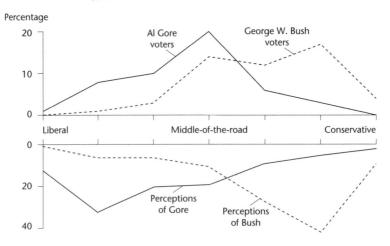

Source: 2000 National Election Study. Data provided by the Inter-university Consortium for Political and Social Research.

voters' positions on abortion and vote choice. George W. Bush's support was higher on the pro-life side of the issue; Gore drew more votes from the pro-choice side.

Figure 8-3 looks at vote choice in a somewhat different manner by illustrating the electorate's perceptions of the ideological positions of George W. Bush and Gore, as well as the relationship between the voters' own ideological positions and their vote choices between the two candidates. In the 2000 National Election Study survey, voters were asked to locate each candidate on a seven-point scale ranging from "extremely liberal" to "extremely conservative." In Figure 8-3 the frequency distributions in the lower half of the chart illustrate the voters' perceptions of the two candidates' ideological positions. For example, 12 percent of the respondents labeled Gore as extremely liberal, and only 2 percent labeled him extremely conservative. Nine percent placed George W. Bush in the most extreme conservative position. Most voters placed Gore on the liberal end of the scale and placed George W. Bush on the conservative side.

Voters were also asked about their own ideological position using the same seven-point scale. The distributions in the upper half of Figure 8-3 indicate the self-placements of those who voted for George W. Bush and Gore. They show that George W. Bush drew most of his support from conservative voters, and Gore received most of his from liberals. It is significant that Gore also gained the lion's share of the votes of those in the middle of the ideological spectrum.

A number of factors must be present for issues to have an impact on vote choice: First, voters must be informed and concerned about an issue; second, candidates must take distinguishable stands on an issue; and third, voters must perceive the candidates' stands in relation to their own. These conditions often are not achieved. Voters may be unable to locate themselves or the candidates on one or more issues. In 2000, 17 percent of the electorate had no opinion on the issue of cutting government services and spending versus increasing government spending and services. About 15 percent were unable to locate the position of either George W. Bush or Gore on this issue. Similar proportions of the electorate could not locate themselves or the candidates on the issue of defense spending. Voters may misperceive the candidates' positions. For example, a few voters viewed Gore as an extreme conservative or George W. Bush as an extreme liberal, although most perceptions appeared accurate.

It is also possible that a weak relationship between an individual's issue positions and vote choice may result from the fact that the analyst chooses the issues for analysis, and these might be issues that are not important to the individual. If the voter is allowed to define what he or she sees as the most important issue, a somewhat stronger relationship between his or her position on issues and voting decisions is found.[6] Others have argued that a rational and issue-oriented voter judges the past performance of the candidates rather than simply comparing the candidates' promises for the future.[7]

This analysis also does not tell us what causes these relationships. Perception of issues may cause an individual's vote choice; alternatively, a preference for a candidate on other grounds may lead individuals to adjust their perceptions of issues in support of their vote choice. No data are available that would conclusively resolve this question. Regardless of the causal relationship, it is significant that, although many voters lack opinions on issues or on the candidates' positions, those who do have opinions show considerable consistency between issue positions and vote choice.

Determinants of Vote Choice

The preceding sections considered candidate images, party images, and issues as short-term forces that either reinforce or deflect voters from their long-term party loyalty. An interesting, but far more difficult, question is the relative impact of these various factors on vote choice. Because all these factors are strongly interrelated and almost certainly all influence each other, it is virtually impossible to disentangle their effects with the kind of data available in nationwide surveys. If one assumes that issues are all-important in determining vote choice, most voting behavior can be accounted for by issues alone, ignoring other factors. On the other hand, if one assumes that party identification and a few social characteristics are all-important, most voting behavior can be accounted for with these variables, ignoring issues. The conflicting conclusions that are reached are largely a matter of the theoretical assumptions with which one starts.

In light of these difficulties, some analysis of the impact of short-term forces has focused on the unique impact of each element in the presence of others. One of the best examples of this mode of analysis is Donald Stokes's effort to measure attitudinal forces influencing presidential vote choices.[8] Following Stokes's method, Arthur Miller and Martin Wattenberg have analyzed the nine presidential elections from 1952 to 1984 (see Table 8-5).[9] Negative values indicate a factor that helped the Democratic candidate; positive values indicate a benefit to the Republican candidate. The perception of group benefits is a consistently large pro-Democratic element in all nine elections. Foreign policy matters have almost always helped the Republican candidate, with the exception of Goldwater in 1964 and Reagan in 1984. The impact of foreign affairs and domestic policies was unusually strong and pro-Republican in 1980. This reflected the strongly unfavorable reactions to Jimmy Carter's handling of the economy and the Iranian hostage crisis. At the same time, the candidates' personalities had an unusually weak influence on vote choice in 1980. In contrast, in 1984 foreign and domestic policy considerations had declined in importance, but the personalities of the candidates had become significantly pro-Republican factors.

Merrill Shanks and Warren Miller published a much more complex analysis of the 1988 and 1992 presidential elections in *The New American Voter*. Their results cannot easily be compared with the work of Stokes and others in Table 8-5, but overall they argue for the importance of longstanding predispositions and retrospective evaluations in contrast to issues and personality traits.

In Table 8-6 we offer an analysis of the determinants of the choice between George W. Bush and Gore in 2000. For simplicity, we consider only seven possible determinants of vote choice. The first column of the table shows the strength of the relationship between the variable and vote choice. The higher the coefficient is, the greater the impact on the individual's choice. The second columns are the net benefits of that variable to a candidate, similar to the estimates given for earlier elections in Table 8-5.

As can be seen in Table 8-6, party identification is the factor most strongly related to the choice between George W. Bush and Gore. This

TABLE 8-5   Net Impact of Six Attitudinal Components in Determining Vote Choice, 1952–1984

	1952	1956	1960	1964	1968	1972	1976	1980	1984
Domestic policy	-1.3	-0.9	-0.5	-2.4	1.1	1.4	-0.7	3.1	1.5
Foreign policy	3.3	2.5	1.8	-0.3	1.0	3.2	0.4	2.8	-0.3
Party management	5.4	1.2	1.2	-0.3	1.5	0.0	0.2	0.6	0.5
Group benefits	-4.3	-5.5	-4.0	-2.6	-3.6	-4.6	-4.5	-4.5	-5.6
Democratic candidate	-1.2	0.2	-2.0	-4.0	0.9	4.3	-0.1	-0.4	1.3
Republican candidate	4.4	7.6	5.7	-2.6	1.6	4.0	2.2	-0.5	1.5

Sources: For 1952–1980, Arthur H. Miller and Martin P. Wattenberg, "Policy and Performance Voting in the 1980 Election," cited in Controversies in Voting Behavior, 2d ed., ed. Richard Niemi and Herbert Weisberg (Washington, D.C.: CQ Press, 1984), 91; for 1984, Martin P. Wattenberg (personal communication).

Note: Positive values are pro-Republican effects; negative values indicate a Democratic advantage. The values can be interpreted as the percentage of the vote moved in one partisan direction or the other.

TABLE 8-6   Determinants of Presidential Vote Choice, Al Gore versus George W. Bush, 2000

	Strength of relationship	Net shift of votes	
		Pro-Gore	Pro-Bush
Party identification	−.34	2%	
Ideological identification	.14		3%
Clinton's handling of the economy	−.20	4%	
Clinton's handling of foreign affairs	−.15	4%	
Policy positions			
Government services and spending	.14		3%
Abortion	−.05	2%	
Defense spending	.01		1%

Source: 2000 National Election Study. Data provided by the Inter-university Consortium for Political and Social Research.

Note: Standardized partial regression coefficients are used to represent the strength of relationship between each variable and presidential vote choice controlling for the other variables. The signs of the coefficients are arbitrary; a vote for Gore is coded 0 and a vote for Bush is coded 1. Multiple R-squared is .60. These variables correctly predict 86 percent of the votes.

indicates a high degree of party loyalty at work in the 2000 election. At the same time, because party identification is so evenly balanced, it produced only a small net gain for Gore. Obviously the voters' views of President Clinton affected the choice between George W. Bush and Gore. Attitudes toward Clinton's handling of the economy are the second strongest determinant of the vote. Because the public had a highly favorable view of Clinton's handling of the economy, this factor moved votes in Gore's direction. Clinton's handling of foreign affairs was the third strongest determinant and along with his handling of the economy had the greatest net impact in moving the vote. Ideological identification and a specific form of ideology, attitudes toward government services and spending, account for most of the remaining influence on the choice between George W. Bush and Gore. The distributions of both these attitudes in the electorate are in a conservative direction, so they benefited George W. Bush. The issue of defense spending also helped move voters in George W. Bush's direction. Opinions on abortion helped Gore, but like defense spending had a relatively small impact.

During the conventions and the brief period of the general election campaign, political parties cannot do much about the basic strength each party commands; therefore, they concentrate on presenting candidate images and issue positions calculated to have greatest appeal to the uncommitted voters. Even if the outcome of an election is not substantially affected by party strategies, the content of the campaign and the meaning the election comes to have for leaders and the public are created by these strategies. The information in Tables 8-5 and 8-6 can be viewed as measures of the content of the campaign and its meaning for voters.

The Popular Vote and the Electoral College

In 2000, for the first time in more than one hundred years, the electoral college chose a president who was not the winner of the popular vote. In a system that purports to be a democracy, this is a significant occurrence. How did this happen and what, if anything, is likely to be done to change the system that produced such an outcome?

Under the constitutional system adopted in 1787, the president is selected by the electoral college, with each state having electoral votes equal to the combined seats that it has in the U.S. House of Representatives and Senate. Voters cast a ballot for one or the other party's presidential and vice-presidential nominees. Legally, however, the voter is casting a ballot for that party's slate of electors, which was certified months before by the party's formal submission of the slate to a state official. The electors of the winning party in each state meet in their respective state capitals on the Monday following the second Wednesday in December and cast their votes for president and vice president. Almost without exception they respect their pledge and vote for their party's nominees. A majority of the electoral votes is required to elect a president—270 electoral votes at this time.

To understand how the electoral college could produce a winner who is not the popular vote winner it is important to remember that all states (except Maine and Nebraska) use a winner-take-all procedure for deciding who wins the states' electoral votes. In other words it does not matter whether a candidate wins the state narrowly or by a wide margin, all of the electoral votes go to the winner. If one candidate wins many states narrowly and the other candidate wins states by a wide margin, the first candidate can win in the electoral college while the second candidate can have more popular votes. Usually we say that the second candidate "has wasted" votes by winning by a larger margin than needed to carry the state.

In 2000 Gore won by large margins in a number of big states such as California and New York, accumulating a huge number of popular votes, while George W. Bush won some big states, like Florida, narrowly. In 2000 another factor was at work to a degree. George W. Bush won a large share of the small states where the two electoral votes assigned to every state to represent their seats in the U.S. Senate create something of a bonus. If turnout is comparable, each electoral vote in a small state represents a lot fewer voters than in a large state. In 2000 each electoral vote in Wyoming represented 70,000 popular votes and in California each electoral vote represented more than 200,000 popular votes.

Although only rarely does the electoral college produce a winner who has not won the popular vote, the consequences of a winner-take-all system are well known to campaign strategists in presidential elections. The electoral college arrangement strongly influences presidential campaign strategy. The closer the expected margin in a state and the larger the number of electoral votes available, the more resources the campaigns will put in the state and the more aggressively the candidates will attempt to respond to the political interests in the state. These are the "battleground states" where both candidates have a chance to win and much is at stake. In contrast, "safe states" are relatively unimportant to both candidates in a general election campaign—taken for granted by one and written off by the other—although they may be visited by one or both candidates to raise funds to spend in competitive states. The 2000 presidential election is deceptive in making every state appear crucial because the result was so close, but, in fact, a winning strategy in this and other presidential elections calls for slighting most states.

In retrospect, it may seem odd that the Founders created such a peculiar scheme for selecting a president. Their main concern, of course, was to devise a method for selecting the president that would result in the selection of George Washington as the first president. The allocation of electoral votes simply combined the state representation in the Senate and the House of Representatives, an easy decision after the Great Compromise had been reached. In the context of the Constitutional Convention, the electoral college had another virtue: It treated the states as they viewed themselves—as sovereign entities. In the current climate, retaining the states as meaningful units in a federal system is one rationale for maintaining the electoral college.

The fact that the electoral college was extremely indirect democracy was not a concern for the Founders; most of the Founders were wary of too much democracy, thus having state legislatures select the electors had appeal. The Founders did not anticipate the emergence of political parties that quickly changed the process of selecting electors into intense partisan conflict. By 1824, most state legislatures had turned the selection process over to the public to avoid the political hassle.

Over the years there have been various proposals for changing or abandoning the electoral college.[10] Some proposals are quite modest, such as getting rid of the slate of electors (who occasionally do not vote the way they are pledged) and have the secretary of state simply certify each state's electoral votes. Though in itself quite noncontroversial, the proponents of greater change have resisted this proposal for fear that adopting it would reduce the incentive to make more substantial changes in the system.

The most sweeping proposal, and the one most commonly discussed by political commentators, would be the substitution of a nationwide popular election for the electoral college. This is an obvious alternative method of selecting the president, and, indeed, the main criticism of the electoral college is the potential (which was realized in 2000) that the popular vote winner may not be the electoral college winner. A nationwide popular election, however, has problems of its own. It is generally believed that a national popular election would attract more and more candidates—third-party candidates, independent candidates, and major-party candidates who failed to get their party's nomination. Candidates with a small but crucial constituency could threaten to take votes away from the major-party nominees as a way to win concessions. But presumably more and more would actually stay in the race to demonstrate their strength. So gradually the percentage of the vote needed to win would shrink. The popular vote winner could have 35 or 25 percent of the total vote, and arguably, this would undermine the legitimacy of the winner. As a consequence, most proposals for a national popular election have included provisions for a run-off election if the winner's percentage was below, say, 40 percent. The prospect of two presidential elections and the political maneuvering associated with run-off elections has reduced enthusiasm for the change.

Two other proposals have been advanced that would not require a constitutional amendment, although a constitutional amendment would be required to adopt them uniformly across the country. The "district method," now used in Maine and Nebraska, allows two electors to be selected statewide and the remainder to be selected within congressional districts. The proposal does not actually eliminate the winner-take-all characteristic, but it does reduce the magnitude of the distortions that can occur. The proportional method would allocate all of the electoral votes on a statewide basis, but through proportional representation rather than to the plurality winner. No individual state is likely to adopt this method because the state would become the least attractive state in the nation for presidential candidates to campaign in.

For years, political scientists and some political commentators have predicted that the electoral college would be immediately abandoned if, in the modern age, it produced a nonpopular vote winner. We might ask, then, why so little has happened to jettison the electoral college since the 2000 election? There are probably a number of reasons why a movement to change the college has not materialized. One is that the election produced new, more pressing issues for reform—notably ballot type and vote-counting procedures. The nationwide popular vote alternative also appears less attractive after the Florida recount, as the possibility of a nationwide recount is contemplated. Most important, perhaps, is the realization on the part of Republicans (in the majority in the House and only slightly in the minority in the Senate in 2001) that the presence of the electoral college produced a Republican president. When a substantial part of the political elite senses a benefit in current arrangements, there is little likelihood that the extraordinary majority needed to change the Constitution could be assembled. Much more likely is the possibility that some individual states will decide to follow the example of Maine and Nebraska and adopt the district method of apportioning electors.

Vote Choice in Other Types of Elections

We have suggested that vote choice can be thought of as the product of a voter's long-term partisanship and the impact of the campaign's short-term forces of candidate characteristics, issue positions, and evaluation of the party's performance. In presidential elections, in which information about the candidates and issues is widespread and easily available, short-term forces often overcome partisanship and cause substantial numbers of voters to defect from a party. As we consider less prominent races, voters make choices with less information and fewer factors influencing their decisions.

In voting for members of Congress, most of the electorate has relatively little information about the candidates, especially candidates challenging incumbents. It is well established that party-line voting becomes stronger for less visible offices, including Congress, because issues and personal attributes of the candidates are less likely to have an impact on the voter in less publicized races.

Another significant factor in congressional elections is incumbency. Studies have shown that voters are about twice as likely to be able to identify the incumbent as the challenger in congressional races, and almost all the defections from partisanship are in favor of the more familiar incumbent.[11] Both Republicans and Democrats seem strongly susceptible to voting for incumbents, with more than one third typically abandoning their usual party for an incumbent representative of the other party. Strong partisans of both parties frequently defect to incumbents of the other party, but on balance support the challengers from their own party more often than not. Both Democratic and Republican weak partisans, in contrast, are more likely to defect for incumbents than to vote for challengers from their own party.

The advantage that incumbents have does not mean that congressional districts are invariably safe for one party, though many are. Rather, it suggests that even in those districts in which the outcome is virtually a toss-up when two nonincumbents face each other, the representatives who manage to survive a term or two find reelection almost ensured. This tendency becomes accentuated as the opposition party finds it increasingly difficult to field an attractive candidate to challenge a secure incumbent. Thus, many incumbent representatives are elected again and again by safe margins from districts that may easily fall to the other party once the incumbent no longer seeks reelection. Put another way, the existence of a safe incumbent in a district may say little about the underlying partisan division in that district. It may simply reflect short-term forces that were at work in the last election in which two nonincumbents faced each other.

A Senate election has relatively high visibility and, unlike most congressional races, is amenable to a mass media campaign using television. The more information about the election that gets through to the voters, the less they rely on either partisanship or the familiarity of the incumbent's name. Indeed, the visibility of a Senate race makes an incumbent senator vulnerable to a well-financed campaign by an attractive opponent; incumbency may, in fact, become a disadvantage in such circumstances because the incumbent has a voting record to defend.

In our companion volume, *Political Behavior in Midterm Elections*, we have analyzed voting in congressional elections at length. Here we will simply update that analysis with a discussion of the 2000 elections. In both House and Senate races there were unusually high levels of party-loyal voting, and the overall outcome left the House and Senate almost evenly divided. The Democrats made a net gain of four seats in the Senate, creating a 50 to 50 deadlock, with Vice President Dick Cheney breaking the tie (although this would change a few months later when the Senate Republicans lost one seat as Senator Jeffords left the Republican Party to become an independent). In House elections Democrats continued gradually to erode the Republican majority with a net gain of three seats.

Incumbents running for reelection in House districts were extremely likely to be returned to office with a 98 percent success rate. Senate incumbents were somewhat more vulnerable with a 79 percent return rate. Still, this was high by Senate standards.

New records were set in 2000 for spending on congressional campaigns, mainly in open-seat contests. This continued the trend of the 1990s. Races that were expected to be close attracted huge amounts of independent expenditures on advertising, especially negative advertising. All of this yielded extremely narrow control of the House and Senate with the prospect of an even more thoroughly divided government.

The Meaning of an Election

Politicians and news commentators spend much time and energy interpreting and explaining the outcome of an election. The difficulties in assigning meaning to election results are easy to exaggerate; the most important element is usually quite clear—the winner. Elections are primarily a mechanism for selecting certain governmental leaders and, just as important, for removing leaders from office and preventing others from gaining office. Nevertheless, an effort is often made to discover the policy implications of patterns of voting and to read meaning into the outcome of elections. This effort raises two problems for analysis: first, the policy implications of the winning and losing candidates' issue stands and, second, the issue content of the voters' decisions.

In both 1980 and 1984 Reagan articulated an unusually clear set of ideological and policy alternatives. Not all elections offer voters a clear choice between a conservative and a liberal candidate, but the 1980 and 1984 races between Reagan and Carter and Reagan and Walter Mondale were widely perceived as doing so. Because Reagan won both elections by wide margins, his administration understandably claimed a popular mandate for a wide range of policies. Similarly, the victory of the House Republicans in 1994 made it easy for them to claim a popular mandate for their so-called Contract with America.

It is perfectly appropriate to attribute policy significance to an election on the basis of the policy preferences of the winning candidates, so long as it is not implied that the voters had these policy implications in mind when they voted. In other words, it is appropriate to observe, particularly in presidential elections, that the election outcome means lower taxes or expanded programs because the victor has pledged to implement lower taxes or to expand programs. But it is very difficult to establish that the voters' preferences have certain policy meaning or that the votes for a particular candidate provide a policy mandate. Several obstacles lie in the way of stating simply what policies are implied by the behavior of the voters. In many elections, the voters are unaware of the stands of candidates on issues, and sometimes the voters are mistaken in their perceptions.

Furthermore, as has been said before, many voters are not concerned with issues as such in a campaign but vote according to their party loyalty or a candidate's personality. Their votes have no particular policy significance but reflect a general preference for one candidate.

Voters who supported Reagan in 1980 had an unfavorable view of Carter's performance as president, especially his handling of the Iranian hostage crisis. The dissatisfaction with Carter was clear enough; however, the expectations about Reagan were quite vague and perhaps limited to the hope that he would strengthen national defense and balance the budget. In 1992 many voters cast a ballot against the elder Bush because of dissatisfaction over the state of the economy, though not for any particular policies. This characteristic of the vote, added to Clinton's low percentage (well below 50 percent) of the overall vote, made it difficult for Clinton to claim any clear mandate. In 1996, the reelection of Clinton, simultaneously with the election of Republican majorities in both the House and Senate, was interpreted, on both sides, as a mandate for bipartisan cooperation. The 2000 election was so close and featured such conflicting signals that no serious claim of a mandate has emerged. The policy significance is undeniable, however, as George W. Bush succeeded in his goal of cutting tax rates (and thereby, by design or inadvertently, eliminating the budget surplus).

Occasionally in a congressional election an incumbent's loss can be traced to a position or action at odds with majority sentiment among the district's constituents. More commonly, election victories say more about the incumbent's attention to constituent service and the advantages of incumbency than about the policy views of the candidates or voters.

A candidate has considerable freedom under most circumstances to interpret a victory with respect to the issues. Obviously, President Reagan felt free to interpret his mandate as requiring a massive tax cut but not dictating a balanced budget. There was no more basis for this distinction in public opinion than a mandate to reduce social programs drastically. Conversely, Clinton chose to interpret his election in 1992 as a mandate for health care reform. As it turned out, the public was not as committed to the idea as he was.

Most election outcomes are just this vague and conflicting with respect to most issues. This partially explains the failure of the American political system to impose policy stands on elected officials. This illustrates as well the opportunities for leadership afforded to electoral victors. If they are perceived as successful in handling their job, political leaders can convert their following to support their policies, and subsequently it will appear as if the public had demanded the policies in the first place.

It is also true that the supporters of a candidate usually do not intensely or widely oppose his or her stands. Voters will often vote for candidates who hold views they do not share, but these views are on matters of little interest to the voters. Presumably, voters seldom support candidates who hold views with which they disagree intensely.

American elections are hardly a classic model of democracy with

202 Political Behavior of the American Electorate

rational, well-informed voters making dispassionate decisions. On the other hand, American elections provide an acceptable opportunity for parties and candidates to attempt to win or hold public office. Although the electorate is capable on occasion of responding to issue appeals both positively and negatively, the electorate does not appear easily moved by most appeals. The electorate offers the parties modest opportunities to gain voters without offering extreme temptations to reckless appeals.

Notes

1. Morris P. Fiorina, *Retrospective Voting in American National Elections* (New Haven: Yale University Press, 1981).
2. J. Merrill Shanks and Warren Miller, "Partisanship, Policy and Performance: The Reagan Legacy in the 1988 Election," *British Journal of Political Science* 21 (1991): 129–197.
3. A good discussion of this topic in a single source is the collection of articles and commentary by Gerald Pomper, Richard Boyd, Richard Brody, Benjamin Page, and John Kessel in *American Political Science Review* 66 (June 1972): 415–470. See also Benjamin I. Page, *Choices and Echoes in Presidential Elections* (Chicago: University of Chicago Press, 1978).
4. Norman H. Nie, Sidney Verba, and John R. Petrocik, *The Changing American Voter* (Cambridge: Harvard University Press, 1976), chap. 10.
5. J. Merrill Shanks and Warren E. Miller, *The New American Voter* (Cambridge: Harvard University Press, 1996).
6. David RePass, "Issue Salience and Party Choice," *American Political Science Review* 65 (June 1971): 368–400.
7. Fiorina, *Retrospective Voting in American National Elections.*
8. Angus Campbell, Philip E. Converse, Warren E. Miller, and Donald E. Stokes, *The American Voter* (New York: Wiley, 1960), 524–531; and Donald E. Stokes, "Some Dynamic Elements of Contests for the Presidency," *American Political Science Review* 62 (1966): 19–28.
9. Arthur H. Miller and Martin P. Wattenberg, "Policy and Performance Voting in the 1980 Election" (Paper presented at the annual meeting of the American Political Science Association, New York, 1981), cited in *Controversies in Voting Behavior*, 2d ed., ed. Richard Niemi and Herbert Weisberg (Washington, D.C.: CQ Press, 1984), 91.
10. See Lawrence D. Longley and Alan G. Braun, *The Politics of Electoral College Reform* (New Haven: Yale University Press, 1972), for a survey of the proposals for electoral college reform.
11. Donald E. Stokes and Warren E. Miller, "Party Government and the Saliency of Congress," *Public Opinion Quarterly* 26 (winter 1962): 531–546.

Suggested Readings

Abramowitz, Alan I., and Jeffrey A. Segal. *Senate Elections.* Ann Arbor: University of Michigan Press, 1992. An extensive analysis of the factors contributing to election outcomes in Senate races.

Bartels, Larry M. *Presidential Primaries and the Dynamics of Public Choice.* Princeton: Princeton University Press, 1988. The best available analysis of public opinion and vote choice during presidential primaries.

Fiorina, Morris P. *Retrospective Voting in American National Elections.* New Haven: Yale University Press, 1981. An important conceptual argument for viewing vote choice as judgments about the past.

Jacobson, Gary C. *The Politics of Congressional Elections,* 4th ed. New York: Addison Wesley Longman, 1996. An authoritative survey of a broad topic and the literature surrounding it.

Niemi, Richard G., and Herbert F. Weisberg. *Classics in Voting Behavior.* Washington, D.C.: CQ Press, 1993. Niemi and Weisberg. *Controversies in Voting Behavior,* 4th ed. Washington, D.C.: CQ Press, 2001. These two collections offer the best readings from decades of research on public opinion and voting behavior.

Shanks, J. Merrill, and Warren E. Miller. *The New American Voter.* Cambridge: Harvard University Press, 1996. A sophisticated analysis of an elaborate model of vote choice.

Internet Resources

The Web site of the National Election Studies, www.umich.edu/~nes/, has extensive data on topics covered in this chapter. Click on "Vote Choice," "Evaluation of the Presidential Candidates," and "Evaluation of Congressional Candidates" for a variety of political items from 1952 to the present. In addition, all of these political items are broken down by social characteristics.

Another Web site, Elections U.S.A. at www.geocities.com/CapitolHill/6228/, has current political information on elections as well as public opinion data. Major news organizations will post results of exit polls on their Web sites. Candidates for office, like the political parties, have Web sites that can be located with search engines.

Survey Research Methods

M ANY OF THE DATA in this book have come from survey research, and most of the analysis cited has been based on findings from survey research. For more than forty years the data from the National Election Studies (NES), as well as from other major survey projects in political science, have been available through the Inter-university Consortium for Political and Social Research and have formed the basis for countless research projects in many fields by scholars, graduate students, and undergraduates. Given this widespread use of survey data, it is appropriate to give some description of the data collection methods that underlie them.

During the past seventy years, social scientists have developed an impressive array of techniques for discovering and measuring individual attitudes and behavior. Basically, survey research relies on giving a standard questionnaire to the individuals to be studied. In most major studies of the national electorate over the years, trained interviewers ask the questions and record the responses in a face-to-face interview with each respondent. A few studies depend on the respondents themselves filling out the questionnaires. Recently, the rising costs of survey research, the pressure for quick results, and the availability of random-digit telephone dialing have led both commercial and academic pollsters to rely increasingly on telephone interviewing. As we mentioned in the introduction, the 2000 NES used both face-to-face and telephone interviewing.

There are four data-collection phases of survey research: (1) sampling, (2) questionnaire constructing, (3) interviewing, and (4) coding. In most instances, the methods of the Survey Research Center at the University of Michigan will be described.

Sampling

It may seem inappropriate to analyze the entire American electorate using studies composed of fewer than two thousand individuals, which is about the average number of respondents in the studies used in this book. But it would be prohibitively expensive to interview the entire electorate, and the only way to study public opinion nationally is by interviewing relatively few individuals who accurately represent the entire electorate. Probability sampling is the method used to ensure that the individuals selected for interviewing will be representative of the total population. Probability sampling attempts to select respondents in such a way that every individual in the population has an equal chance of being selected for interviewing. If the respondents are selected in this way, the analyst can be confident that the characteristics of the sample are approximately the same as those of the whole population. It would be impossible to make a list of every adult in the United States and then draw names from the list randomly, so the Survey Research Center departs from such strict random procedures in three basic ways: the sample is stratified, clustered, and based on households.

Stratification means that random selection occurs within subpopulations; in the United States the sample is customarily selected within regions to guarantee that all sections are represented and within communities of different sizes as well. *Clustering* means that relatively small geographical areas, called "primary sampling units," are randomly selected within the stratified categories so that many interviews are concentrated within a small area to reduce the costs and inconvenience for interviewers. Finally, the Survey Research Center samples *households* rather than individuals (although within households individuals are randomly selected and interviewed); this means that within sampling areas households are enumerated and selected at random. (This sampling procedure means that no respondents are selected on military bases, in hospitals, hotels, and prisons, or in other places where people do not live in households. However, after the enfranchisement of eighteen-year-olds the Survey Research Center began to include college dormitories as residences to be sampled.)

Increasingly, the commercial polling organizations have turned to telephone interviewing as a faster and cheaper alternative to field interviewing. Random-digit dialing is typically used by these polling operations to select both listed and unlisted numbers and to give each residential number the same chance of being called. There is a sampling advantage over field surveys in that telephone sampling does not require clustering.

Obviously, telephone sampling ignores individuals without telephones, but there are no major obstacles to drawing an excellent sample of telephone numbers. The problems begin at that point. Success in finding someone at home and completing a telephone interview is uneven, and failures may run as high as 50 percent. Some polling organizations make repeated callbacks, and of course, the chances of getting an answer increase with the number of callbacks. Repeated callbacks, however, slow the data collection and increase the costs. Because an important reason for using the telephone is speed and low costs, most polling organizations do not call back.

Once the telephone is answered, it is necessary to select a respondent from the household. Some randomizing procedure is typically used to select the respondent. There are two methods for selecting respondents, and they have quite different consequences. The most common method of selection identifies the respondent among those eligible who are at home and the interview is conducted immediately. This further compromises the sample, making it a selection among those people who happen to be at home when the interviewer calls. A superior sampling procedure (but a more costly and time-consuming one, similar to methods used to select respondents for a face-to-face interview) is to identify all the eligible members of the household and select one at random. If the respondent selected is not at home, an appointment is arranged for a callback. In a high-quality survey like the 2000 NES, many attempts are made to interview the individual randomly selected, but no substitutions are made. Quick, less thorough telephone surveys allow a huge proportion of their respondents to be substitutes for the respondents who should have been interviewed.

The more often respondents are lost in this way or refuse to be interviewed, the more the sample departs from its original design. Probability samples, with either face-to-face or telephone interviews, can result in unrepresentative samples if the *nonresponse rate* is high. The nonresponse rate refers to the number of respondents originally selected who, for whatever reason, are not interviewed and thus do not appear in the sample.[1] Should these nonrespondents share some characteristic disproportionately, the resulting sample will underrepresent that type of person. For example, if residents of high-crime neighborhoods, the elderly, or busy people refuse to be interviewed at higher rates than others, the sample will have fewer of these people than occur in the population and thus the sample will be biased. All the polling organizations take steps to counter these tendencies by weighting the results to compensate for various demographic biases.[2] This is a difficult problem to solve, however. Currently, survey organizations have the greatest difficulty getting interviews in the inner cities of the largest metropolitan areas. The likelihood is high that the people who consent to be interviewed in these areas are different from, and therefore not representative of, those who refuse. If this is the case, counting those who are interviewed more heavily (which is essentially what weighting the sample does) does not really eliminate the bias.

Questionnaire Constructing

In survey questionnaires, several types of questions will ordinarily be used. Public opinion surveys began years ago with forced-choice questions that a respondent was asked to answer by choosing among a set of offered alternatives. For example, forced-choice questions frequently take the form of stating a position on public policy and asking the respondent to "agree" or "disagree" with the statement. The analysis in Chapter 6 was based in part on the answers to forced-choice questions on public policy that were used in NES questionnaires in which respondents were asked to "agree strongly," "agree," "disagree," or "disagree strongly." Some respondents either gave qualified answers that did not fit into these prearranged categories or had no opinions.

A major innovation associated with the Survey Research Center is the use of open-ended questioning. Open-ended questions give respondents the opportunity to express their opinions in their own way without being forced to select among categories provided by the questionnaire. Questions such as "Is there anything in particular you like about the Democratic Party?" or "What are the most important problems facing the country today?" permit the respondents to answer in their own terms. Interviewers encourage respondents to answer such questions as fully as they can with neutral "probes" such as "Could you tell me more about that?" "Anything else?" and similar queries that draw forth more discussion. There is no doubt that open-ended questions are a superior method of eliciting accurate expressions of opinion.

There are two major disadvantages to open-ended questioning: (1) It places more of a burden on interviewers to record the responses; and (2) the burden of reducing the many responses to a dimension that can be analyzed is left for the coders. For example, if Americans are asked, "Do you think of yourself as a Democrat, a Republican, or an independent?" almost all the responses will fit usefully into the designated categories:

1. Democrat
2. Independent
3. Republican
4. Other party
5. I'm nothing; apolitical

6. Don't know
7. Refused to say
8. Not ascertained

If a relatively unstructured, open-ended question is used, however, such as "How do you think of yourself politically?" some people would answer with "Democrat," "Republican," and so forth, but many others might give answers that were quite different, such as "liberal," "conservative," "radical," "moderate," "pragmatic," "apathetic"—and these could not easily be compared with the partisan categories. Analysts often intend to force responses into a single dimension, such as partisanship, whether the respondents would have volunteered an answer along that dimension or not. This is essential if researchers are to develop single dimensions for analytic purposes. Modern survey research includes questions and techniques considerably more complex than these examples for establishing dimensions.

Interviewing

The selection of the sample depends in part on the interviewer, but even more important is the role of the interviewer in asking questions of the respondent and in recording the answers. Motivated, well-trained interviewers are crucial to the success of survey research. The interviewer has several major responsibilities. First, the interviewer must select the respondent according to sampling instructions. Second, the interviewer must develop rapport with the respondent so that he or she will be willing to go through with the interview, which may last an hour or more. Third, the interviewer must ask the questions in a friendly way and encourage the respondent to answer fully without distorting the answers. Fourth, the interviewer must record the answers of the respondent fully and accurately. To accomplish these tasks with a high level of proficiency, a permanent staff of interviewers is trained and retrained by survey organizations.

A technological innovation used in telephone interviewing is the Computer-Assisted Telephone Interview (CATI) system. The interviewer sits at the telephone, with the questionnaire appearing on a computer screen. As the interviewer moves through the questionnaire, responses are entered directly into the computer and automatically coded (discussed later). Complicated branching to different questions, conditional on the responses given to preceding questions, is possible.

There are some real advantages in telephone interviewing. The travel costs of a field staff are eliminated. Within-interview "experiments" are possible with the CATI system. It is also easy and inexpensive to change the content of the questionnaire during the course of the study. The great disadvantage is that face-to-face interviews yield higher quality data.

Coding

Once the interviewers administer the questionnaires to respondents, the verbal information is reduced to a numerical form, according to a code. Numeric information, unlike verbal information, can be processed and manipulated by high-speed, data-processing equipment. The coder's task may be simple or complex. For example, to code the respondent's gender requires a simple code: 1 = male, 2 = female. A data field that contains information on the respondent will have a location designated for indicating the respondent's gender. A value of 1 will indicate male, and a value of 2 will indicate female. The list of partisan categories shown previously gives the coding numbers that would stand for various responses. Printed questionnaires for face-to-face interviews are precoded for many of the more straightforward questions and, as we saw, the CATI system allows precoded categories to be assigned automatically as the interviewer records the respondent's answers.

Some coding is complicated, with elaborate arrays of categories. For example, coding the responses to a question such as "Is there anything in particular you like about the Democratic Party?" might include hundreds of categories covering such details as "I like the party's farm policies," "I like the party's tax program," and "I've just always been a Democrat." Some codes require coders to make judgments about the respondents' answers; in political surveys these codes have included judgments on the level of sophistication of the respondents' answers and judgments about the main reason for respondents' vote choices.

After the verbal information has been converted into numbers according to the coding instructions, the data are ready for analysis by computer. At this point, the survey research process ends; the political analysts take over to make what use of the data they can.

Validity of Survey Questions

A frequent set of criticisms directed at public opinion research questions the validity of the responses to survey items. *Validity* simply means the extent to which there is correspondence between the verbal response to a question and the actual attitude or behavior of the respondent that the question is designed to measure. There is no one answer to doubts about validity, because each item has a validity applicable to it alone. Some items are notoriously invalid; others have nearly perfect validity. Many survey items have not been independently tested for their validity, and for practical purposes, the researcher is forced to say that he or she is interested in analyzing the responses, whatever they mean to the respondent. In other instances the sample result can be compared with the known population value.

The items with the most questionable validity in political studies come from those situations in which respondents have some incentive to misrepresent the facts or when their memories may not be accurate. Questions about voter turnout or level of income are noteworthy in this regard; validity checks reveal that respondents are about as likely to underestimate their income as overestimate it, and a noticeable percentage of respondents claim to have voted when they did not.[3]

Recall of past voting behavior falls victim to failing memories and intervening events. Changes in party identification, past votes cast, the party identification of one's parents—all may contain substantial error. For example, during November and December immediately after the 1960 election, respondents were asked how they had voted for president. Most remembered voting for either John Kennedy or Richard Nixon, and, as shown in Table A-1, they were divided about evenly between the two. (The slight deviation of 1 percent from the actual results is within sampling error by any reasonable standards.) The 1962 and 1964 sample estimates of the 1960 vote reveal increasing departures from the actual outcome. Granting that some change in the population over four years may affect vote-choice percentages, a substantial pro-

TABLE A-1   Recalled Vote for President in 1960,
             1962, and 1964

Recalled vote	1960	1962	1964	Actual vote in 1960[a]
Kennedy	49%	56%	64%	49.7%
Nixon	51	43	36	49.5
Other	[b]	[b]	[b]	.7
Total	100%	99%	100%	99.9%
(N)	(1,428)	(940)	(1,124)	

Sources: National Election Studies. Data provided by the Inter-university Consortium for Political and Social Research; Office of the Clerk, U.S. House of Representatives, clerkweb.house.gov.

[a]There are a number of ways to tally the popular vote from 1960, including ways that show Nixon with a slight popular vote majority. No matter how the votes are counted the election was very close.

[b]Less than 0.5 percent.

portion of the 1964 sample gave responses to the question of 1960 presidential vote choice that misrepresented their actual vote. The validity of this item always declines over a four-year period, but President Kennedy's assassination in the intervening years created an unusually large distortion in recalled vote.

Validity versus Continuity

One of the important features of the NES is its continuity over a fifty-year time span. Samples of the American population have been asked the same questions during every national election campaign throughout this period, offering an extraordinary opportunity for studying trends in the attitudes of the American electorate. The development of this valuable, continuous series does have one unfortunate aspect, however. Because the value of the series depends on the comparability of the questions, researchers are reluctant to alter questions, even when doubts about their validity arise. Improving the questions undermines comparability. Therefore, a choice between continuity and validity must be made.

The NES's questions concerning religious preference provide a recent example where validity was chosen over continuity. For years, respondents were simply asked, "What is your religious preference?" Although a small percentage in each survey answered "None," it was clear that a significant number of those answering "Protestant," and fewer numbers citing other religions, had in fact no meaningful religious affiliation. In the 1992 survey, the NES began asking the question differently. Respondents were first asked, "Do you ever attend religious services, apart from occasional weddings, baptisms, and funerals?" Those who answered "no" were asked an additional question about their religious preference: "Regardless of whether you now attend any religious services, do you ever think of yourself as part of a particular church or denomination?" Those who did not answer "yes" to one of these two screening questions were not asked the traditional question about religious affiliation that then followed. As a result, the percentage of the population categorized as having no religious affiliation increased dramatically. This new question more validly reflects the religious sentiments of the American public, but it is now impossible to compare these later results with those of previous years. We cannot infer a large drop in religious affiliation on the basis of the responses to these new and different questions. In this instance, continuity has been sacrificed in favor of validity.

Despite inevitable concerns about validity, survey research provides the best means of investigating the attitudes and behavior of large populations of individuals such as the American electorate.

Notes

1. See John Brehm, *The Phantom Respondents* (Ann Arbor: University of Michigan Press, 1993).
2. *Public Opinion* 4 (February/March 1981): 20.
3. Paul Abramson and William Claggett, "Race-Related Differences in Self-Reported and Validated Turnout," *Journal of Politics* 46 (August 1984): 719–738.

Suggested Readings

Asher, Herbert. *Polling and the Public,* 5th ed. Washington, D.C.: CQ Press, 2001. A good discussion of how polls are conducted and how they are used.
Backstrom, Charles H., and Gerald D. Hursh-Cesar. *Survey Research,* 2d ed. New York: Wiley, 1981. A good introduction to survey research methods.
Kish, Leslie. *Survey Sampling.* New York: Wiley, 1965. By far the most authoritative work on sampling.
Mann, Thomas E., and Gary R. Orren, eds. *Media Polls in American Politics.* Washington, D.C.: Brookings Institution, 1992. An excellent collection of essays on the use of polls in contemporary media analysis.
Survey Research Center. *Manual for Interviewers* and *Manual for Coders.* Ann Arbor: Survey Research Center, University of Michigan. A simple, thorough introduction to the interviewing and coding processes.
Weisberg, Herbert F., Jon Krosnick, and Bruce D. Bowen. *An Introduction to Survey Research and Data Analysis.* San Francisco: W. H. Freeman, 1989. A good, methodological textbook on survey research and the interpretation of statistical analysis.

Internet Resources

The Web site of the NES at www.umich.edu/~nes/ has extensive information on survey research methods. Click on "Studies, Data, and Other Resources" to examine NES questionnaires and codebooks for recent studies. The codebooks also have discussions of the NES sampling design and the selection of respondents.

Some other Web sites with methodological information are The Gallup Poll at www.gallup.com; The Pew Research Center for The People & The Press at www.people-press.org; the General Social Survey at www.icpsr.umich.edu/gss/; and the Institute for Research in Social Science at www.irss.unc.edu/data-archive/.

Index